The Philosophy of Anne Conway

Also available from Bloomsbury

Finding Locke's God, by Nathan Guy
God, Existence, and Fictional Objects, by John-Mark L. Miravalle
Kant's Transition Project and Late Philosophy, by Oliver Thorndike
Natural and Artifactual Objects in Contemporary Metaphysics,
edited by Richard Davies
The Bloomsbury Companion to Robert Boyle, edited by Jan-Erik Jones

The Philosophy of Anne Conway

God, Creation and the Nature of Time

Jonathan Head

BLOOMSBURY ACADEMIC
LONDON • NEW YORK • OXFORD • NEW DELHI • SYDNEY

BLOOMSBURY ACADEMIC
Bloomsbury Publishing Plc
50 Bedford Square, London, WC1B 3DP, UK
1385 Broadway, New York, NY 10018, USA

BLOOMSBURY, BLOOMSBURY ACADEMIC and the Diana logo
are trademarks of Bloomsbury Publishing Plc

First published in Great Britain 2021

Copyright © Jonathan Head, 2021

Jonathan Head has asserted his right under the Copyright, Designs and
Patents Act, 1988, to be identified as Author of this work.

For legal purposes the Acknowledgments on p. vii constitute an
extension of this copyright page.

Cover design by Charlotte Daniels
Cover image: Artist, Ruisdael, Jacob Isaacksz, van (1628/29–1682).
(Photo by Fine Art Images/Heritage Images/Getty Images)

All rights reserved. No part of this publication may be reproduced or
transmitted in any form or by any means, electronic or mechanical, including
photocopying, recording, or any information storage or retrieval system,
without prior permission in writing from the publishers.

Bloomsbury Publishing Plc does not have any control over, or responsibility for,
any third-party websites referred to or in this book. All internet addresses given
in this book were correct at the time of going to press. The author and publisher
regret any inconvenience caused if addresses have changed or sites have
ceased to exist, but can accept no responsibility for any such changes.

A catalogue record for this book is available from the British Library.

Library of Congress Cataloging-in-Publication Data
Names: Head, Jonathan, author.
Title: The philosophy of Anne Conway : God, creation and
the nature of time / Jonathan Head.
Description: London ; New York : Bloomsbury Academic, 2020. |
Includes bibliographical references and index.
Identifiers: LCCN 2020027571 (print) | LCCN 2020027572 (ebook) |
ISBN 9781350134522 (hb) | ISBN 9781350134539 (ePDF) |
ISBN 9781350134546 (eBook)
Subjects: LCSH: Conway, Anne, 1631–1679. | Conway, Anne, 1631-1679.
Principles of the most ancient and modern philosophy.
Classification: LCC B1201.C5534 H43 2020 (print) |
LCC B1201.C5534 (ebook) | DDC 192–dc23
LC record available at https://lccn.loc.gov/2020027571
LC ebook record available at https://lccn.loc.gov/2020027572

ISBN:	HB:	978-1-3501-3452-2
	ePDF:	978-1-3501-3453-9
	eBook:	978-1-3501-3454-6

Typeset by Integra Software Services Pvt. Ltd.

To find out more about our authors and books visit www.bloomsbury.com
and sign up for our newsletters.

To my parents, Kathryn and Michael

Contents

Preface	viii
Note on References	ix
Introduction: Anne Conway's life and letters	1
1 The inner light	21
2 God, spirit and body	45
3 Creation and the infinity of time	69
4 God, Christ and Creature	95
5 Christ, salvation and the end of time	115
6 Freedom	133
7 The constitution of creatures	151
Conclusion	183
Notes	185
Bibliography	197
Index	203

Preface

This book is the product of a five-year study of Anne Conway and her philosophical circle, though most of the manuscript was written during the summer months of 2018 and 2019. Since reading Conway's *Principles of the Most Ancient and Modern Philosophy* on a whim, it has been an incredibly rewarding experience to get to know something of her ideas and her world, and I sincerely hope that others will be inspired by this work to read Conway for themselves if they have not done so already. Just as worthwhile has been getting to know other scholars interested in Conway, many of whom have been kind of enough to discuss their work with me and comment on draft material, including Sarah Hutton, Jasper Reid, Julia Borcherding, Jacqueline Broad, John Grey, Emily Thomas, Jessica Gordon-Roth and Christia Mercer. I have also benefited from the comments of numerous anonymous peer reviewers – my thanks to them, whoever they are! I must also thank Peter Kail for showing me, when I was an undergraduate, just how rewarding scholarly work in early modern philosophy can be.

I have also been fortunate enough to spend the last seven years teaching and researching at Keele University, first as a PhD student and now as a faculty member. I have many wonderful colleagues there, but I would particularly like to thank the other members of the Philosophy programme for their advice and support during this time: Sophie Allen, Sorin Baiasu, Guiseppina D'oro and James Tartaglia. I must also thank Bloomsbury Publishing for supporting my work, particularly my editors, Colleen Coalter and Becky Holland. Some of the chapters of this book in earlier versions have appeared as journal articles and I would like to thank the relevant editors for their permission to reuse that material here (the salient details are to be found at the beginning of these chapters). Cambridge University Press must also be thanked for their permission to use quotes from the 1996 translation of *Principles of the Most Ancient and Modern Philosophy*, edited by Allison P. Coudert and Taylor Corse.

Finally, I would like to thank my family and friends for their love and support. Though I count myself exceedingly blessed to have the time to devote myself to research projects such as this one, there are nevertheless challenges they bring that would be insurmountable without the help of those I care about. This book is dedicated to my parents, Kathryn and Michael, who have done so much to ensure that I was able to pursue my ambitions of being a philosopher.

Note on references

Conway's *Principia* is referred to by chapter and section number, followed by a page reference to the translation by Coudert and Corse, published by Cambridge University Press in 1996.

The Conway Letters (revised edition, published by OUP in 1992), edited by Nicolson and Hutton, is referred to with the letter L, followed by a page reference.

The Latin edition of *Principia*, edited by Peter Loptson and published in 1982 by Martinus Nijhoff, is referred to by chapter and section number, followed by a page number with the designation 'P2'.

Quotations from the Bible are taken from the King James Version.

Some quotes from seventeenth-century sources have been modernized in terms of spelling, in order to ensure readability for the modern reader. However, great care has been taken to not change the meaning of the original passage. Original punctuation and capitalization have been retained.

Introduction:
Anne Conway's life and letters

This book is an exploration of the philosophy of Anne Conway (1631–79), as found in her extant correspondence and her only published work, *Principles of the Most Ancient and Modern Philosophy* (*Principia Philosophiae antiquissimae et recentissimae*)[1] (1690). My intention is to systematically expound the details of her thought in a manner that not only contributes to the growing scholarly debate on her work but is also accessible for non-specialist university teachers and students. Whilst I will mostly focus on the details of her arguments, and the interconnections between various claims she makes (both theological and philosophical), I will also at points consider the various influences that had an impact on her work, including Cambridge Platonism, Quakerism and Kabbalism. In this way, I will seek to provide some of the historical and intellectual context that will illuminate her philosophical aims, methods and arguments.

This introductory chapter is going to focus on Conway's life, her philosophical development (which can be tracked to some extent in her correspondence) and some of the textual issues surrounding the publication of the *Principia*. As we shall see, the *Principia* had a rather tortured route to publication, including the loss of the original notes on which the text is based, and so this may affect how we read the text as we go along. We will then be able to begin considering her thought in more detail in Chapter 1, focusing first on the question of religious epistemology and Conway's intellectual engagement with Cambridge Platonism and the early Quaker community.

Life and education

On 14 December 1631, a daughter was born to Lady Elizabeth Finch and the late Sir Heneage Finch at the family residence in London, Nottingham House (now known as Kensington Palace, following its sale to the Royal Family in 1689).

The child, named Anne,[2] was born into an extensive family, including one sister and numerous half-siblings from the first marriages of both her mother and father.[3] Very little is known of Anne's education during the early period of her life, but she certainly received no formal instruction at a school or university. However, by the time she came to write the notes that would constitute her philosophical corpus, in the latter half of the 1670s, she was (as the writer of the Published Preface to the *Principia* states), 'a woman learned beyond her sex, most skilled in Greek and Latin literature, and especially well versed in every sort of philosophy' (7).

Anne's intellectual curiosity at eighteen is evident, at least, in the earliest correspondence that we have addressed to and from her. One such exchange of letters is with her father-in-law, Edward, 2nd Viscount Conway. Anne had married Edward Conway (who would later be titled as the 1st Earl of Conway) on 11 February 1651. Her new father-in-law had an extensive library and wide-ranging intellectual interests that he was happy to discuss with her over a series of letters. Another early correspondent of Conway was the philosopher Henry More, who had been at Christ's College, Cambridge since 1631, first as a student and then Fellow. More came to know Anne through her half-brother, John Finch, who studied under More. John and Anne both became close to More and they often met and exchanged letters over the following decades. From the extant correspondence, we can see that More seems to have adopted the role as a philosophical mentor to Anne from 1650 onwards. At the time, More had yet to write many of the texts with which he would make his name, but he was already playing a part in some of the major intellectual debates of the age and was contributing to the Platonist revival that would dominate Cambridge in the mid-seventeenth century. We will see throughout this work that the Neoplatonism of More would go on to have a major intellectual impact on Conway, but she was very much unafraid early on to establish her own philosophical viewpoint.

After marrying Edward, Anne moved to Ragley Hall in Warwickshire. She would also spend periods of time in London, as well as staying in Ireland from 1662 to 1664, where Edward had an estate. In 1658, she had her first and only child, Heneage, but her joy, and that of her family and friends, would very quickly lead to despair: he died of smallpox in 1660 whilst she was also battling the disease. Anne spent increasing amounts of time at Ragley Hall, which became the centre of an informal intellectual network. Instrumental in constructing this complex of philosophers, theologians and scientists was another notable character from Conway's life: the physician, writer and alchemist Francis Mercury van Helmont. He first met Conway in 1670, having been referred to her by Henry More for his medical abilities. At the age of twelve, Conway had suffered a significant illness that she survived but had nevertheless left her with recurring, severe headaches that would continue throughout the rest of her life. Numerous physicians were consulted in an attempt to cure her of this illness, but to no avail. When Henry More met van Helmont at Christ's College, Cambridge on 12 October 1670, he was impressed by what he saw and soon asked him to consult with Conway, with a view to finally curing her debilitating illness. More also wrote a letter to Conway the next day, commending van Helmont to her and praising his 'very good plaine and expert humour' (L 323). Intrigued by the case, van Helmont put off his return to Continental Europe in order to visit Conway at Ragley Hall in November 1670. Though van Helmont would not be able to cure Conway of her medical ailments, they struck up a close intellectual friendship, discussing philosophical and theological issues at great length, and the impact of this collaboration can be seen upon the philosophy presented in the *Principia*. Following this initial visit, van Helmont spent much of the rest of the 1670s staying at Ragley Hall, until Anne's death.

Through the intellectual activities of Conway and van Helmont, Ragley became the meeting point for numerous thinkers during the 1670s. As Byrne notes, van Helmont's vast array of connections opened up Conway's intellectual world to a substantial degree:

> Some thinkers are important not because they have original ideas or write influential treatises, but because they serve as conduits and synthesizers. F.M. van Helmont is such a figure. One of the most travelled men of his age … van Helmont linked Ragley with the Continent. He and More were probably two of the most intellectually well-connected men of their time, assuring the remarkably cosmopolitan nature of Ragley. Contacts between the Royal Society and Continental natural philosophical trends were rare, but at Ragley, ideas from across Europe converged.
>
> (2016: 45f.)

In particular, van Helmont's study of Kabbalist texts from the mystical Jewish tradition, in which there was a growing interest in Continental Europe, seems to have played a newly significant part of the discussions taking place at Ragley during this time. His interest in Kabbalism led him to contribute to the publication of the *Kabbala Denudata* in 1677, co-edited with his friend, Christian Knorr von Rosenroth. Both were interested in the ideas of Isaac Luria (1534–72), a Kabbalist teacher and mystic who had lived in the Ottoman

Empire. The *Kabbala Denudata* includes a variety of different Kabbalist texts, but those written by Luria's followers dominate. The tradition of Kabbalism was not entirely new to Conway, in that Henry More had a longstanding interest in that school of thought, on the basis that (supposedly) ancient Jewish texts may have secret esoteric teachings that show the hidden links between Judaism and Christianity and ultimately vindicate the truth of the Gospel message. In 1653, More had published a book entitled *Conjectura cabbalistica*, which had attempted to uncover different levels of meaning within the creation story that begins the Book of Genesis. However, as Hutton argues (2004: 160f.), it was unlikely that Conway had direct, detailed access to Jewish Kabbalist sources until she met van Helmont in 1670. We will consider the potential influence of Kabbalist ideas upon Conway's philosophy as we explore her work.

The 1670s saw another major change in Anne's life, as she became interested in the growing movement of Quakerism. It seems that it was van Helmont who first enthusiastically embraced the movement, attending meetings in the area local to Ragley Hall from 1675: Conway writes in November of that year that 'Monsieur Van Helmont is grown a very religious Churchman; he goes every Sunday to the Quakers meetings' (L 409). However, even before that point, it is possible that Conway already had links to prominent Quaker figures, and how these contacts developed is somewhat unclear. Hutton suggests that Conway's interest in Quakerism may have begun before her first meeting with van Helmont, through her companion, Elizabeth Foxcroft, who began staying at Ragley Hall from 1664 onwards. Foxcroft was the sister of another Cambridge Platonist, Benjamin Whichcote, and had her own intellectual interests, particularly in mystical thought, such as that of the German theologian, Jacob Boehme (1575–1624). Meetings with prominent Quakers at Ragley Hall commenced in 1666, with the visit of Thomas Bromley, but intensified particularly in the late 1670s, beginning with a stay by George Keith, who met with Conway following an invitation to William Penn, and culminating with visits from the founder of the Society of Friends, George Fox, in 1678. Henry More also began having his own meetings with various Quaker figures during this time (see L 404).

In a letter to Henry More from 1676, Conway defends the presence of Quaker visitors at Ragley Hall. She argues that she is not unaware of their faults, including that there are 'many bad people amongst them' and that they may require intellectual guidance from someone like More 'for the clearing up of their understanding, and advancing their progress towards the best things' (L 421). However, on the other side, she emphasizes the severity of her illness and the comfort they bring to her as she battles it:

They have been and are a suffering people and are taught from the consolation that has been experimentally felt by them under their great trials to administer comfort upon occasion to others in great distress ... The weight of my affliction lies so heavy upon me, that it is incredible how very seldom I can endure anyone in my chamber, but I find them so still, and very serious, that the company of such of them as I have hitherto seen, will be acceptable to me.

(L 421f.)

To push her case even further, Conway argues that their example and presence at Ragley Hall have a beneficial effect on her faith: 'The particular acquaintance with such living examples of great patience under sundry heavy exercises, both of bodily sickness and other calamities... I find begets a more lively faith and uninterrupted desire of approaching to such a behaviour in like exigencies, then the most learned and rhetorical discourses of resignation can do' (L 422). Conway ends by denying that she identifies as a Quaker, though 'their principles and practices (at least most of them) as far as I am capable are Christian and apostolical' (L 422), and stating that she has decided to take some Quaker women on as servants.

The position of the Quakers at Ragley Hall in the final years of Conway's life becomes even more clear in a letter from Anne's husband, Edward, to his friend, Sir George Rawdon, following a visit to his residence from June 1676. Edward complains that van Helmont entertains numerous Quakers at Ragley, to the extent that when he is not there, 'the house is as full of them as it can hold' (L 535). However, in the face of growing rumours that Anne herself had become a Quaker, Edward issues a stark denial: 'How long this will last I know not, for I have not yet seen my wife since I came, but both from my own knowledge and from Dr More I can assure you that my wife is no Quaker' (L 535). How Edward could be entirely sure of this, given that he had not been able to see his wife on this visit and that he now spent most of his time away from Ragley, is not clear, but we have no reason not to take his word on this. However, things had certainly changed by the following year, with Henry More reporting to Anne's brother, John Finch, that she had now adopted the Quaker practice of addressing all people as 'thee' or 'thou', disregarding the usual practice of adapting address according to societal rank (see L 534n.). So, it seems that Conway did indeed die a Quaker, confirmed by her desire for a simple funeral, entirely unbefitting someone of her social rank, and the epitaph of 'Quaker Lady' scratched on her coffin (a detail provided by Nicolson in L 452). However, in terms of the philosophy presented in the *Principia*, the significance of these events in the final years of her life for our interpretation is unclear, insofar as the dating of the notes that make up the text is not entirely settled. Were the notes written before Conway had committed herself to Quakerism or after? Even if the notes were written in her very final years, it is by no means clear that her philosophy would reflect Quaker theology to that great an extent, as Quaker thought was generally unformed at the time anyway. This is an issue I will return to in the following chapter, as we discuss the potential influence of Quaker ideas on her philosophy and throughout this work.

However, the personal impact of Quakerism upon Conway in her final years is clear from an examination of her will. The main part of her will dates from 1673, two years before regular contact with the early Quaker community began. Clearly, at this point, her health had deteriorated again to a point where it was felt that death might be near: she is 'continually expecting that the good Hand of God will put a period to [her] trouble and afflictions by a blessed death', given her 'being very sickly and apprehensive of [her] daily dangers' (L 480). Conway then goes on to express her wishes with regard to the disposal of her body in fairly predictable terms for a good member of the Church of England at the time:

> I give up and resign my soul into the hands of Almighty God, from whom it came, trusting to be saved, and to partake of a blessed Resurrection only by the Merits and through the satisfaction of Jesus Christ my Saviour and Redeemer: And I give my body to the Earth to be decently interred according to the Rites of the Church of England in such convenient place as my dear husband shall choose.
>
> (L 480)

The will, however, has a codicil appended to it, which was clearly added some years later.[4] In it, Conway begins by explaining that her religious convictions since the time of the writing of her will had undergone a significant revolution:

> Since the writing [of the will] God Almighty having more enlightened my understanding (in convincing me of the vanity and evil of using those Rites and ceremonies and all other pompous shows and formalities commonly used in burials) I find myself obliged to clear my conscience in the sight of God to confess to the truth, which the Lord has made known to me in bearing my testimony against all such things.
>
> (L 481)

Having asked for a burial in alignment with the traditions of the Church of England in her will, she now rescinds that request, repudiating entirely the formal liturgy associated with funerals in the established Church. Conway makes this request on the basis that she has achieved a new religious understanding that significantly undercuts the formal structures of the Church and the outward 'show' that these activities involve. This is exactly the kind of request that someone wholly committed to Quakerism would make, including a substantial and scornful critique of the religious authorities and their activities.

Conway ends the codicil by repeating her request 'that all those rites and ceremonies of the so-called Church of England may be wholly forborne at my burial; and all other superfluity whatsoever. This being writ with my own hand may give sufficient assurance to any concerned that they were all omitted upon my desire' (L 481). On the basis that the notes that make up the *Principia* date from these final years of her life, we would do well to approach the text with this context in mind, namely, that Conway's religious beliefs had recently undergone radical revision following what she understood to be divine intervention that had 'enlightened' her understanding, and that this had led her to emphatically reject the Church of England, with its beliefs and liturgy, and move towards a more radical standpoint. As we shall see, this change in Conway's life is reflected in the philosophy found in the *Principia*, insofar as we find an ambitious and radically non-conformist religious system of thought.

Conway eventually succumbed to the illness that had plagued her throughout her adult life at the age of forty-seven on 23 February 1679. Her final hours, under the care of van Helmont, are described in a letter by Charles Coke (her secretary) to Lord Conway, who was visiting Ireland at the time: he writes, 'Between 7 and 8 of the Clock at night My Lady parted this life, having her perfect understanding and senses to the last minute, giving up her Spirit very peaceably without any perceivable motion and keeping a very sweet face, her pain have held her to the last' (L 451). Following news of her death, Henry More is reported to have written in a suggestive note that reflects his deep respect and affection for Conway:

> I perceive, and bless God for it, that my Lady Conway was my Lady Conway to her Last Breath; the greatest example of Patience and Presence of Mind, in highest Extremities of Pain and Affliction, that we shall easily meet with: Scarce anything to be found like her, since the Primitive Times of the Church. Of her Supernatural Comforts and Refreshments after some of her greatest Agonies and Conflicts, and of her strange Pre-visions of things future, I might here also make mention.
>
> (Ward 2000: 126)[5]

There are some remarkable biographical details here that give food for thought for someone approaching Conway's philosophy. For one thing, this note suggests a mystical dimension to Conway's religious and philosophical reflection that is only hinted at in the *Principia*. Reflecting the crucial role that experience of suffering will have to play in her metaphysical system, Conway seems to have claimed that her particularly extreme bouts of ill-health gave her religious insight, even to the extent that she could prophesy about the future. The extent to which these experiences did shape Conway's philosophy will always be a matter of speculation, but we would do well to keep these aspects of her own self-understanding in mind as we approach the text of the *Principia*. At the very least, we may have to bear in mind that Conway perhaps is not just the rationalist that she has sometimes been labelled as; rather, there may be a multitude of different philosophical traditions and approaches that have an interlinking impact upon the development and exposition of her philosophy.

The text that we will be focusing upon, the *Principia*, was not published in Conway's lifetime. Indeed, she published nothing during her life, despite her many years of philosophical study. Women authors were certainly rare, but not entirely unknown, during this period. One prominent example of a woman philosopher at this time is Margaret Cavendish (1623–73), who published prodigiously in a number of different forms, including poetry, novels, plays and philosophical works.[6] Conway shows no indication of wishing to publish during her lifetime, and that may be understandable given her ongoing battles with ill-health, as well as the ridicule publicly directed at Cavendish, despite her many contemporary admirers. Conway had first-hand experience of the ridicule that Cavendish attracted due to a letter from More, where he writes that Cavendish 'is afraid some man should quit his breeches and put on a petticoat to answer her in that disguise' (L 237). Conway, for her own part, was happy to pursue her studies in privacy, keeping up correspondence with other intellectuals and religious thinkers, and working out her own ideas in note form. It is these notes that form the basis of her posthumous publication, the *Principia*.

Publication history of the *Principia*

In 1690, a book was published in Amsterdam, entitled *Opuscula Philosophica*. It was a collection of three texts by various authors in Latin. One of them was a Latin translation of van Helmont's *Two Hundred Queries*, originally published in English in 1684.[7] Another was a text entitled *Philosophia vulgaris refutata* (Popular philosophy refuted), an attack on scholasticism by Jean Gironnet. The final text of the collection was entitled *Principia Philosophiae antiquissimae et recentissimae* (Principles of the most ancient and modern Philosophy). The Preface provided to the text makes its remarkable origins clear, being 'written a few years ago by an English Countess', who 'was taught the principles of Descartes, [and] having seen their faults, she later discovered so many things from reading certain writings of genuine ancient philosophy that she wrote these few chapters for her own use' (7). The entire text published here is in Latin and is therefore a translation of Conway's notebooks that were written in English. In 1692, the text of the *Principia* was published in an English translation by 'J.C.', identified by Marjorie Nicolson as John Clark, M.D., who worked as a translator on another van Helmont project (L 453). Given that this translation was published, rather than Conway's original writings, we can conclude that her notebooks were lost very soon after her death during the 1680s, presumably never to be recovered.

Though there has been some debate concerning when the notes that make up the *Principia* were written, all scholars agree that they are from the 1670s, the last decade of Conway's life. The main reason for this is the apparent influence of Kabbalist ideas upon the philosophy presented by Conway, and it is unlikely that she would have become familiar with such ideas prior to meeting van Helmont in 1670. In the *Conway Letters*, Marjorie Nicolson states that the text probably derives from the first half of the decade, on the basis that there is no sign of the Quakerism that would become a major part of Conway's life from 1675 onwards (see L 453). Loptson also argues that the *Principia* shows no evidence of 'specifically Quaker views', on the basis that it 'is a metaphysical and theological treatise of the highest abstraction' (1982: 8). However, Hutton disagrees with Nicolson's dating and her evaluation of the nature of the intellectual influences upon the *Principia*, stating that the philosophy Conway presents in that text is a reflection of the 'powerful combination of Helmontianism, kabbalism and Quakerism' (2004: 203) that formed the centre-point of the intellectual circle at Ragley Hall in the late 1670s.[8]

After the two early editions of the *Principia*, there were few substantial publications on Conway and her philosophy until the appearance of a collection of her correspondence in 1930.[9] Edited by Marjorie Nicolson, *The Conway Letters* provides nearly 300 letters written by, to and about Conway throughout her life and in the immediate period following her death. In addition to the correspondence, Nicolson offers extensive background information, including important biographical details concerning Conway and her circle of acquaintances. This remarkable book was improved upon even further by Sarah Hutton, who issued a revised edition in 1992 that includes new material left out of the first edition, such as important early philosophical letters between Conway and Henry More. The only disappointment connected to this volume is no fault of the editors, in that very few of the letters written by Conway herself have survived. *The Conway Letters* contains thirty-eight of Anne's letters, and we often have to use the replies of others to discern something of what she may have been saying to them.

The first appearance of the *Principia* in a modern printing was in 1982 by Martinus Nijhoff, in an edition that includes both the 1690 Latin text and the 1692 English translation, with an extensive introduction and commentary by the editor, Peter Loptson.[10] A second edition of this volume, with a rewritten introduction, was issued in 1998 by Scholars' Facsimiles and Reprints.[11] Perhaps more significant is the first full modern English translation of the *Principia* by Allison Coudert and Taylor Corse, which appeared in 1996 by Cambridge University Press and has become the primary translation used by scholars (including in this work).[12] Since then, interest in Conway's philosophy has grown significantly, with numerous papers published in scholarly journals and a few significant book-length studies, such as Sarah Hutton's intellectual biography, *Anne Conway: A Woman Philosopher* (CUP: 2004), and Carolyn Wayne White's *The Legacy of Anne Conway* (SUNY Press: 2008). However, the process of recovering Conway's philosophy from the shadow of its historical scholarly neglect is still very much starting and there are numerous outstanding interpretive issues that will undoubtedly be discussed for many years to come. The intention of this book is to provide both an accessible and scholarly overview of the key aspects of Conway's philosophy as presented in the *Principia*. Some topics I will consider have been discussed already at some length by scholars and I will seek to build upon this work that has already been done. Other aspects of Conway's philosophy, though, have yet to receive any substantive scholarly consideration and so I hope to shed some new light on these ideas. We will begin this project in the following chapter, in which I consider the possible epistemological foundations of Conway's philosophy. Before that, however, I wish to return to the question of Conway's philosophical development, as charted in an elusive way in her correspondence.

Philosophical concerns in the *Letters*

As I have already stated, this book will focus on the philosophy presented in Conway's only published work, the *Principia*. The only other evidence we have regarding Conway's intellectual development and philosophical thought are clues scattered throughout her correspondence. Though Conway did not receive a formal education in philosophy, she was able to nevertheless engage in substantial philosophical study and discussion. In her seminal paper on women philosophers in the early modern period, 'Disappearing Ink', O'Neill describes the wide arena of philosophy (at least within the upper classes) during this period, which allowed women such as Anne Conway to engage in intellectual pursuits:

> Given the extremely limited access of early modern women to universities and other institutional spheres of scholarly activity, we might be led to think that these women could not have contributed to philosophy in any significant way. But this would be to forget the blossoming of philosophical activity outside of the schools since the Renaissance. Philosophy was being done in convents, religious retreats for laypersons, the courts of Europe, and the salons; philosophical networks, which stretched throughout Europe, communicated via letters, published pamphlets and treatises, and scholarly journals.
>
> (1998: 19)

Through her correspondence and meetings with other intellectuals of the time, Conway was able to play an active role in philosophical discourse outside of the formal confines of the university and the established Church. Unfortunately, the evidence we have of her intellectual contributions through her correspondence does not add up to much (many of her extant letters deal with personal, non-academic matters), but we are able to map, in broad strokes, some of her interests as they grow and develop over her adulthood. We are thus left in the position that, unless more evidence comes to light, we are unable to detail precisely how Conway came to develop the ideas presented in the *Principia*. Nevertheless, in this section, I will provide a brief overview of the extant correspondence to and from Conway, in an attempt to give some sense of her intellectual interests that arise over the years from just before her marriage to the final part of her life.

One of the first major epistolary exchanges we find in *The Conway Letters* is with Anne's father-in-law, Edward. We can see that Anne's correspondence with him very quickly turned to philosophical matters, following her marriage. In a letter dated 1 July 1651, Lord Conway offers a criticism of the new Cartesian philosophy, comparing it unfavourably with the genuine learning offered by the ancient sources, as far as he sees it. Edward claims that Descartes and others

> have written as their fantasy did persuade, and done as a man must do that goes on hunting in a thick, enclosed country, leave his horse behind him and

scramble over hedge and ditch and tear his clothes, so do they leave the ancient rules, and set up new opinions for the maintenance of which, they are forced into great inconveniences, in their reason.

(L 30)

Lord Conway portrays the Cartesians as setting up their own modern irrational fantasies: something that is particularly damning given the possibility of engaging with the rationally grounded teaching of the ancients. They are, further, portrayed as offering desperate arguments in defence of the new irrationalities that they are proposing.

That Anne was only too happy to engage with her father-in-law in these matters can be seen in his next letter to her, dated 8 July of the same year. Here, he returns to the question of modern versus ancient sources, having praised her engagement with the issue in her previous letter (now lost): 'Because I see your judgement is good, I will tell you some conceptions of mine concerning new books, all being either written according to the rules of former writers in the same subject, or else being totally new, or in part differing from former rules' (L 31). Lord Conway goes on to reflect upon the differing reactions to new philosophies depending upon the extent to which they reflect ancient wisdom:

> They live or die according to their complexion or spirit, some of those that are written according to old rules are thought worthy to live so long as the world lives, others never outlive their first impression, those that are writ contrary to or besides the old rules, have their fates according to the affection of their readers or their real truth as it will be found upon experience.
>
> (L 31)

He goes on to complain that some, like Copernicus, are followed 'not because his opinion is true but because the opinion is different from what all men in all ages ever had' (L 32). Lord Conway argues that intellectuals are swayed more by the promise of something new and cling to their preferred speculations, rather than hewing to the time-tested, rationally grounded theories of the ancients.

The debate with Anne concerning ancient and modern teaching continued, with her robustly defending emerging scientific and philosophical theories. Lord Conway seemingly concedes some ground to his daughter-in-law in what is presumably his next letter in the exchange, dated 22 July: 'I am of your opinion that many concealed truths are discovered in these latter times' (L 32). However, the concession that Lord Conway is willing to make is limited: 'Without doubt in many particulars, knowledge is much increased, and although knowledge do thus increase yet it is true that nothing is found out new in philosophy since Aristotle, that is considering it according to his grounds and principles and in the general, not according to every particular' (L 33). So, as far as he is concerned, nothing has yet superseded Aristotelianism in its broad terms, though particular details of that system would now have to be amended in light of the advances in knowledge there have been.

Lord Conway then moves on to the more specific question of the possible conflict between religious tradition and new advances in the sciences and philosophy, arguing that Christian scripture warns against the pretensions of philosophers and of the need to recognize the limitations of the human intellect apart from divine revelation:

> St. Paul who spake by the Spirit … gives a great diminution to the estimation of philosophy, saying that it does falsely brag of knowing things by the cause, which is a most certain way of knowing if that way be known, and a most uncertain if it be not known. It is most fit that we should be thus ignorant of the natures of things in this world … [Instead] the knowledge of Christ shall make us wise in all things.
> (L 33)

The debate finishes with a letter written by Anne in early October, which may have only survived because it appears to be a draft. In the letter, she comments on the growth of knowledge in ancient times and concedes to her father-in-law that the ancients did indeed possess great knowledge, but this was a result of their learning and experience, in the same manner that modern scholars formulated their theories. She admits that Biblical figures from the Book of Genesis had something of an advantage in gaining wisdom, though not because they had some mysterious access to deeper truths, but simply because they lived longer lives than are enjoyed now and all people could converse with each other in the same language:

> That the learning of [the ancients] before the flood was very great is no wonder because Adam who certainly was an excellent natural philosopher as appears by his giving names to every beast and bird according to their natures was contemporary with them for above 900 years, and the men at that time having all but one language to frame their conceptions by, had an unspeakable advantage of all that succeeded them, whereas we are now forced to spend a great part of our age in attaining to the shell of learning mere words; when as they had nothing but the kernel offered to them. Then the extraordinary length of their lives gave them leave to make infinite experiments, and experience is the mother of all knowledge.
> (L 36f.)

So, in line with the general tenor of the debate that we have seen so far, Anne is giving some ground to her interlocutor but is nevertheless maintaining the general thrust of her position. Though the ancients did have scientific and philosophical knowledge, they nevertheless had to learn in the same way that the moderns do, through experience and experiment. The ancients did have their own distinct advantages in terms of gaining knowledge, but this is perhaps outweighed by the compensations we have in the modern period, in being able to build upon the collective experience of centuries of scientific and philosophical progress. The letter reveals, then, that the young Conway is very much on the side of the moderns in terms of their advanced learning, whilst recognizing the intellectual achievements of the ancients. Another notable aspect of this letter is the breadth and depth of the learning she has already gained at this age, despite having received no formal education, including knowledgeable discussions of ancient philosophy, history and scripture.

Part of Anne's admiration for the moderns in her exchange with Lord Conway is perhaps to be attributed to the fact that, by this point, she had already entered into her correspondence with Henry More, which would perhaps be the most important intellectual influence upon her. One major topic of discussion in the early correspondence between More and Conway was the philosophy of Descartes, who had proposed a theory of substance dualism, according to which there exist two completely distinct types of substance (mind and body) with their own principal attribute (thought and extension, respectively) that cannot be had by the other kind of substance. Conway would go on to criticize this view at great length in the *Principia*.

The first hint we have of Conway's response to Descartes comes from a letter (from More to Conway) from September 1650, which is clearly a response to a letter by Anne proposing two objections to Cartesianism, focused on his sceptical arguments and his philosophical approach to God. One of her objections is to Descartes's ontological argument for the existence of God, which argues that we can establish that God exists on the basis of the nature of our idea of God: we clearly and distinctly perceive that our idea of God involves necessary existence, and given that clear and distinct ideas can be trusted, there must be a necessarily existent being, namely, God (for a necessarily existing being cannot fail to exist) (see 1968: 144–7). In response to this argument, Conway questions the inference from an idea to existence: can the idea of something really imply that thing's existence? In addition, if one can argue from the idea of a fully perfect being to the existence of a fully perfect being, why can we not pursue analogous reasoning and argue from the idea of a fully imperfect being to the existence of a fully imperfect being (see L 484)?

Conway also seems to have attacked Descartes on the supposition that there is no way of distinguishing between dreams and our waking life, though the exact details of her argument are not clear from More's letter (see L 484f.). Further letters touch on entirely different matters related to Cartesian philosophy, such as whether there can be a vacuum (see L 486–9), the possibility of uncreated matter (see L 491f.) and the subjectivity of the experience of colour (see L 493f.). So, even at this early stage of her philosophical correspondence with More, Conway clearly already has wide-ranging philosophical interests and the willingness to take an independent approach that challenges the authority of both Descartes and More.

Conway's severe medical issues throughout her adulthood also seem to have directed her philosophical and scientific reflections. As the 1650s continues, her correspondence with More increasingly focuses on medical matters, reflecting her declining health during this time. We can see that the search for a cure for Conway's debilitating headaches included research into contemporary medical theories and the prominent medical practitioners of the day, not only on the part of Anne, but also her husband, Edward, her brother, John, and Henry More. Part of her research into the alleviation of her illness led her to France (in 1656), accompanied by More, in order to undergo trepanning. In the end, the trip was something of a disaster: the physicians eventually refused to give her the treatment, and Edward was kidnapped by the Dutch during his crossing over the English Channel and held hostage (he was eventually released following the payment of a ransom).[13] The expertise that her medical interests gave her can be seen in a letter from Conway to her husband, in which she dispenses medical advice to him, as well as criticizing a particular doctor who had treated him:

> It was matter of no small amazement, as well as trouble to me, to find you should be so suddenly and violently surprised with sickness, and though I cannot certainly conjecture the cause of it, yet I do much suspect that it may proceed from what you took of Dr Pridian to apply outwardly to your fester, for I never knew it held safe to use any such thing to repel a humour that appeared upon the flesh without first preparing the body for it by purging and other physicke which you did not, I should be glad therefore if you would discontinue the use of it now.

(L 132)

Conway's comments here bespeak her continuing efforts, through research and dealing with different doctors, to seek effective treatment for her health issues. Unfortunately, whatever afflicted her was beyond the help of seventeenth-century medicine and she does not seem to have found anything that substantially relieved her illness.

As a result of her bouts of ill-health, the subject of her correspondence with More often turns to questions concerning religious faith and the role of suffering. More describes suffering as a God-given trial and thus an opportunity to grow in faith:

> While it shall please God to exercise you with so great an affliction, I question not but that your Ladyship will make the best and most proper advantage of it, being assured that all things whatsoever tend to the good of those that are good even those that seem for the present to the greatest evils. For the pious and virtuous come out of them, as gold purified out of the fire ... we are thus moulded in the furnace of affliction.
>
> (L 154)

Following the death of her son, More later writes to Conway about the importance of facing life's difficulties by lifting one's attention from worldly things and orienting your reflection towards the divine: he counsels Conway 'not to indulge to any content but such arises out of the sense and conscience of living according to the light of that eternal Reason that is everywhere ready to heal and rectify the minds of men, not to drink deep of any joys but such as are holy and intellectual', and that when 'our affections [are] sinking too far into any perishable object ... they necessarily expose us to Fate, and leave us too sadly in the lurch through their entanglements' (L 501). More is not advising Conway to disengage with the world, but rather to engage with it in a measured way that takes into account the divine ground of all things and the transitory, accidental nature of this life.[14]

Conway responds to this letter by stating that the response to misfortune that More recommends 'to get our reason so fortified by principles of philosophy and Religion as to be able to withstand all the calamities' is 'a thing very desirous', but 'I find my proficiency in these so small, and my weakness so great, that though such considerations may enable me to bear lesser crosses, yet I lie open to receive the assaults of greater' (L 181). Though Conway concedes the value of philosophical and religious reflection in re-orientating our perspective away from a bodily life filled with trials and tribulations, she rather heartbreakingly denies that she will be able to do this during her grief for her son. These kinds of reflections upon philosophy and overcoming hardship will not be explicitly discussed in the *Principia*, but we will see that suffering comes to a play a distinctive and wide-ranging role in her philosophical system, and this was almost certainly shaped by her life experiences, including her own medical issues and the loss of her only child.

Despite her illness, though, there is clear evidence that Conway's general philosophical studies continued, as her relationship with More evolved from mentor-student to intellectual equals. We hear of her studying Descartes's letters, in which he discusses his philosophy with various leading intellectuals of the day (see L 145), Euclid (which she studied along with her husband – see L 148) and theories associated with the early Church father, Origen (see L 192–4). As we shall see, echoes of Origen's ideas can be seen in Anne Conway's philosophy, probably via the influence of Henry More, and we can see the seeds of this in the correspondence. An anonymous publication in 1660 by George Rust (a friend of More), *A Letter of Resolution Concerning Origen*, occasions a series of letters between More and Conway that touch on Origen, including the rather controversial doctrine of the pre-existence of the soul, prior to birth. Though we do not have Anne's replies to these letters, she was clearly interested in learning more about Origen and was keen to discuss his ideas with More. For his part, More tries to defend the orthodoxy of Origen against the charge that the pre-existence of the soul conflicts with the Incarnation (the view that Christ, as the only Son of God, was both fully God and fully human in a 'hypostatic union'), stating that he does not see where the conflict would be: he argues, 'I confess I do not see how a pre-existence soul is not as capable of incarnation as a newly created one, or they all pre-existing, how the Messiah's soul may not enter a body as well as the rest' (L 194). It is unfortunate that we do not have Conway's replies to these letters concerning Origen, but it certainly shows that she was eager to engage in deeply controversial topics in theology, including in both contemporary and ancient theological literature. We will return to the question of Origen, and Henry More's possible influence upon Conway, later on in this work.

As her studies continued throughout her adult life, Conway's sphere of correspondence steadily increased to encompass numerous figures, in addition to close family and friends, though ill-health prevented her from writing at times. As an example, we can see that Conway had instigated correspondence with leading Quakers from a letter addressed to her by William Penn (1644–1718) from 1675. Conway clearly wished to learn more about Quaker beliefs and Penn spends much of the letter summarizing their claims, as well as describing their stance towards other Christian denominations (which probably reflects Conway's interest in the ecumenical project, shared with van Helmont, of undermining denominational differences within Christianity). Despite giving a harsh critique of other Christian groups, Penn nevertheless gives a sign of hope for reconciliation on the basis that 'they have formerly felt some touches of the divine power, that raised up the soul above formality' (L 402). He describes non-Quaker Christians as having been led astray, but still in a position in which they could be led back to the pure truth of the Christian message, encapsulated in the life and teaching of Jesus Christ. Penn describes what he perceives to have been their downfall as follows: 'None of them knew a stay, to their mind, where to wait for a daily supply of power and life, but instead of waiting for less mixture of their own spirits, they became careless, and grew literal, earthly, formal: and fell to mans-worship: and held their faith by Traditions of men' (L 402). Waiting for inspiration from the spirit, other denominations grew impatient and began to focus on worldly concerns (including the practice of a formal liturgy), instead of focusing on the transcendent. Penn sees the Quaker movement as a message from God, offering testimony with regard to the follies of other Christians, tempered with the hope that they can and will listen to the spirit within them again. He finishes the discussion with an exhortation to Conway to engage in the inner journey of the Quaker to retrieve the true Christian spirit:

> If thou watch unto the light of Jesus, give not way to the roving and wanderings of thy mind, and This blessed inward yoak, burden, and cross has been my preservation, with thousands. I cannot but admire it, speak honourably of it, and earnestly recommend it, as that which leads back to innocency by redeeming the soul from evil, and strengthening it against temptation. This is more noble than crosses of silver or gold, or dead religions: this inwardly slays and mortifies.
> (L 403)

As discussed earlier, it appears that Conway enthusiastically embraced this message, and we will be able to see traces of it as we consider her work, including questions of ecumenism that concern how to bring those of different faiths together.

Reading the *Principia*

Before we begin our detailed examination of the *Principia*, there are some important features of the text that should be noted. To begin with, we must remember throughout that we are not working with the original notes that the text of the *Principia* is based on. At the very best, we can work with a Latin translation of the original manuscript, and there is simply no way of knowing how reliable that translation is. If we focus on one of the two English translations, then we are working with a translation of a translation, where even more unreliability may have crept in (though at least in that case, we can check the translation against the Latin edition). We must be careful, then, to not rely too heavily on specific phrases and terminology in our interpretation of Conway's philosophy, as the text in question may have been translated in a manner in which the original meaning has been obscured to some extent. In addition, it may be the case that the notes on which the text is based are taken from different time periods, and so we may find contradictory passages in the text that reflect Conway changing her mind on a particular question over time. Such a possibility is certainly worth bearing in mind, but given the historical uncertainties involved, my approach is to treat *Principia* as a coherent text that expresses a singular philosophical vision. Thus, if I come across any apparent internal contradictions, I will seek to provide an interpretation that resolves them.

Another aspect of the text to bear in mind is the possibility of editorial intervention. It is highly likely that some elements of the text are editorial additions to the original material of Conway's notes, but the extent to which this took place is something that will remain uncertain.[15] For one thing, we find throughout the *Principia* numerous references to the second edition of *Kabbala Denudata*, a collection of Kabbalist texts produced by Christian Knorr von Rosenroth, with help from van Helmont, and published in 1684 (after Conway's death). Though Conway may have consulted early drafts of this edition, she would not have been able to make these specific references herself, and so these are clearly editorial additions. There are other elements of the text that we may consider as possible editorial changes. For example, given that this material was written for her own use, it is unlikely that she would have divided the text into neat, topic-based chapters in the manner we find in the *Principia*. As such, it seems likely that the ordering of the material into chapters as well as the summaries of the sections provided at the beginning of each chapter are editorial interventions. It is also entirely possible that the editors may have added or modified passages in the main body of the text itself. Given that van Helmont helmed the translation project, it is unlikely that any changes would have been significant, insofar as he would not have wished to misrepresent the work of his close friend. However, it is impossible to rule out minor changes here and there, such as the possible addition of references to Kabbalist ideas, such as can be found in the 'Annotations to the First Chapter', which is a section that is a leading candidate for an editorial addition in the text. My approach to the *Principia* through this work is as a text that can be trusted as reflecting, at least in broad strokes, the philosophy of Anne Conway, but we should maintain a level of hermeneutic suspicion at the same time, particularly with regard to Helmontian and Kabbalist aspects of the text.

Something we must also bear in mind is that the *Principia* does not give us the entire text of Conway's manuscript remains. The Preface tells us that only parts of the notes were transcribed in preparation for the translation 'because the rest were hardly legible' (7). As such, in the *Principia*, there may be important elements of Conway's philosophy missing or presented in an incomplete fashion. We may have to at points use what we have in the text, as well as our knowledge of her philosophical influences and milieu, to make an educated guess about how we could fill in some of the missing details of her system. This kind of 'best fit' approach, where we attempt to provide an overall view of her metaphysics that incorporates as much of the text as possible, is something that we should use sparingly, but may be unavoidable at points. However, I will endeavour throughout to depart from the text of Conway's *Principia* as little as possible, in order to give what I see as the most accurate and plausible interpretation of her remarkable philosophy.

1

The inner light

We begin our examination of Conway's philosophy with a consideration of its epistemological underpinnings. Throughout the *Principia*, Conway makes a number of claims about the nature of God, Christ, the world and the soul. However, the question of just how Conway knows these things is one left largely unanswered in the text. Much of what she claims could, perhaps, be reasonably deduced from the statement concerning God's nature that begins the book, but that still leaves the question of what justifies this starting point from an epistemological perspective. In order to answer this question, we need to look at Conway's intellectual context: in particular, we will examine the account of divine illumination suggested by her philosophical mentor, Henry More, as well as the doctrine of 'inner light' that was prevalent in the religious sect that she identified herself with during the period of the writing of the *Principia*, namely, the Quakers (known officially as the Religious Society of Friends).

I will argue that it is likely that More's Platonic-inspired view that one could receive insight into God and the soul through divine illumination paves the way for a later acceptance of something like the Quaker notion of the inner light. In addition, on this basis, I will seek to explain why Conway might not have discussed epistemological matters in the notes that came to be the *Principia*. We will also see that it is likely that the doctrine of the inner light, due to its egalitarian implications, played a major role in provoking Conway's interest in Quakerism. As such, this chapter will help to clarify the impact of More's philosophy upon the metaphysical system found in the *Principia*, as well as giving some insight into why Conway may have been drawn to the Quakers in her later life. We will also start exploring some of the controversies surrounding the early Quaker community, including their perceived threat to the political powers of the time, including the Church, and the way in which this shaped the intellectual response to early Quaker theology, particularly with regard to their doctrine of the inner light. Some of the implications of this implicit epistemology for our understanding of other important aspects of her philosophy, particularly her Christology and theory of salvation, will be explored later in Chapter 4.

God, the 'inner light' and the Quakers

The *Principia* begins with a simple statement about the nature of God: 'God is spirit, light, and life, infinitely wise, good, just, strong, all-knowing, all-present, all-powerful, the creator and maker of all things visible and invisible' (1.1; 9). This list of divine attributes is pretty unremarkable in one sense, as these are attributes that all theists would agree to. However, there is some oddity about this list, particularly regarding the prominent position of 'spirit, light, and life', but we will leave this to one side until the next chapter. The list is also remarkable because it is the founding statement of Conway's philosophy: many of the philosophical and theological claims to come will be established on the basis of this list of divine attributes. We will see many arguments of the form 'God has *x* attribute, so *y* must be true', be it establishing conclusions about God or the universe he created.

However, before we start exploring the outlines of Conway's metaphysical system, we may wonder just how Conway thinks she knows all these things about God. There are no arguments offered for God's existence or for attributing these attributes to God. Conway simply assumes that God exists and has all these attributes, and the rest of her philosophy follows from this. Though Conway never explicitly tells us how we are supposed to know such things about God, there are hints that we can perhaps pick up on in the *Principia* as to what epistemological assumptions are being made here. We can also look to Conway's intellectual context for some clues: if we know that Conway was influenced by certain figures and traditions, and perhaps even influenced them in turn, then exploring the religious epistemologies of these thinkers may help us to detect the underlying assumptions here.

As we saw in the previous chapter, the *Principia* was written at a time in Conway's life that followed a fundamental change in her religious viewpoint. From brief remarks in her will and correspondence, it seems that Conway believes that, through the intercession of God and her experience of suffering, she is able to come to a deeper religious understanding beyond the doctrinal confines of the established Church. As we saw earlier, Henry More cryptically refers to the fruits of Conway's religious reflection as 'Supernatural Comforts and Refreshments' and 'strange Pre-visions of things future' (Ward 2000: 126).

We find a truly radical religious philosophy in the *Principia* and given the dating of the text, it seems likely that the arguments and ideas contained within are at least partly inspired by Conway's deeply felt religious experiences, inspired by the emphasis on immediate experience found in the religious community that she now identified with, namely, Quakerism.

We will be helped, then, by investigating the religious epistemology of the early Quakers. As noted previously, the *Principia* (or at least the notes that were edited to form this text) was almost certainly written in the late 1670s, by which time Conway had seemingly become part of this radical religious sect.[1] We know that Conway discussed issues related to religious epistemology with leading Quakers around this time. In a letter to Conway from William Penn dated 17 February 1675, we find an outlining of some of the key claims that Quakers were making with regard to knowledge of the divine: 'My friend, we preach not our selves, but the light of Christ in the conscience, which is gods faithful and true witness… So dear friend, that thou mayst retire thy mind to that tender spirit of truth which god hath sent into our hearts to convince us of sin, of righteousness, of judgement' (L 402).

In the same letter, Penn speaks of this divine 'inspiration' as 'the true foundation of all right knowledge, hope, faith' (L 402). Penn is writing here of the Quaker doctrine of the 'inner light' as a source of divine revelation, thus a foundation of reliable, even infallible, knowledge about God, the soul and the world around you.

It is important to note at this point that it is very difficult to talk about the theological commitments of the early Quakers with any degree of exactitude. Given the disparate nature of the Quaker community at the time, the fact that there is no founding text that all Quakers looked to for their doctrinal commitments, that very few Quakers published any theological texts and that those that did write such works often made contradictory claims, we are left in a difficult position in determining any definite 'early Quaker theology', and this includes the doctrine of the inner light that I discuss here. In addition, as a community under attack from a powerful religious establishment, much of the Quaker writing of this period is defensive in tone, emphasizing that they do not deny certain key aspects of Christian thought, rather than explaining more positively precisely where they may in fact diverge from strict Anglican orthodoxy.[2]

However, there are broad theological strokes across Quakerism that we can trace from this period, and we can focus on the theologies of those figures (such as William Penn and George Keith) that we know Conway had contact with around the time of the writing of the *Principia*, particularly relating to the notion of the 'inner light'. The underlying theological commitments for the 'inner light' were not settled, and often, for example, involved different persons of the Trinity. Fouke notes this confusion, situating it in the practical context of a desire to promote a confrontational crisis of faith in professed believers, at the expense of the need to formulate a clear, consistent theology: 'The early Quakers were less interested in formulating a clear theology than in bringing individuals to a moral and religious crisis. Seldom careful to develop their thought with an eye towards Trinitarian distinctions or a clear Christology, the "Inner Light" was various described as the Christ within every person, an impersonal force, the Holy Spirit, or the Father' (1997: 136). However, despite the theological confusion, the general features of the inner light were largely uncontested, based around the claim that there is an aspect of each individual that can participate in the divine, and such participation can bring insight not only into the nature of God, but also into the moral health of the individual and wider society.

The notion of the inner light places emphasis upon the impact of potential self-knowledge that can be garnered by an individual, apart from the teachings of the Church. With the help of the divine, we are able to see our depravity in much greater focus than we have before, and the shock of such knowledge is able to bring about a radical transformation towards true piety on the part of the individual. We are brought to a moment of crisis, in which we feel despair at the depth of our sinful depravity, the prospect of God's judgement upon us and hope for a purified individual and society. In the Quaker literature of the time, the experience of the inner light is described as bringing a realization that first provokes great terror and despair at the state of our sinful nature, followed by a positive transformation into a purified individual at one with God and Christ.

These two stages are clearly outlined in an autobiographical text by Francis Howgill (1618–69), one of the earliest prominent Quakers. Of the first stage, he writes,

> I was ignorant what the first principle of true religion was: but as I turned my mind within to the light of Jesus Christ wherewith I was enlightened ... I saw it was the true and faithful witness of Christ Jesus, and then my eyes was opened, and all things was brought to remembrance that ever I had done ... [The] dreadful power of the Lord fell upon me, plague and pestilence, and famine, and earthquake, and fear, and terror, for the sights that I saw with my eyes ... I would have run away to have hid my fear, but nothing but weeping and gnashing of teeth, and sorrow, and terror, and I roared out for the disquietness of my heart.
> (1656: 11f.)

The reference to 'weeping and gnashing of teeth' is an allusion to the eschatological explanation given for the parable of the sower in Matthew 13. In this passage, Jesus describes the fate of those who have fallen into sin: 'The Son of Man shall send forth his angels, and they shall gather out of his kingdom all things that offend, and them which do iniquity; And shall cast them into a furnace of fire: there shall be wailing and gnashing of teeth' (Matthew 13: 41–2).[3] Howgill's reference here to a key eschatological Gospel passage illustrates the devastating significance of the transformation that takes place when the inner light is recognized within the individual and reflects the understanding that the Quaker community had at the time of their own world-changing significance, as bringing the Kingdom of God to earth.

After this deep despair and terror at the recognition of the depths of his sinful nature, Howgill then goes on to describe the feelings he then experienced in the acceptance of the divine judgement upon him, and the concomitant realization of the possibility of his radical purification and transformation:

> In all that I ever did, I saw that it was in the accursed nature, and then something in me cried, *Just and true is his judgement*, my mouth was stopped, something rejoiced… and as I did give up all to the Judgement, the captive came forth out of prison and rejoiced, and my heart was filled with joy… and the new man was made.
>
> (1656: 12f.)

In texts such as these, early Quakers attempted to describe their own apparent experiences of the inner light, involving both knowledge of God and the sinful nature of the individual, as well as a deep transformation of one's character. It is likely that Conway will have gone through similar experiences as she joined the Quaker community.

Tensions with the church and women writers

The notion of the inner light soon brought the early Quaker community into conflict with the established Church. What was particularly worrying for the religious establishment of the time was the claim that the inner light brought reliable insight into the divine to the individual, apart from the teachings of the Church and the reading of scripture. The Quakers departed from a general Protestant emphasis on the Bible as having primary doctrinal authority, with the claim that scripture has to be approached within the more fundamental and significant perspective of the inner light. The Quaker historian Adrian Davies explains that, in the view of the Quakers of the time,

> The indwelling light displaced the Bible as the cornerstone of the Christian faith... The Friends did not dismiss the Bible as the source of authority; but they held that it possessed no superior authority which limited the inspiration of the indwelling light. They were convinced that the Spirit which guided them was the same as that which inspired those who wrote the original scriptures.
>
> (2000: 17)

For the Quakers, the inner light held the doctrinal veto over the teachings of the Bible, whilst the Church would assert that apparent individual revelation should be measured against the yardstick of scripture and rejected if it departed too far from the revelation encapsulated in Biblical teachings.

As far as the Church was concerned, any notion that someone could come to theological knowledge without any guidance from the clergy or from scripture was very dangerous, leading to superstitious practices, religious enthusiasm and the promulgation of heretical doctrines. If everyone could potentially come to religious truth without the aid of officially endorsed theological education and the guidance of clergy, then the necessity of even having an organized church (and certainly one with a strict hierarchy) would be greatly undermined. There was also something worrying, for the authorities, about the inherent egalitarianism of the doctrine: in principle, all individuals, regardless of class, background and gender, could receive the fruits of the inner light. Such a doctrine, surely, could only serve to dissolve the carefully constructed social structures that held society together and stopped matters from degenerating into chaos and anarchy. However, for someone who had second-class status at the time (including even a woman with such a high social position as Anne Conway), the inner light opened up their opportunities to engage in religious reflection, apart from the overbearing and constraining ecclesiastical authorities, who wished to hold to a strict set of doctrines and a formal liturgy.

Whilst the status of some women in England at the time was improving in some aspects, their role in organized religion was minimal: as Lloyd notes, in his study of early Quaker social history, 'However intelligent and capable women might be in business, they were in church affairs "that simple and weak sex." They had no share at all in the government of the church, they might not even meet together for prayer. "If she worships in assemblies," wrote Bunyan, "her part is to hold her tongue, to learn in silence'" (1950: 107). The egalitarian implications of the inner light were not fully reflected in the Quaker community of the time, but nevertheless they paved the way for the women of that community to play a more active role[4] and express their own religious experiences and insights. The Quaker historian Christine Trevett explains that

> [from] its inception Quakerism offered to women occasions of greater autonomy. Its teachings offered a rationale for what some women had known instinctively but had never acted upon and for some, Quakerism, itself born in a time of social and religious upheaval, allowed them to break through the bonds of 'femininity' so that by adopting the biblical (primarily male) prophetic role, they might transcend the very, womanly, self.
>
> (1991: 41)

The Quakers claimed Biblical authority for their opening up of the religious hierarchy in this way, pointing to the Letter to the Galatians, in which Paul paints an unmistakable picture of an egalitarian religious community:

> But after that faith is come, we are no longer under a schoolmaster. For ye are all the children of God by faith in Christ Jesus. For as many of you as have been baptised into Christ have put on Christ. There is neither Jew nor Greek, there is neither bond nor free, there is neither male nor female: for ye are all one in Christ Jesus.
>
> (Galatians 3: 25–8)

Women have the same need as men to respond to the inner light, and such an opening was grasped by Conway and other women Quaker writers of the period as an opportunity to express what they saw as their own religious insights (though it is not always clear just how much autonomy they claimed for themselves in this process, for it is possible to see oneself as merely a passive vehicle for the revelation of the inner light[5]).

The egalitarian assumptions underlying the doctrine of the inner light had a decisive impact upon the literary life of the early Quaker community, particularly with regard to the contributions of women writers. Women Quakers were able to write much more broadly and with an entirely different tone than many other women authors of the time were able to, due to the recognized authority of the inner light acting with them. In a study of early Quaker literature, Catie Gill notes,

> Female Quakers wrote and spoke from a position of connection to the godhead, and their sense of revelation was due, in large part, to the community's method of writing about the spirit's immediacy within the believer, whether they be male or female. Women could write forcibly and confidently of their personal understanding of the godhead, achieving a vigorous prose style that was rarely other than assertive.
>
> (2005: 123)

Women writers felt driven to share their experience of the inner light within them with others, and the theological underpinnings of the inner light being available equally to all in the community gave what they had to say a legitimacy that was rarely afforded to women at that time. Of course, Conway's *Principia* is quite different from much Quaker literature of the period, which tended to be less concerned with strictly theological and philosophical matters; rather, the emphasis was on conversion narratives and the experience of the workings of the inner light.

However, it is worth remembering that the *Principia* is edited from notebooks that were presumably not intended for widespread public consumption and certainly were not written to proselytize for the Quaker community, unlike the work of most other Quaker writers. These notes were probably written for Conway's own benefit, to set out her own ideas clearly to herself, as well as for discussion with close friends, such as More and van Helmont and the leading Quakers who regularly visited Ragley Hall. Nevertheless, the point remains that the doctrine of the inner light bestowed a powerful social legitimacy on the ideas and writings of women amongst the Quaker community, and it is likely that this realization had an impact upon Conway herself, perhaps partly playing a role in enticing her into the community in the first place. We have no evidence of other theological or philosophical writings by Conway (apart from scraps in her correspondence), and so it is also an open question whether it was the openness for, and example of, women writers in the Quaker community that drew her to start making these notes (even though, as we have noted, they do not concern the usual topics of Quaker literature). It is certainly striking that after so many years of philosophical study, Conway should decide at the time of joining the Quaker community to note these ideas down on paper.

The Quakers, apocalypticism and revelation

Another common topic amongst women writers of the time from different radical Protestant sects, in addition to their own religious experiences and the workings of the inner light, was apocalyptic matters related to the end of the world. Those who made prophetic claims were viewed with great suspicion by the religious establishment and wider society, especially if they were a woman. Partly fuelling the antipathy towards women prophets was the fact that there are a number of 'false' women prophets excoriated in the Bible, including in the apocalyptic Book of Revelation: 'I have a few things against thee, because thou sufferest that woman Jezebel, who calleth herself a prophetess, to teach and to seduce my servants' (Revelation 2:20). The attitude of the Church was that they had been given fair warning in scripture about the dangers posed by women prophets, who should be met with suspicion and resisted.

Trevett explains that women were thought to be particularly liable to false and dangerous prophecy due to their 'weak' nature: in the seventeenth century, '[it] is the prevailing view that where there is heresy there too will be women.... Women, so runs the prevailing wisdom, are easily disposed to error and are prey for seducers, as was their foremother Eve; they are vulnerable because of their lustful natures and drawn to offers of power and knowledge which are not rightfully theirs' (1991: 3). However, despite such social pressure, publications by religious women writers multiplied, including those dealing with matters of prophecy, and the Quaker community, once firmly established in the 1650s, continued this tradition amongst the Protestant sects in England of the time. The tumult of the Civil War, the Interregnum and the Restoration gave rise to a more liberal atmosphere for religious writers and those women in the Quaker community who felt compelled to share their experiences and prophecies with others did so.

The legitimacy of women's prophesying was affirmed from the very beginnings of Quakerism and by some of the most important figures in its founding. Such authority was often conferred on the basis that the women involved were mere vessels for God or Christ speaking through them, and so they were not seen, at least by some, as autonomous, active writers of their own experiences and knowledge (see Gill 2005: 133). This view is echoed, for example, by the Quaker prophet Dorothy White (c. 1630–86), who claims an ultimately subordinate role in prophecy to the will of God: 'the Lord hath spoken, and therefore I will speak, for God hath unloosed my tongue, to speak to the promise of his name' (White 1661: 2). Nevertheless, the opening was still there in an unprecedented way for religious women writers to express their faith, even if they had to accommodate themselves in some ways to the norms of the time.[6]

Looking to the *Principia*, we do not see any prophesying with regard to events of the time (along the lines of 'Person X is the Antichrist' or 'Event Y is a sign of the end-times'), but nevertheless Conway does address eschatological matters, if somewhat indirectly. As we shall see, Conway's philosophy has far-reaching eschatological implications, regarding the possibility of salvation, divine judgement and the end of the world, that sets her at odds with the official theology of the Anglican Church. Though there are, undeniably, great differences between the *Principia* and Quaker prophetic works of the time, there is a shared sense of legitimacy and authority amongst women writers that led to a willingness to fundamentally challenge the religious establishment and this is exemplified in pronouncements upon eschatological matters, a topic that male writers had largely reserved for themselves for centuries.

The doctrine of the 'inner light' further undermined the Church by emphasizing the significance and power of revelation immediately available to each individual, even in the modern period, so far after the events described in scripture. Part of the Church's status was linked to its self-appointed role as the safeguard of the special revelation granted to the Jewish community in Biblical times and then the early Christian Church. Church authorities pointed to Matthew 16:18–19 as testimony of the moment in which Jesus had established the Church, nominating the disciple Peter as both the head of the Church and the vehicle by which the Gospel message would be passed on through history:

> And I say also unto thee, That thou art Peter, and upon this rock I will build my church; and the gates of hell shall not prevail against it. And I will give unto thee the keys of the kingdom of heaven: and whatsoever thou shalt bind on earth shall be bound in heaven: and whatsoever thou shalt loose on earth shall be loosed in heaven.

There was general agreement within the Church that the kind of revelation made accessible to the Jewish community at the time of the Hebrew Bible, and that which the early Christian community received, was no longer available, leaving the Church to maintain and promote the Gospel message, whilst rejecting any new claims to special revelation from unapproved exterior sources.

The Quakers undermined the Church's role in this regard by arguing that the revelation of the past is just as accessible and significant now as it was back then and is available to everyone. The Church was no longer held to be a unique receptacle of the special revelation of the past, and the religious authorities knew that this was a serious attack on their status. Due to this, the nascent Quaker community was widely attacked both in print and through the legal system, with many Quakers being imprisoned for long periods of time. The Quakers also came under attack by the state, as those who had power understood the function of the established Church in maintaining an ideology that kept those in the lower classes in their place: those who had little were persuaded to accept their lot in life, with their struggles painted as a God-given opportunity to fulfil their ordained role in the world and to work towards their salvation in Christ. The growing popularity of the Quakers was seen as potentially fermenting political instability, with chaos and anarchy the potential consequence. The destabilizing effect of the Quakers was realized in behaviour that explicitly undermined the social hierarchy, such as using the more informal 'thee' when addressing social superiors, rather than the more proper 'you', as well as refusing to show any other signs of deference, such as bowing (see Reay 1985: 58). As such, both the Church and those who had political power had great interest in attacking and undermining the Quaker community, including the use of philosophical and theological attacks on the doctrine of the inner light.

More, Neoplatonism and knowledge

Given how they were viewed by the religious and political establishment of the time, it was highly controversial for Anne Conway to start associating with the Quaker community: inviting them into her home, discussing philosophy and religion with prominent Quakers and taking others as her servants.[7] However, if we consider Conway's philosophical education through her correspondence with the Cambridge Platonist, Henry More, it is perhaps not all that surprising that she was later drawn to Quaker notions concerning the inner light (even if More himself, as we shall see, was very suspicious of the Quakers), partly because it certainly has Neoplatonic elements to it. As Fouke explains, the notion of the inner light

> draws upon the metaphysics of light which was central to Neoplatonism as a model of causal relations. The Quakers were not Neoplatonists in any robust sense of the word… They did however use the language of participation which (as it depicts lower realities as completed, perfected, and filled by higher realities of which they are images) was well-suited for expressing divine immanence.
> (1997: 134)

Participation, as generally understood by the Neoplatonists, is intended to note the manner in which higher realities have presence within lower ones, without thereby taking on a lower form of being. As images of higher levels of being, we are able to participate, in an imperfect manner, in these higher levels to some extent, as the higher things of which we are an image are present in us.

So, for example, something which is beautiful can be said to participate in the perfect Form of Beauty, and the Form is thereby imperfectly present in its image, namely, that object.

Participation, then, gives us a model by which we can understand how a divine being could be present in an imperfect, created universe: as we are beings created in the image of God (as maintained within the Christian tradition), it can be held that, in some sense, we can participate in the divine and God can be present within us. The imagery of light is often used here as human beings are seen as an imperfect reflection of the perfect light that emanates from God. The model also safeguards against having to say that these divine beings are brought into the imperfect, created universe in a manner which undermines their perfection, for all that is within the world is a mere reflection of them. We can think of it along the lines of a mirror that gives an imperfect reflection: when we stand facing this mirror, we are not affected in ourselves; rather, it is merely our reflection that becomes distorted. In the same way, the perfection of divine beings is not affected by participation in the imperfect created world.

In his early Platonic poem *Psychozoia*, More himself offers a narrative of the journey of a soul through a process much like that described by the Quakers of an individual being confronted with the inner light. More sees his early philosophical works as an attempt to describe his own spiritual journey and the insights he has gained along the way, and he found a Platonic model (most closely following the Neoplatonist Plotinus) the best way of expressing his religious experiences in a philosophical manner, whilst holding to his fundamental Christian faith. Later on in his life, More claims that he wrote *Psychozoia* 'by some *Heavenly Impulse* of *Mind*; since I did it at that time with no other Design, than that it should remain by me a private Record of the Sensations and Experiences of my own Soul' (Ward 2000: 21). The emphasis in these early poems is just as much on describing More's own personal religious experiences as following a more familiar model of philosophy for us today: in fact, direct experience ultimately trumps philosophical argumentation on this view, though this is not to say that arguments are dispensed with entirely. Robert Crocker captures the spirit of these early poems well when he describes them as 'a profoundly religious document, a "confession" in verse, describing in sometimes obscure allegorical detail a quite unique illuminist revelation' (2003: 17). As such, the poems should not be approached straightforwardly as philosophical texts, in that they are a complex mixture of philosophical and religious concerns, including elements of contemplative and devotional literature that attempt to reflect the deep religious experiences of the author in a manner communicable to a reader who themselves have not had such an experience (but will ideally be exhorted to pursue such practices that would prepare them to have such experiences).

David Leech notes that, at this early point in More's works, his conception of philosophy follows the ancient model of involving both praxis and theory:

> More imbued the ancient conception of philosophy as spiritual practice which was conspicuously absent in the late scholastic literature he had grown disenchanted with as an undergraduate… In Plotinus he encountered a model of philosophy as a cultivable form of life, involving purification and a general disciplining of the self, culminating in a knowledge by acquaintance of the soul's immortality of God as infinite spirit.
>
> (2013: 41)

In his reading of the Neoplatonists, More discovered a way of doing philosophy that spoke to his desire to immerse himself in philosophical and religious contemplation, more along the lines of an ancient mystic than a modern philosopher. Such an approach might include, for example, withdrawal from everyday interactions and complete focus on the life of the mind. This model of doing philosophy would be widely shared by the Cambridge Platonists, who followed the ancient model of philosophy as involving praxis, in particular cultivating virtue largely through practices of self-denial[8] and gaining fundamental religious and philosophical insights. Conway herself, who suffered so much in her life, seems to have believed that her experience of pain and ill-health, including the isolation this brought, had given her metaphysical insights into the nature of things.

From More's early philosophical perspective, then, philosophy is ultimately used for religious ends, leading to a kind of 'second birth' or salvation, in which the believer has achieved something of the deification that is open to them as images of God. As Charles Taliaferro explains, the Cambridge Platonists generally see the quest of knowledge for God as a kind of internal inquiry, involving becoming more like God themselves:

> In what may be called external inquiry, one need not have or seek to exemplify the property of the thing looked for: you do not have to be watery or even thirsty to seek water… But if you are inquiring into the nature of love, justice, goodness, and the like, it will not help if you are spiteful, unjust, and bent on ill will.
>
> (2005: 43)

By becoming, say, more wise, we become more acquainted with wisdom and thereby gain greater insight into it, and in the same way, by becoming purified and more like God, we gain knowledge by acquaintance of God. Greater perfection and greater knowledge thereby develop together. We can also think about this by returning to Platonic notions regarding participation: by making ourselves more like God, we increase our participation in him, in the sense that we become more like the images of God that we were created to be, and this brings great epistemic benefits, such as greater insight into God and the nature of the soul.

More's early philosophical approach therefore bears striking resemblance to later Quaker theory and practice that we explored previously. Quaker writings of the time often focus on the description of personal religious experiences and emphasize the need to undergo a transformation in character in order to achieve insight into God. The goal of such literature was to persuade the reader to engage in such a journey of development themselves and this is something that More also attempts to achieve with his Platonic poems. The idealized reader of these works is not simply a passive recipient of ideas; rather, they are exhorted to actively respond to these accounts of religious experiences and to engage with the same practices so that they can also achieve a strengthening union with, and insight into, God.

The notion of a difficult, even painful journey as one becomes closer to God is also shared with More's early works. In the narrative of *Psychozoia*, the soul begins mired in sinfulness, allowing its animal nature to dominate the will and then undergoes a painful struggle with itself, resulting in divine illumination and deification. As Crocker notes, the individual undergoing this process of deification feels a painful conflict between their spiritual and material aspects: '[The] immediate aim of More's allegory is to convince the reader of the importance of recognizing the powers characterizing the material and the spiritual realms, and their respective sympathetic influences over the soul. Thus a primary spiritual and moral choice confronts the embodied soul, a choice of identification with its spiritual or material nature' (1997: 133). Nevertheless, despite the difficulty involved in this process, More follows the Platonic claim that the soul holds memories of previous existences and thus has a sense that it has a higher calling than simply being bound to an imperfect, material body: the soul is ineluctably drawn back towards the divine, though backsliding towards greater embodiment is always possible.[9]

The use of inner epistemological resources with regard to accessing fundamental religious truths is a topic raised by Henry More in an early letter to Conway from 1652. We find More discussing a passage from 1 Corinthians 3, which Conway had evidently been enquiring as to the proper interpretation.[10] The passage is as follows:

> According to the grace of God which is given unto me, as a wise masterbuilder, I have laid the foundation, and another buildeth thereon. But let every man take heed how he buildeth thereupon. For other foundation can no man lay than that is laid, which is Jesus Christ. Now if any man build upon this foundation gold, silver, precious stones, wood, hay, stubble; Every man's work shall be made manifest: for the day shall declare it, because it shall be revealed by fire; and the fire shall try every man's work of what sort it is. If any man's work abide which he hath built thereupon, he shall receive a reward. If any man's work shall be burned, he shall suffer loss: but he himself shall be saved; yet so as by fire.
>
> (1 Cor 3: 10–15)

More emphasizes that the passage should be read as an extended metaphor concerning the manner in which the core Gospel message has been added to in the history of the early Christian church, as far as the writer, St Paul, sees it. More interprets the wood, hay and stubble as referring to 'any unwarrantable opinions and concernings that men would in a self-humouring way of religion and in them of greater holiness, or for an escape from the more indispensable points of holiness [religion[11]] add to the plain and sincere fundamentals of Christianity' (L 68). There are combustible elements included in the list of materials, More argues, because these can be removed by fire, which can be interpreted in two ways: (1) the 'unwarrantable opinions' can be removed, but only in a potentially hazardous way or (2) the 'unwarrantable opinions' can only be removed by the Holy Spirit (as the Holy Spirit is often symbolized as fire in scripture). It is clearly the latter interpretive option that More prefers, leading him to a description of the epistemological role played by the Holy Spirit: 'While it burns in our hearts with a sincere affection after the simplicity of the life of Christ, and unsophisicate truth of the Gospel, will purge away and burn up in us, all assumptitious follies, whether in opinion or precept. Whether they be of our inventing or others' (L 68).

More certainly believes that divine activity plays an inner role in maintaining religious truth and focusing the individual on the salvific core of the Gospel message, and so this is an idea that Conway is certainly aware of early on in her philosophical reflections. However, More emphasizes that this does not necessarily lead to the kind of egalitarian religious epistemology later propounded by the Quakers and others, insofar as the Holy Spirit 'does most naturally and properly respect those that are teachers and doctors in the Church' (L 68), and so ecclesiastical authority on doctrinal matters should still be respected, even though the inner activity of the Holy Spirit (including removing those ideas that detract from the core Gospel message) takes place in all.

More's epistemology also has sceptical elements that could help prepare the way for an acceptance of Quakerism. He holds that most potential sources of knowledge do not give us certainty: for example, our senses sometimes deceive us, and even the teachings of the Bible should be checked for error against the dictates of our reason, despite the inspiration underlying the Biblical authors. It would be wrong to claim, though, that More is a sceptic per se. He is neither a global sceptic (denying all knowledge) nor is he a sceptic about specific types of knowledge; rather, he speaks of scepticism as 'a thing rather to be pitied or laughed at, than seriously opposed' (1659: 5). Nevertheless, he is a sceptic insofar as he holds that *certainty* in our beliefs is only available from one source, namely, through the intervention of the Holy Spirit. Crocker writes that, for Henry More, 'truth in religion, and truth generally, could never be communicated to others with any exclusive or absolute certainty, but depended for its recognition upon the Holy Spirit, which was experienced as an "inner sense" by the believer' (2003: 37). Given the need to measure our beliefs against this participation of the Holy Spirit in our souls, other sources of epistemic authority should be approached with caution and appropriate suspicion. Significantly, such scepticism extends to the Church and scripture as two potential sources of religious truths.

Even with regard to such a central religious commitment as the immortality of the soul, More recommends a healthy scepticism regarding such teaching, as long as one has not attained a clear inner sense:

> Seeing our most palpable evidence of the soul's immortality is from an inward sense, and this inward sense is kept alive the best by devotion and purity, by freedom from worldly care and sorrow, and the grosser pleasures of the body… [Therefore] it is better for us that we become doubtful of our immortal condition when we stray from that virgin-purity and unspottedness.
>
> (1647: Preface to the Second Edition, B4)

Here we see an implicit threat to the doctrinal authority of the Church that would be echoed, just a few years later, in the Quaker community. For one thing, More is arguing that one cannot be sure of the immortality of the soul on the basis of the teachings of the Church alone, which is something that many in the clergy would reject; regardless of your inner condition, they would say, you can and should accept the Church's teaching in this matter.

Further to this, More holds that the remedy for appropriate scepticism towards the teachings of the Church is to engage in practices that improve one's inner character, so that the individual can then strengthen the inner sense within them and gain certainty with regard to some religious truths such as the immortality of the soul. We thus have an account of the possibility of attaining religious truths with certainty that relies entirely on the individual alone, apart from any epistemic authority or even supervision from the Church. In its broad strokes, then, More's religious epistemology (and related claims concerning praxis) lies very close indeed to that of the early Quaker community: there is a shared sense of the unreliability of the teachings of the Church, and an emphasis on the inner light and what the individual can and should do by themselves to come to religious insights. When considered from this perspective, it may then seem unsurprising that a philosopher mentored by Henry More for such a long period of time may find the teachings and practice of the Quaker community of great interest, and perhaps even worthy of adoption.

More, Conway and the Quakers

More's early philosophy, then, includes an account of religious illumination, an epistemological spark within each individual that grants insight into the nature of the soul and of God. However, as we shall see, More often criticizes claims to subjective revelation by others, such as those made by religious sects like the Quakers. We may wonder, then, why More thinks that he can legitimately criticize others who claim a subjective source of revelation, when he seems to posit his own.

More is aware of such a potential criticism and even allows that there are (at least surface) similarities between his views and those who claim the benefits of the inner light, such as the Quakers:

> There are those great *Spiritualists* that talk so much of *The Light within them*, and *the power within them*; and boast that they want nothing without to be their Guide and Support, but that they can go of themselves without any external help. For keeping to *the Light within them*, the Power of God and the Spirit of God will assist them, and will lead them to all truth. And truly I cannot but say Amen to what they declare.
>
> (1660: 408)

More makes it clear that he is happy to follow the Quakers with regard to the inner light, insofar as they claim that God has granted them a subjective capacity with which the Holy Spirit guides them to insights about God and the soul.

However, he seems to struggle to provide any kind of standard by which we can easily judge whether any purported divine illumination is legitimate or whether it is the result of the false enthusiasm of the Quakers and other sects, other than to say that their claims do not 'keep to *Reason*[12] and *Conscience*', but are rather the results of a *'reprobate sense* ... [that exposes] a man's self to all the temptations that either the Devil or a man's own Lust or a sordid Melancholy can entangle him in' (1660: 408).[13] More claims that illumination must be understood as the workings of a human capacity rather than as the direct participation of the divine, arguing that claims of the latter are a matter of 'false enthusiasm'. It is not clear how we are supposed to tell whether a purported illumination arises from 'reason and conscience', rather than a 'reprobate sense', other than by seeing those who have fallen into error being led astray from Christian orthodoxy, and by identifying claims of the direct participation of the divine, apart from any usual human capacities.

As an example, More sees those religious sects who wish to subjectivize and allegorize the story of Christ, rather than affirm the literal truth of the Gospel message, as having fallen under the spell of false enthusiasm:

> I hold it well worth our observation, how giddy and injudicious those persons are that are so mightily taken with the *Mystical* sense of such parts of the *History* of Christ as are most profitable in the belief of the *mere Letter*: such as his *Passion, Resurrection, Ascension*, his *Session at the right hand of God*, and *his coming again to Judgement*... For making this a mere Representation of something to be performed within us... such *Allusions*, I say, and *Similitudes* as there have no more force nor efficacy to urge us, or to help us on to those Accomplishments they represent, then if the *History* of Christ were a mere Fable.
>
> (1660: 252)

More argues that it can only be a false illumination that leads some to denigrate the literal truths concerning Christ, as it is only true faith that involves belief in the life and resurrection of the historical figure of Christ. False illumination leads one to a position where it does not really matter anymore whether there was an historical Christ or not, as all of the significant work with regard to knowledge of God and the purification of the individual is left to the subjective workings of the inner light alone. There is no straightforward standard of true illumination versus false enthusiasm here; rather, More points to a sign of the latter, namely, a departure from Christian orthodoxy or, at least, undermining the importance of the Gospel message to the extent that one can no longer legitimately claim (in his eyes) to be a Christian.

In his Preface to *An Antidote against Atheism*, More argues that features of false enthusiasm are shared with atheism and that false enthusiasm can be identified by its relative inconstancy, in comparison with a true faith built more securely upon a proper foundation: 'For as dreams are the fancies of those that sleep, so fancies are but the dreams of men awake. And their fancies by day, as those by night, will vary and change with the weather and present Temper of the body' (1653: Preface, A). More wishes to strike a contrast between the waxing and waning of false enthusiasm, and a true enthusiasm that is more stable over a longer period of time. From observation of the characteristics of the behaviour of those who are false enthusiasts, it is clear that their faith is based on mere imagination (which creates unstable and inconstant dreams or fancies) and emotion. True enthusiasm will not necessarily be accompanied by such emotional peaks and troughs, instead looking more like the sustained periods of quiet contemplation practised by More himself. Further to this, More argues that the clearly irrational and emotional basis of false enthusiasm leads others to reject faith altogether: 'the Enthusiast's boldly dictating the careless ravings of his own tumultuous fancy for undeniable principles of divine knowledge, confirms the *Atheist's* [view] that the whole business of religion and [a] notion of a God, is nothing but a troublesome fit of overcurious *Melancholy*' (1653: Preface, A2).

In this way, false enthusiasm not only leads people astray from Christian orthodoxy, but can ultimately lead them to atheism, as they turn away from the emotional and irrational spectacle of false enthusiasm in practice.

More's scepticism with regard to the Quaker inner light seems also to have been heightened by the sheer number of transformative experiences claimed within the community during that period: in a letter to Conway from 1670, he claims that a 'motion from the Lord' is 'very cheap amongst them' (L 306). For More, so many claims of divine illumination amongst the community were an unmistakable sign of an irrational, superstitious fervour that had no basis in genuine divine illumination. In contrast to Quaker claims, the process of gaining divine illumination is a long and arduous one, and few are genuinely successful in this task. In an autobiographical note, More speaks of his own difficult quest for divine illumination as a young man for a number of years, in which he immersed himself in Platonic and mystical literature, strove to lose the desire for knowledge for its own sake, and felt a conflict between the animal and the divine within him: he writes, 'I aspir'd after nothing but this sole *Purity* and *Simplicity* of *Mind*, [and] there shone upon me daily a greater *Assurance* than ever I could have expected... Insomuch that within a few Years, I was got into a most *Joyous* and *Lucid* State of *Mind*' (Ward 2000: 20), which led to his description of the journey of the soul towards deification in his *Platonic Poems*. More's biographer, Richard Ward, speaks of this period as a 'time of *Holy Discipline* and *Conflict*, [which] let him in, it seems, wonderful *Communications*; and open'd, as it were, the Gates of *Paradise* to Him' (Ward 2000: 21). The apparent ease with which the Quaker community attained illumination by the inner light simply did not cohere with More's own experience of a difficult, arduous path towards illumination in his youth.

We will return to the conflict between the religious establishment and the Quakers over the question of the historical Christ later (in Chapter 4). What we can note here is that it would be entirely unsurprising, given More's theory of divine illumination and his apparent inability to give a straightforward standard by which we can determine between true and false illumination, if Conway came across the discussion of the inner light amongst Quakers and found it amenable to her way of thinking. More's early philosophy, which continues to have a great intellectual influence upon her, as can be seen at various points throughout the *Principia*, has ideas concerning religious illumination and practice that are remarkably similar to those found in the theology of the Quaker community of the time. Thus, it is likely that her early tutelage with Henry More played a major role in paving the way for her later adoption of Quakerism.

Further to this, Conway is much less concerned than More is with keeping to the strict orthodoxy of the Anglican Church in England at the time, and so any apparent departure from this orthodoxy on the part of the Quakers, brought about by their belief in the inner light, would be unlikely to stop her from giving serious consideration to their views: she certainly would not use the criterion More proposes between true and false illumination, linked to the orthodoxy of the claims coming from them, to assess the veracity of what the Quakers were claiming. Given her desire to be known as a Quaker in the last few years of her life, it would be very strange if the key doctrinal claims made by this community, all concerning the inner light, did not play at least an implicit role in how she understands her philosophizing, particularly the epistemological underpinnings of her system.[14]

So, how do we know that 'God is spirit, light, and life, infinitely wise, good, just, strong, all-knowing, all-present, all-powerful, the creator and maker of all things visible and invisible' (1.1; 9)? We know about the divine attributes through the kind of illumination postulated by More, as a Christian Platonist, and by the Quaker community. We can also come to understand why Conway does not explain this to us in the *Principia*, in that her self-identification as a Quaker should lead us to immediately recognize an implicit claim to the existence and veracity of the inner light with regard to knowledge about God and the soul. The notes that make up the *Principia* should be read with an eye on the context of what was taking place in Conway's life at the time, and her convincement[15] is surely the most significant event during this period, including both intellectual and practical commitments. As such, it is not too much of a stretch to attempt to read the *Principia* within the intellectual context of the early Quaker community and this primarily includes a commitment to some kind of notion of the inner light.

Of course, it could be that there were reflections on the inner light and epistemological matters in the notes, and they were simply edited out by van Helmont. However, this seems highly unlikely, as it is not clear why he would have done so. It cannot have been due to any possible controversy such a notion might bring, as there are plenty of controversial claims, both philosophical and theological, made in the *Principia*, including that Christians may have to significantly amend their own understanding of the Trinity in order to make Christianity more amenable to Jews (an incredibly controversial, and potentially dangerous, thing to say at the time – see 1.7; 10 and Chapter 5 of this work). It is also unlikely that van Helmont would have taken out such references because he disagrees with such a notion: for one thing, as mentioned in the previous chapter, van Helmont was highly active in Quaker circles and seems to have converted to the sect himself. In addition, there are claims in the *Principia* that seem to put Conway and van Helmont at some distance, which the latter clearly did not edit out of the text. The most likely scenario, then, is that Conway simply did not write about the inner light and that it functions as an implicit epistemological framework that we can reasonably read into the text, given her full embrace of Quakerism at the time of the writing of these notes.

In addition, van Helmont himself is a likely source of Quaker and mystical ideas that we find in the *Principia*. As we shall see, Conway's philosophy has clearly been shaped by her intellectual engagement with van Helmont throughout the 1670s. van Helmont had a longstanding association with the Quakers[16] and he was also profoundly shaped by the ideas of his father, whose mystical work straddled alchemy, medicine, philosophy and religion. Jan Baptist van Helmont (Francis Mercury's father) had established his own distinctive epistemology, shaped by numerous different sources, as noted by Coudert: 'The elder van Helmont developed a theory of knowledge that contains elements of the Platonic conception of innate ideas blended with a firm scepticism reminiscent of Montaigne, and a mystical emphasis on divine illumination' (1999: 15). In his Platonic-inspired epistemology, J.B. van Helmont prioritized immediate intuition at the expense of empirical investigation and the use of reason by itself. In his *Oriatrike*, he claims that reason 'doth generate nothing but a dim or dark

Knowledge', compared to the insights gained by 'the intellectual light of the Lamp or Candle [of God]' (1662: 18). The fundamental source of all genuine knowledge is the mystical foundation of the intellectual light granted to us by God. Francis Mercury van Helmont largely follows his father in epistemological matters, again by prioritizing mystical intuition over the teachings of reason alone (see Coudert 1999: 157f.). Given that Conway's thought is shaped so thoroughly by her collaboration with van Helmont, we have further evidence in favour of her adopting some form of implicit Neoplatonist-inspired epistemology that posits inner illumination as the ultimate source of knowledge about God, the soul and the world. All this is not to say that reason does not have a role to play: indeed, we shall see that much of Conway's system follows from her reasoning concerning what can be deduced about the world from the nature of God. However, the building blocks of this knowledge will ultimately be furnished by our participation in the divine.

Conclusion

In this chapter, we have explored the likely epistemological underpinnings of Conway's claims concerning the nature of God and of the soul. Given the impact of Henry More's mentorship upon her philosophy, as well as her embrace of Quakerism at the time of the writing of the *Principia*, it is highly probable that there is the assumption of some kind of notion of divine illumination or inner light underlying Conway's metaphysical claims. The case for this position will be strengthened as we proceed through our examination of the text, particularly as we note numerous Platonic elements to her thought, for a philosophy that shows the deep influence of Neoplatonism is likely to bring with it a Neoplatonic-inspired epistemology of illumination. We have also started glimpsing Conway's willingness to engage with controversial ideas, to the point where she may depart from the teachings of the Church at that time. The radical nature of her thought during the last few years of her life, during the height of her interactions with the Quaker community, will surface throughout the *Principia*.

Why, though, this diversion into epistemological matters that Conway does not explicitly address in the text? We will see, in Chapter 4, that this implicit epistemology has significant implications for our understanding of other key aspects of her metaphysics, such as her Christology and theory of salvation. The Quaker's 'inner light' is often taken in literature of the time to be a Christ Within, a term which generated much controversy and raised questions about the role of

Christ in early Quaker theology. I will argue that Conway's Christology is made much clearer by reading it within its Quaker-inspired context, along the lines of the shared notion of the Christ Within, as outlined in the work of George Keith.[17] However, before we go on to this, we need to explore the metaphysical fundamentals of her philosophy, including her account of the nature of God and his creative action, of time, and the created universe.

2

God, spirit and body

In the previous chapter, we completed our preliminary look at the background of the *Principia* by considering the question of Conway's religious epistemology, alongside some aspects of her intellectual contact with Henry More and the Cambridge Platonist school on the one hand, and the early Quaker community on the other. We will have cause to revisit these links as we proceed. For now, we will begin considering the details of Conway's metaphysical system, as it is presented in the *Principia*. In this chapter, I will introduce her concept of God and her theory of reality as both essentially spiritual and alive. As part of this, we will continue considering the possible influence of Neoplatonism on her thought as well as the manner in which she departs from the philosophy of Henry More.

In the next section, I will outline how Conway's theory of the distinction between communicable and incommunicable attributes leads to her theory of spiritual monism: the claim that there only exists one type of thing in creation, namely, spirit in various forms of corporeality. Following this, I will analyse Conway's various arguments against substance dualism, a view most prominently held at that time by Descartes. Substance dualism claims that there exist two fundamentally different types of things in the world, spirit and matter, which contradict monist positions such as Conway's spiritual monism, as well as the materialism of Hobbes and others. In the final section of the chapter, I will also introduce Conway's vitalism, which, as Marchant puts it, 'affirm[s] the life of all things through a reduction of Cartesian dualism to the monistic unity of matter and spirit' (1979: 255). The remarkable claim that all things are fundamentally alive is one of the most important aspects of Conway's thought, and will be discussed at points throughout the rest of this work.

God and monism

The foundational claim of Conway's philosophy is encapsulated in the very first sentence of the *Principia*, namely, that there is a God who is 'spirit, light, and life, infinitely wise, good, just, strong, all-knowing, all-present, all-powerful, the creator and maker of all things visible and invisible' (1.1; 9). No argument is offered for this claim throughout the *Principia*, and it is simply assumed that this is the case, perhaps given the kind of religious epistemology that we considered in the previous chapter. The argumentative structure of the work as a whole then largely proceeds from this claim. Conway asks, given that such a God exists, what we can infer about the nature of the world and all the things that exist in it.

Part of the explanatory power of this argumentative strategy for Conway lies in her distinction between communicable and incommunicable attributes, as well as an understanding of creation that in some ways departs from a traditional Christian account and instead reflects an approach more indebted to the Platonic tradition. Conway will use this argumentative strategy to move from God's ontological status as pure spirit to the claim that all things are spirit. 'Spiritual monism' is the claim, made by Conway, that all things are spirit. This position conflicts with at least two mainstream metaphysical theories of the time: first, materialism, which claims that all created things are essentially material (Hobbes's metaphysical philosophy was a particularly prevalent example of this theory from the period), and second, substance dualism, which split the created world in two by postulating two fundamentally different kinds of substance, physical body and spirit.

Conway offers an account of creation that is inspired by the Neoplatonists. This approach is introduced in Chapter II, with imagery reminiscent of that tradition:

> God is infinitely good, loving, and bountiful indeed, he is goodness and charity itself, the infinite fountain and ocean of goodness, charity, and bounty. In what way is it possible for that fountain to not flow perpetually and to send forth living waters? For will not that ocean overflow in its perpetual emanation and continual flux for the production of creatures?
>
> (2.4; 13)

The Neoplatonic model revolves around the notion of emanation that Conway mentions here. Whilst there are great overlaps between the Neoplatonic and Christian models of creation, there are nevertheless significant differences in details and emphases. One notion we can focus on is that of the principle of plenitude, which is the claim that there are as many created things as there could be. Whilst a Christian would not necessarily disagree with this principle, it is nevertheless consistent with Christian thought that this may not be the case, as it could potentially be that the best possible world (which God must create) is not 'full' in the sense committed to by the Neoplatonist. What is particularly important here is the notion of divine causation that underlies the account of creation proposed by the Neoplatonists.

First, note that it is consistent with Christianity that the created world be nothing like God. At least in principle, it is possible for God (given the scope of his omnipotence) to create a world that is nothing like him, or at least significantly removed from the divine nature. Such a difference can be multiplied once we take into account the doctrine of the Fall, which has been taken to imply that the entire created world essentially fell away from the goodness of God due to the first sin undertaken by Adam: so, whilst creation may have been closer to the nature of God prior to the first sin, it has since become further estranged from the perfect goodness of the divine being. Neoplatonism, on the other hand, has a distinct account of divine causation that implies necessarily deeper similarities between God and creation. The roots of this account go back to Plato and his theory of Forms. Plato postulated a realm of objects that transcend the world of our everyday experience.[1] These objects, the Forms, exist at a more fundamental level than the world we ordinarily experience and are beyond time. The things we experience are merely imperfect reflections of these more fundamental, perfect objects, and there is nothing in this world that is not a manifestation of the Forms. The important point to take away for our purposes is that the world of our experience is a *reflection* of the transcendent realm of the Forms, albeit an imperfect one, and so it will inescapably bear a significant trace of the Forms. In the manifestation relation between Forms and the world, then, there will always be some form of essential similarity that is maintained between the two.

The model provided by the Forms in Plato's dialogues was built upon by the Neoplatonists to form their notion of emanation. Reality as a whole is made up of different levels, some more fundamental than others. The lower levels of reality emanate from the higher levels, and in the manner of the Form–world relation, these levels imperfectly reflect that which is more fundamental than them. Remes describes this hierarchical emanationist view of causation as follows:

> The caused and thus the metaphysically posterior in the hierarchy is always dependent on its cause and origin, while the prior is independent of the posterior. This dependence also holds for the content or character of what is created. The cause bestows its own character to the effect. The cause does not create another thing identical to itself, but the Neoplatonists believe that if the effect did not communicate anything of the cause, it would not be capable of arising from that particular cause.
>
> (2014: 44)

As Remes notes, the Neoplatonist notion of causation necessarily involves some relation of substantial similarity between cause and effect: going back to Plato's theory of the Forms, the Form of Beauty bestows beauty (albeit an imperfect version of it) on to all beautiful things in the world, whilst the Form of the Good bestows goodness upon anything that is good, and nothing can be beautiful or good through any other means.

We can now start to detect the possibilities of a tension between the Neoplatonist and Christian viewpoints concerning the creation of the world, for whilst Christian creation could in principle be entirely estranged from divine nature, a Neoplatonic world necessarily retains something of the more perfect level of reality above it. Some features of the world will be a reflection of the higher levels of reality, whilst other features will be novel aspects that appear as part of its relative imperfection: so, whilst any beauty in the world will be a reflection of a higher principle of beauty, any ugliness in the world will be a mere feature of its imperfection and will not have a direct source from elsewhere. This naturally leads to a distinction between those features of the world that are a reflection of a more perfect, higher level of reality and those that are not. With regard to the divine attributes, there will be those that can be found in an imperfect version in creation and those that cannot be.

We find this Neoplatonist idea reflected in Conway's thought, as she builds on her emanative account of creation by striking a distinction between communicable and incommunicable divine attributes. Communicable attributes are those divine attributes that can be shared with creatures, whilst incommunicable attributes are those that cannot. She strikes the division as follows: 'The incommunicable [attributes] are that God is a being subsisting by himself, independent, immutable, absolutely infinite, and most perfect. The communicable attributes are that God is spirit, light, life, that he is good, holy, just, wise, etc.' (7.2; 45). The distinction is to supposed to capture the idea that the nature of creation reflects something of the nature of God (these are the communicable attributes shared by God and creatures), though there are limits to this, insofar as having some of the divine attributes would entail that you are also God (the incommunicable attributes) and there are other attributes (what Conway calls 'differentiating attributes') that God cannot have, such as hardness, shape, motion and mutability.

The incommunicable and differentiating attributes reflect the assumption that anything created by God must exist at a lower level of reality. God 'is not able to multiply himself' (2.4; 13) and create other Gods, and so any of his attributes that are infinities in any way (those attributes that are necessarily without limitation, such as absolute independence, having necessary existence or being self-caused, unchanging, perfect) are not communicable to created beings. However, some of the divine attributes can be found in a limited form, and these are the attributes that can be communicated (so, for example, it is possible to be good, but to fall short of perfect goodness).

So, how do we get from the distinction between communicable and incommunicable attributes to the theory of spiritual monism? Conway argues that all created beings must have all the communicable attributes in at least some limited sense. As a consequence, all things will partake of spirit in at least some way, as part of their fundamental nature, in virtue of being a creation of God. Conway argues that 'there is no being which is in every way contrary to God' (7.1; 42) and so there cannot be anything so unlike the infinite spirit, God, that it is not itself spirit. Material beings are things that have fallen away from God, moving away on the ontological scale from infinite spirit to matter, with the implication that there is no strict ontological distinction in the manner claimed by dualists: '[The] crasser [body] becomes, the more it is removed from the condition of spirit. Consequently, the distinction between spirit and body is only modal and incremental, not essential and substantial' (6.11; 40), 'nor is there any difference between body and spirit, ... except that the body is the grosser part and the spirit the more subtle ... [Truly] there is no body anywhere which does not have motion and consequently life or spirit' (7.4; 51).

So, given this, how we do we explain the fact that some things in the created universe appear to be merely material? There are two strands in Conway's answer to this question: namely, (1) nothing is just how it appears to you in your experience and (2) matter *is* spirit. We will focus on the latter claim for now, before returning to the former later. At first glance, the claim that matter is spirit may seem contradictory, but this is only the case if you accept the dualist premise that matter and spirit are fundamentally different kinds of thing. Conway establishes her spiritual monism with the claim that matter is a kind of spirit, namely, spirit that has condensed – 'spirit is able to become more or less corporeal in many degrees' (7.1; 43) – in an analogous manner to how water vapour (water in the form of a gas) condenses and solidifies into liquid water. In the same way that you can have water in different states, some more 'gross' than others (solid, liquid, gas), spirit can be in more rarefied and more corporeal forms. God is the unique example of the most rarefied spirit (in fact, we can say that he is infinitely rarefied), and everything is less than God due to being more corporeal than him. So, whilst it may appear on the surface that there are two fundamentally different types of things in the world (spirit and matter), they are the same thing in different forms: matter *is* spirit.[2]

In what sense, then, is nothing just how it appears in our experience? Without going into too much detail here, the world is much more complex than it seems on the surface, being filled with an infinite number of incorporeal and infinitesimally small spirits that we are unable to experience directly. What both substance dualism and materialism miss is the sheer complexity of the world beyond how it appears to us, with a complex intermingling of different spirits at different degrees of corporeality at a miniscule level. Materialism falls into the trap of thinking that the material things that make up the objects of our experience are all there is, whilst substance dualism does not take into account the complex system of intermingling spirits that exists beyond the limits of our experience.[3]

Another mistake of dualists and materialists is to claim that only matter can be extended (i.e. can take up space in the world). Following More (see 1995: 38–40), Conway holds that spirit can be extended as well as penetrable, which is why it can appear in both the ontological state that Cartesians conceive of as spirit and that which they conceive of as matter. The argument against the Cartesian separation of extended matter and thinking mind on the basis of Neoplatonic assumptions concerning creation has been examined in detail by John Grey: he sums up the argument thus,

1 Two substances have different natures only if they ultimately depend for their existence upon different things.
2 All created substances ultimately depend for their existence on the same thing or things.
3 So, no two created substances have different natures (2017: 13).

This argument is reconstructed from a passage in which Conway argues that all things can be distinguished into kinds on the basis of 'their original and peculiar causes' (6.4; 30): if two things are different in nature, then they must have a different original cause. However, Descartes wishes to claim that both mind and matter are of different natures and that they have the same original ground in God. As both Conway and Descartes would agree with (2), and (3) is the conclusion of Conway's argument, it is claim (1) (referred to by Grey as the 'dependence thesis' (2017: 12)) that we are interested in. Why would we think that any two things that depend upon a common source for their existence necessarily must share their essential nature? We would certainly have reason to believe this if we think along Neoplatonic lines that all things must have some shared fundamental similarity on the basis of their creation in the same being, but Descartes could surely just reject the 'dependence thesis'.

However, Grey goes on to argue that Descartes's view of substance commits him to at least some version of the dependence thesis, and thus Conway's argument will not be so easily avoided. Descartes defines substance in terms of existential independence: in other words, a substance is that which can exist independently apart from the ontological sustenance of any other thing (1985: 210). Clearly, given that all created things depend upon God for their existence in at least some sense, we need to temper how strictly we define existential dependence. Indeed, as Grey notes, the manner in which we understand the independence of created beings will be different from how we understand the existential independence of God: 'On the one hand, we can construe substance as an entity that is totally independent, in which case there is only one: God. On the other hand, we can construe substance as an entity that is independent of anything *except for God*, in which case (Descartes thinks) there may be many of them: all minds and bodies will count' (2017: 14). On this basis, it may seem natural to suppose that God and created substance can be distinguished on the basis of the manner in which they are existentially dependent: God is fully existentially independent, and so has a different nature from his creatures, who are existentially independent in a more limited sense. However, Descartes would then be left in the position that he is unable to distinguish essentially between mind and matter, as they are existentially independent in the same way (of all things, apart from God), and so Cartesian dualism fails.

However, I would argue that it is not clear at all that Descartes is indeed committed to the dependence thesis. The question 'what makes a substance a substance?' is quite separate from 'how can we distinguish one kind of substance from another?' The answer to one does not necessarily shape how we answer the other. So, even if existential independence is what allows us to identify something as a substance, there is no reason why we have to look to existential independence to determine one kind of substance from another. As such, I do not believe it is obvious that Descartes is in fact committed to the dependence thesis. It is beyond our scope of interest here to examine in more detail whether Descartes really is committed to some form of the dependence thesis, but at the very least, we can see that Conway thinks that her Neoplatonic assumptions concerning causation and creation pose a significant challenge to the Cartesian distinction between spirit and matter. However, the *Principia* does not entirely rely upon a Neoplatonic framework to establish spiritual monism. In the next section, we will consider some of Conway's other arguments against substance dualism and for spiritual monism.

Love and the interaction problem

In the previous section, I briefly mentioned two possible competitor theories to Conway's spiritual monism from that period, namely, materialism and substance dualism. Conway seems to think that materialism can be quickly sufficiently dispatched through an argument based on her account of creation and the divine attributes: anything that would be merely material would be too ontologically remote from God for him to possibly create. Such an argument would dispatch substance dualism too, in that this theory also posits the existence of a purely material substance. Nevertheless, given the hold that substance dualism had over the philosophical and theological tradition at the time, it is understandable that Conway would wish to offer as many arguments as she can against such an influential theory, and these dominate Chapters VII and VIII of the *Principia*.[4] As Mercer notes (2019b: 709–11), Descartes had been roundly criticized with the claim that his attempted explanation of mechanical phenomena purely in terms of matter in motion failed to explain all observable events in the physical world. Whilst mechanical explanation for physical events should not be discounted (as Conway states, 'it cannot be denied that Descartes taught many remarkable and ingenious things concerning the mechanical aspects of natural processes and about how all motions proceed according to regular mechanical laws' (9.2; 64)), a complete explanation of them could not be provided in these terms. Accordingly, a different kind of metaphysics that was able to offer other avenues of explanation of observable phenomena was required and this is precisely what Conway offers in the *Principia*.

In the arguments she provides against dualism, Conway appeals to a number of different sources for reasons to believe in spiritual monism instead. One major argument she provides draws from our experience of 'that great love and desire which spirits or souls have for bodies, and especially for those bodies with which they are united and in which they dwell' (7.3; 46). Given the importance of this argument for her thesis, we would do well to first consider what exactly Conway means by 'love'. From the discussion found here, it seems that Conway understands love amongst creatures as an overwhelmingly favourable psychological or behavioural attitude towards something on the basis of perceived similarity. In defence of this view, she points to the Biblical example of Adam and Eve, arguing that their love for each other 'comes not only from the unity of their nature but also because of their remarkable similarity to each other' (7.3; 47). Here, we can look to Genesis 2:23, where Adam is reported to say of Eve, 'This is now bone of my bones, and flesh of my flesh: she shall be called Woman, because she was taken out of Man.' Conway argues that this Biblical passage grounds the love of Adam and Eve not only in the fact that they share the same kind of being (to the extent that she was developed from one of his ribs), but also in their similarity, for his joy at Eve is intensified due to the fact that up to that point, 'among all creatures he saw no one like himself with whom he could associate' (7.3; 47).

Furthermore, with regard to love between creatures, Conway allows that goodness can be a reason for such an attachment, but it is still fundamentally on the basis of similarity that we love others: 'One must concede that goodness is the great, indeed the greatest cause of love and its proper object. This goodness is not, however, a reason distinct [from similarity] ... For the reason why we call something good is because it really or apparently pleases us on account of its similarity to us, or ours to it' (7.3; 47). Conway uses the same model of actual or apparent similarity as the ground for love in explaining the love of God for his creatures and vice versa. Again, though we could also understand love as grounded in the fact that one has given being to another thing, this is ultimately subsumed under the similarity model, given Conway's commitment to the Neoplatonic view of creation that there are limits to the dissimilarity between creator and the created. So, God's love for creation is fundamentally grounded in the similarity between him and his creation, and given that all creation retains some similarity to him, it follows that he loves all of creation. As a corollary, God could not love his creation if the things he created were nothing like him in any way, as is allowed at least in principle by the Christian account of creation.

Going the other way, Conway argues that the love of creatures for God is also predicated on perceived similarity. As rational creatures, there 'is a certain divine law and instinct' (7.3; 47) within us for God that presumably gives us a sense of our similarity to him through our goodness and this love is intensified as we become more similar to him, by becoming more good. As we shall see, this growing similarity is not only moral but ontological, insofar as we become more spirit-like (and thus closer to the infinite spirit, God) as we morally better ourselves.

Returning to the question of love between creatures, Conway argues that spirits show love for particular bodies to an extent that is only explicable if they are fundamentally constituted of the same kind of substance. The first set of experiences that she appeals to is the partial love that creatures show for certain other creatures, for example, the love of parents for their children, the love within romantic relationships and the preferential treatment that animals show to those who are of the same species as them (see 7.3; 46). It is perhaps not immediately clear that these examples of particular love necessarily show the love of spirits for bodies, for the object of an individual's love for their children and those who are of the same species could simply be the spirit of these beings, rather than their respective bodies. It is possible, however, that Conway is appealing to the fact that we only experience the bodies of others and so our love for them *in the first instance* must be the love of a spirit for a body. To further reinforce this point, she claims that similarity in bodily appearance can increase the love of a parent for their child, something that would only be possible if mere body is the possible object of love.

The love that the spirit of an individual has for its own body is also taken as evidence for spiritual monism. Conway argues that this love can be seen in the example of spirits who remain close to the body that they inhabited after their death: 'I ask, then, for what reason does the soul or human spirit so love the body and so unite with it and so unwillingly depart from it that, as is widely known, the souls of certain people remain with their bodies and their power after the death of the body and until it decomposes and turns to dust' (7.3; 48). For modern readers who may be surprised by such an appeal to ghostly apparitions, the existence of ghosts was very much taken for granted at the time, and Henry More himself was a keen investigator of the paranormal, avidly collecting ghost stories throughout his life (see Crocker 2003: 127–33).

However, even if one were willing to accept the existence of ghosts and that they do indeed remain close to their bodies after death, there are still ways of challenging Conway here. It could be that spirits act in this way for a variety of reasons: for example, the spirit may become psychologically attached to its material body (in the way that we can become attached to any of our material possessions), and thus it finds it difficult to leave the body behind after death. It could also be the case that the spirit's attachment to the body can be explained in terms of its prior generation of the body as an organic system, in an analogous way to how parents are attached to their children. Conway rejects this possibility, though, on the basis that the spirit would only love in this way if it gave 'a distinct being to the body', but that is not case 'for this would be creation in a strict sense' (7.3; 48) and only God gives being to things in this way.

Conway does not only claim particular instances of love as evidence for monism, but also speaks of 'a certain universal love in all creatures for each other, in spite of that great confusion which resulted from the Fall' (7.3; 47). It is not entirely clear what Conway means by this 'universal love', though it may be that she is appealing to a certain harmony in nature that allows the natural environment as a whole to flourish as a self-sustaining system, rather than descending into the chaos that could have resulted from the metaphysically deleterious results of the Fall: it is a testament to the universal love between all things that the natural system as a whole did not entirely collapse into disharmony. Of course, one could challenge Conway here by questioning just how harmonious nature really is and certainly, given the bloodshed that dominates the natural world, it does not seem obvious that creatures do have a universal love for each; rather, the individual's Darwinian struggle to survive always seems to prevail. At the least, though, it is possible to take such an abstract viewpoint that one nevertheless sees suffering and bloodshed in nature as part of an overall harmonious system and perhaps this is simply what Conway is appealing to here.

In addition to her argument from love, Conway also offers an argument against dualism based on our experience of pain. She points out, first of all, that the dualist is committed to the view that it is the soul that feels pain, not the body (which is denied any perceptive qualities). However, Conway argues that the dualist cannot then explain just why the soul feels the pain of the body: 'If when united to the body [the soul] has no corporeality or bodily nature, why is it wounded or grieved when the body is wounded, whose nature is so different? For since the soul can so easily penetrate the body, how can any corporeal thing hurt it?' (8.2; 58). Conway's argument involves the view that the soul does not feel the pain of the body in a disconnected manner, like I might feel pity when I observe someone else suffering; rather, the soul feels the pain of the body in such an intimate way that the only possible explanation is that they are not two fundamentally different things, as posited by the substance dualist. When the body is hurt, the soul is hurt too, and this is why we feel the pain following injury to our body so keenly. The soul 'suffers with [the body] and through it' (8.2; 58), suggesting a kind of intermingling and interpenetration that the dualist cannot explain.

As Borcherding points out, Conway does not only ask *why* the mind feels pain in the way it does, but also asks *how* it can, given the dualist commitment to their dissimilarity. Otherwise, Descartes could attempt to offer his own dualist explanation of why the mind might feel sympathy for the body, based on a relation of emotional identification: 'The soul ... despite being so different in nature, identifies the body's good with its own by means of the passions, and thereby lets its self-love extend to the whole of which both it and the body are parts. Consequently, if the body is injured and this ability decreases, the soul is grieved by it and feels pain' (2019: 30). We might find some plausibility in this Cartesian claim, given our experience of feeling sympathy for others. As such, it is certainly a persuasive account of what is going on when we feel pity or compassion for others that we are identifying ourselves with those people. So, Descartes's claim that the mind feels pain because it is so emotionally attached to the body is not immediately implausible.

By moving on to the more fundamental question of *how* the mind feels pain, though, we can read Conway as offering a version of the wider 'problem of interaction' that the substance dualist traditionally faces. The success of the dualist model of mind and body relies upon a bidirectional flow of information from one to the other. So, in the case of my hand accidentally brushing a hot stove, my mind needs to sense that my hand is in pain, and then in turn will that my hand be pulled away from the surface. Both stages of this instinctual response to sudden pain require some kind of process between mind and body and it seems that this would be best understood as a kind of causal relation between the two. However, as the objection goes, the dualist cannot explain how such interaction between mind and body can be possible: given the assumption that they are two fundamentally different kinds of things, how can they have any kind of impact upon each other? With regard to causal relations between material objects, we have a fairly clear idea of how they can have an impact upon each other due to their impenetrability: two snooker balls cannot share the same physical space, and so when the white ball hits the black ball, the former displaces the latter, which then moves across the table into the pocket. However, the Cartesian dualist claims that the soul is not impenetrable and so it is not clear how it can have any kind of causal impact upon the material body, in the manner that one snooker ball can have causal impact upon another. Going back to Conway's argument from pain, the claim seems to be that the way in which the mind feels pain at the injury of the body suggests the kind of intimate connection between them that is not possible on the dualist view. The best way out of this difficulty, Conway argues, is to switch to a monist standpoint, according to which mind and body are not fundamentally different types of things, but in fact stand on a continuum of penetrability and can thus interact with each other.

Conway also draws upon the interaction problem for dualists when she considers the question of how the mind is able to move the body. Henry More had struck a dualist position, particularly in his later works, that focused on the question of penetrability as the key distinguishing feature of spirit and matter: whilst spirit is able to occupy the same space with some bodies, no body is able to occupy the same space as another body. Conway argues that such a position makes (at least conscious) bodily action difficult to explain, in that it is not clear how a spirit that forms part of me would be able to move my physical body. As mentioned already, when it comes to impenetrable objects, like snooker balls, it is easy to understand how one object can have an impact upon the other (precisely because they cannot share the same physical space). However, the case of a penetrable object moving an impenetrable object is more problematic. Indeed, Conway raises the challenge to the dualist position by asking, 'If spirit so easily penetrates every body, why, when it moves from place to place, does it not leave the body behind since it can so easily pass through it without any or the least resistance?' (8.1; 57) Let's say you want to raise your hand in the air: given the penetrability of spirit, when it tries to move your hand upwards, it will simply float through your hand with no impact upon it. Conway uses the imagery of a ship to explain her point, arguing that the influence of a penetrable spirit upon the impenetrable body would be as little as that on a ship that sailed with a net, rather than with a sail. With Conway's system of mediating spirits, she holds that this difficulty of explaining bodily movement can be resolved: an incorporeal spirit can move a material body indirectly through a series of spirits at different levels of grossness on the spirit–matter continuum.

Having made this point, Conway anticipates a potential objection to her argument, in that she seems to have ruled out all possibility of any spirit having influence upon matter. The problem is that, within the theistic framework, she would presumably want to allow that God (who is pure spirit) can have such an influence, despite being entirely impenetrable. At the very least, if God cannot have an effect upon matter, then that seems to rule out any possibility of miracles, and though there is no mention of miracles in the *Principia*, this is presumably not something that Conway would wish to exclude. In response to this potential problem, Conway argues that God is essentially a special case, insofar as divine spiritual action is able to move matter in a unique way that is unavailable to the spirits of creatures. God is the 'author of motion', the being whose will allows all other beings to move. Thus, if God wills that the waters of the Red Sea part in order to facilitate the escape of the Israelites, then the waters will part, and this is an entirely different process to what occurs when the spirit of a creature moves their physical body. Conway emphasizes the importance of God's status as the ground of all motion, as opposed to the particular situations in which creatures can bring about individual movements:

> Motion and being come from the same cause, God the creator, who nevertheless remains unmoved himself and does not go from place to place since he is equally present everywhere and bestows motion on creatures. But it is a very different

case when the soul moves the body, for the soul is not the author of motion but merely limits it to this or that particular thing.

(8.2; 58)

Conway takes it for granted that her reader will agree with her with regard to God's status as the first cause of motion and so may be inclined to accept that the question of God moving matter is distinct from that of other spirits moving matter. Whilst the process by which God moves things may remain a divine mystery, and thus something ultimately beyond our ken, we might think that the question of movement by creaturely spirits is rather more within our purview and thus is suitable for the kind of metaphysical explanation that Conway offers.

In addition, Conway points out that theists are used to thinking of God's role in motion in a different manner from how we consider the motion of creatures, in that they would have God play a complementary role in our actions, whilst disavowing any divine responsibility for the sinful acts we undertake. Again, Conway uses nautical imagery to illustrate her point:

> If, for example, a ship is moved by wind but is steered by a helmsman so that it goes from this or that place, then the helmsman is neither the author nor cause of the wind; but the wind blowing, he makes either a good or bad use of it. When he guides the ship to its destination, he is praised, but when he grounds it on the shoals and suffers shipwreck, then he is blamed and deemed worthy of punishment.

(8.2; 58)

It is the wind that moves the ship, but it is up to the helmsman to use that wind in a productive way, and so it is with God and creatures: we are provided with the possibility of motion by God, and it is up to us to make the best use of it. We thus have two different ways of thinking about motion, focusing either on God as the ground of the possibility of motion or on creatures who are able to make use of that motion. Thus, Conway argues, we can naturally see that her argument concerning the dualist failure to explain creaturely movement does not threaten the possibility of divine motion. So, her version of the interaction argument against dualism still allows for God to have a causal impact upon creation.

Now that we have considered both the arguments from love and pain, we can briefly reflect on the nature of these arguments. I have presented them so far as arguments to the best explanation: namely, arguments that have the form, 'given the data that we have, which hypothesis (out of the many available) best fits that data'? In this respect, I have followed other scholars such as McRobert (see 2000: 34) and Broad (see 2002: 75f.). Borcherding, on the other hand, presents both as arguments from conceivability (2019: *passim*). Such arguments rely on the assumption that what we can conceive is a good guide to what is possible and impossible: if we can conceive it, it is possible, and if we cannot conceive it, it is impossible. Such an argumentative approach would cohere well with Conway's general rationalist approach, which assumes that reason is a powerful cognitive tool that can reveal fundamental metaphysical truths apart from our experience. However, such a reading of Conway does commit her to the rather strong claim that similarity is the *only conceivable basis* for love and mind–body interaction. In order to pursue this argumentative strategy, Conway would have to rule out all other possible explanations as inconceivable, and thus as impossible, and she certainly does seem to attempt this to at least some extent, by going through and dismissing competing dualist claims in a reasonably systematic way, though this is compatible with attempting an inference to the best explanation (as one would need to argue that other hypotheses are not as explanatorily powerful as yours).

With regard to this question, I would argue that the text is ultimately inconclusive. Borcherding points to a particular passage in defence of her reading of the love argument as an argument from conceivability, where Conway states that love '*necessarily* occurs because of the similarity or affinity between their natures' (7.3; 15 – my emphasis). Due to the reference here to necessity, Borcherding claims that Conway is committed to the view that similarity is the only possible explanation for love (see 2019: 12). However, there seems to be a significant problem with relying upon this passage, as Conway here allows that we can conceive of *two* possible grounds of love: namely, similarity and having given being to an individual, in the sense of divine creation. So, taking the passage in a wider context, Conway's claim is, given that the ground of love is not the fact that one creature has created another, it must necessarily be grounded in similarity. To read Conway as providing an argument from conceivability here, we must take her as at least committed to the view that it is inconceivable that one creature could create another, given that she seems to allow in principle these two possible grounds of love. It very well may be that Conway does not think such a thing is conceivable, but she does not clearly state this, and so I think the text is ultimately ambiguous between the 'conceivability' and 'best explanation' readings.

We can also consider Borcherding's interpretation of the pain argument as an argument from conceivability, according to which Conway is committed to the claim that similarity is the only conceivable explanation for the interaction between mind and body. However, this is not obviously the argumentative line that Conway takes here, in that her purpose is more negative, namely, establishing that any possible dualist explanation for mind–body interaction fails, rather than positively arguing that similarity is the only conceivable explanation for it. Again, I would argue that Conway is not clearly committed to either argumentative strategy, and regardless, little of substance hinges upon whether she is relying upon arguments from conceivability or inferences to the best explanation.

To conclude this section, Conway's arguments against dualism from love and interaction tie neatly together, as they both challenge a perspective upon nature that splits it into two realms that can largely operate independently of each other. Through the theory of spiritual monism, and other aspects of the philosophy of the *Principia*, Conway proposes a more integrated view of nature that stresses the harmony and intertwining of all created beings, regardless of the kind of being they are. We can further see this in her argument against dualism from spontaneous generation, which we shall consider in the next section.

Affinity and the argument from spontaneous generation

Another of Conway's arguments for spiritual monism uses an appeal to empirical data concerning the generation of organic bodies. She follows some scientific opinion of the time that organisms can be spontaneously generated from apparently dead matter, asking, 'Does not rotting matter, or body of earth and water, produce animals without any previous seed of those animals?' (6.6; 34)? As evidence for this claim, Conway points to pools of water in which fish appear, seemingly without any normal process of reproduction having taken place. On this basis, she argues that 'the spirits of all animals are in the water' (8.4; 60). As further scriptural backing for this claim, she appeals to the Genesis creation story, which begins with God '[moving] upon the face of the waters' (Genesis 1:2), and argues that all living things that God goes on to create come out from those waters.

However, Conway recognizes that this is by no means a knockdown argument for spiritual monism at it stands, for the claimed scientific data is wholly consistent with substance dualism. Even if we admit the spontaneous generation of organic beings, that does not necessarily imply that all things are essentially spirit; rather, it could be that the body of water or earth in question 'contains', or is in some way attached to, particular living spirits, from which organic beings can be spontaneously generated (in the way that the material body is attached to a mind). As such, nothing in the possibility of the spontaneous generation of organic beings from dead matter necessarily leads to the supposition that these things are essentially spirit. It is also worth noting that Conway's argument would not concern Descartes because he claims that animals do not have anything like a soul. As Boyle notes (2006: 185f.), Conway's target here cannot be Descartes, as he would feel no need to explain how the souls of animals can arise out of mere matter; rather, it is most likely Henry More, who had supported claims concerning spontaneous generation and the souls of animals, whilst maintaining a dualist framework (see More 1925: 83f.). So, in this argument at least, Conway has More's dualism in mind as her philosophical target, though this is not to say that Descartes is not part of her critique elsewhere.

In expounding her argument, Conway first points out that the substance dualist is committed to bodies actually having, rather than merely potentially having, the spirits of all animals within them. She argues that accepting that bodies have potentially all spirits gives way to spiritual monism, because it leads to the interchangeability between spirit and body that substance dualism cannot explain: 'If one says that all spirits are contained in every body in their different essences, not actually but potentially, then one must concede that the body and all those spirits are the same; that is, that body can be changed into them, as when we say that wood is potentially fire … and water potentially air' (8.4; 60). The substance dualist cannot allow such interchangeability, given that spirit and matter are supposed to be fundamentally different types of things and thus cannot be changed into the other. The objection put by the substance dualist, then, must be committing them to the claim that bodies can *actually* contain the forms of all animals.

Conway attempts to answer this potentially worrisome objection by referring to her theory concerning interactions between more spirit-like and more material beings, using this account to show how her spiritual monism can avoid the problem of interaction faced by substance dualists. As we saw earlier, the challenge to dualists is to explain how two fundamentally different kinds of things (indeed, things that are so different that they are defined in opposition to each other) can have any sort of interaction between them. Conway's answer to the problem is to claim that spirit and matter are not in opposition, but rather on a continuum: you can have more gross beings, on the one hand, and more incorporeal beings, on the other. The idea is that one being could have an impact upon another being that is close enough to it on the spirit–matter continuum, so an object that is at one level of grossness could have a direct impact upon another object that is slightly less or more gross and so on. Even if two beings are set quite far apart on the continuum, there is nevertheless the possibility of interaction between them, as long as there are beings in the middle that can act as mediators: 'The most subtle and spiritual body can be united with a very gross and dense body by means of certain mediating bodies, which share the subtlety and crassness in various degrees between the two extremes. These median bodies are truly the ties or links through which such a subtle and spiritual soul is connected to so crass a body' (8.3; 59). We can then start to get a sense of the complexity of beings, as Conway understands it. To take the example of a human being, they are not exhausted by one mind and one physical body (as the substance dualist would have it). The mind and the body, standing apart on the spirit–matter continuum, require an immense number of mediating spirits that can interact with each other in order to fill that gap, and it is only in this way that a mind can be present in a body.

One objection we could consider with regard to Conway's theory of interaction focuses on the claim that beings close enough to each other on the spirit–matter continuum can interact with each other. We can ask whether Conway has really solved the interaction problem, for how is it that beings close to each other on the spirit–matter continuum *can* interact? Conway assumes that bodies at different levels of corporeality can interact with each other (she asserts that 'things of one or of a similar nature can easily affect each other' (8.3; 59)), but this is potentially just as difficult a problem of interaction as the one we started with. Though Conway could now point to the fact that we are now dealing with one type of substance, rather than two, it is not clear that the problem is solved by invoking beings that are at different levels of corporeality (no matter how close they might be on the spirit–matter continuum). Also, how close on the continuum is close enough, and how much is too far? Why is the ontological line drawn there? These are all issues that Conway's theory faces, and it is not immediately clear to me how she would answer them, other than to say that she is providing an argument to the best explanation: given the experience we have of spirit and matter apparently interacting with each other, this is the explanation that best fits the data we have. However, we may feel that the problem of interaction has not yet been solved here.

Accepting Conway's theory of interaction for now, how does she respond to the potential dualist claim that the water actually contains the spirits of all animals within them? Whilst substance dualism allows in principle for any kind of spirit to be connected to any kind of body (leaving the precise nature of this connection aside), there are constraints upon interaction in spiritual monism, as Conway construes it. Spirits can only affect each other insofar as they have 'that true affinity which one has for another in its nature' (8.3; 59). Whilst we will expand upon what Conway means by 'affinity' between spirits later, when we consider the question of her vitalism and theory of the constitution of creatures, at this point we can take away the claim that it is not the case that just any spirit can be present in any other body: rather, there must be some kind of 'affinity', or shared nature, between them, which is only possible, it is claimed, on the basis that spirit and body sit on a continuum. However, not all beings will have this affinity with each other, and so one will not be able to be present in the other.

Conway seeks to challenge the substance dualist by arguing that, if a material thing can contain spirits in the manner suggested by them, then there is no reason why a particular body, such as a pool of water, could not in principle produce all sorts of different kinds of organic being. However, this is not what we see, in that only water-borne animals are ever found to have been generated in this way: she asks, 'If all kinds of spirit exist in any body, even the smallest, how does it happen that such an animal is produced from this body and not from another? Indeed, how does it happen that all kinds of animals are not immediately produced from one and the same body? This is contrary to experience' (8.4; 60). The fact that there is an order to the spontaneous generation of creatures (water-borne creatures from water, land-based animals from mud) shows that matter does not contain the spirits of all animals in the manner envisioned by the substance dualist. There is nothing to stop any kind of spirit being connected with any kind of body, in principle, under substance dualism, and so if this theory were true, then land-based animals could be generated from water and water-borne creatures from mud. However, this does not happen, as the spontaneous generation of creatures is far more ordered.

Conway argues that this suggests that there is a more complex story to be told here that assumes spiritual monism and explains the experience that we have concerning spontaneous generation. There is a systematic way in which animals arise from matter that suggests a deeper connection between matter and spirit than that posited by substance dualism, so that we find this ordered phenomenon. Conway explains her point in this way: 'If spirits and bodies are so inseparably united ... this is surely a weighty argument that they are of one original nature and substance. Otherwise, we could not comprehend why they would not finally separate from each other in various and startling dissolutions and separations' (8.4; 60f.). Such a unity between spirit and matter, revealed by the orderly process of spontaneous generation, cannot be explained by the substance dualist, and so this points towards the truth of spiritual monism. In addition, Conway argues that she can explain not only why water-borne creatures can be spontaneously generated in water, but also why *only* these creatures can be generated in water (because only in these cases is there the requisite 'affinity' between spirits). In other words, her theories of interaction and spiritual monism can explain both spontaneous generation and its limits in a neat way that is not available to the substance dualist.

The notion of 'affinity' also has a role to play in Conway's critique of the dualist understanding of personal immortality. The dualist, she argues, is committed to some sense of affinity between the mind and body that is somehow lost when the body dies. However, she writes, 'One must first ask in what this vital affinity consists? For if they cannot tell us in what this affinity consists, they are talking foolishly with inane words which have sound but not sense' (8.1; 57). After rejecting the idea that there could be such an affinity between mind and body on the dualist viewpoint (given their fundamental ontological difference), she argues that even if the dualist could sustain such a notion, they would still have some explaining to do with regard to precisely why mind–body affinity is lost at bodily death. The only reason, Conway suggests, that the dualist could draw upon is to argue that mind–body affinity is lost when the body breaks down as an organized system at death. However, she argues, it is not clear why this would necessarily be the case: 'Why does spirit require such an organized body? For example, why does the spirit require a corporeal eye so wonderfully formed and organized that I may see through it?' (8.1; 57) So, the dualist struggles to both explain why body and mind have an affinity throughout life and why that affinity is lost at bodily death, given that there seems to be no reason why the mind requires a particular kind of organized system in the form of the body to remain in affinity with the matter that makes it up ('if some affinity does exist, it would clearly remain the same whether the body is whole or corrupt' (8.1; 57)).

Of course, we now know that Conway's argument concerning spontaneous generation can easily be dismissed on the basis that this scientific theory has now been comprehensively overturned. Such is the fate of many philosophical arguments of the past that rely upon now widely discredited scientific theories for support. However, this is by no means her most important argument for spiritual monism, and so can be lost with little damage done to her overall theory. Conway's appeals to empirical data here should be taken as additional confirmation of her overall system, which can be established much more solidly through purely rational reflection. Conway's related affinity argument does not rely on the outdated theory of spontaneous generation and so is not vulnerable to new empirical data that has been gathered, though it could potentially be philosophically challenged. So, regardless of the progress of science since the writing of the *Principia*, and new discoveries to come, our acceptance of spiritual monism can rest alone on the non-empirical foundations provided by other arguments Conway gives in support of her metaphysical system.

Introducing Conway's vitalism

Conway takes her arguments concerning spiritual monism and substance dualism to establish that all things are not only essentially spirit, but also fundamentally alive. God's communicable attributes include 'life', and so given we established earlier that all creatures have these attributes to at least some extent, it follows that all things are alive to some extent. We are thus brought to the topic of Conway's vitalism, which answers the open question of why she thinks all things are fundamentally alive. The answer she provides is that all things are alive because they are all driven by the same kind of vital force that, in the form of a relatively incorporeal spirit, permeates all nature. In arguing for this kind of vitalist theory, Conway adapts Henry More's account of living matter in a manner that makes it more rigorously monistic, as well as reflecting the influence of the vitalist theories of the van Helmonts (both father and son).

As Jasper Reid points out, More's theory concerning the nature of life shifts throughout his career, but in his earliest writings, he imputes life to all matter: 'Notwithstanding the fact that some bodies might be united to really distinct spirits, [More claims that] they *additionally* needed to be granted some minimal form of intrinsic life, all of their own' (2012: 10). In his early *Philosophical Poems*, More generally follows a Cartesian dualist standpoint concerning the separation of spirit and body, but denies that there is any such thing as 'dead matter', insofar as everything has some semblance of life: he speaks of body as 'nothing but a fixed spirit', one of 'an infinite number of vital atoms ... [which are] the last projections of life from the soul of the world' (1878: 94). It seems that Conway continued to follow More's earlier arguments concerning the possibility of living matter (see Reid 2012: 255–78) and this will appear as something of a trend, insofar as the influence of More's earlier works seems to have been stronger upon Conway than his later ones.

I have not covered all of the anti-dualist points raised by Conway in Chapters VII and VIII of the *Principia*, insofar as some details will be covered when we consider Conway's vitalism and her account of the constitution of creatures in Chapter 7. Before we conclude this chapter, though, it is worth quickly noting that the details of Conway's metaphysics that we have sketched here already suggest a radical approach to other animals and nature as a whole that significantly departs from the mainstream thinking of the time. Although an extreme example, Descartes's philosophical treatment of animals is a reflection of the anthropocentric approach to nature taken at the time. According to the Cartesian view, all other animals could be understood entirely within the confines of the mechanistic approach to nature: other animals were mere mechanically operating physical bodies, without any mind, strictly speaking (see Hatfield (2003: 302–11) for a detailed account of Descartes's mechanist theory of nature). In a letter to Henry More from 1649, Descartes speaks of animals as merely 'automata': 'It seems reasonable since art copies nature, and men can make various automata which move without thought, that nature should produce its own automata much more splendid than the artificial ones. These natural automata are the animals' (Kenny 1970: 244). If animals can be regarded as mere automata, this raises potentially worrisome ethical implications, as seemingly we are given little reason to treat them as anything other than mere tools for our own purposes: for in the same way that I cannot really be said to have ethical duties towards a mere machine, I would not have any ethical duties to other animals either. The same reasoning can also be applied to any other aspect of nature, with the result that it is morally permitted that I act towards nature in any way I see fit, as long as it does not have a deleterious moral impact on any other genuinely moral agent (i.e. any other human being). Such a perspective on other animals and nature conflicts with much ethical reflection today, with claims of ethical duties towards things other than human beings being commonplace.

Conway, in contrast to the Cartesian approach, presents a far more unified, interconnected view of the world. Human beings are an integrated part of nature and are not ontologically special, insofar as they share in the same essential spiritual nature of everything else in creation. Duran emphasizes the substantial impact that Conway's metaphysics would have on our attitude, as human beings, towards the rest of creation:

> Because Conway repeatedly says that the difference between spirit and body 'is only one of degree not essence', and because she refuses to admit that there is matter devoid of spirit, the notion that humans, or other creatures, are entitled to be contemptuous of creation, in any sense, is unsupportable. The degree to which matter is penetrated by spirit is clearly, for Conway, a decision of God, and humans are simply one part of the chain of creation that is the result of divine decision.
>
> (2006: 59)

Conway shifts the place of humankind within nature as a whole. We are no longer the centre of things, nor so important that the rest of creation was really made for our benefit. Though there is still something that places human beings above all other things (and we will go on to explore this in more detail), this is not a position that human beings necessarily will always find themselves in, and so we must approach other animals and the rest of nature in a stance of humility and in recognition of the fact that all things are essentially the same. Admittedly, Conway does not spell out these practical and ethical implications of her philosophical system, but they are nevertheless worth elaborating and reflecting on as we continue our discussion.

Conclusion

In this chapter, I have introduced a number of the most important elements of Conway's metaphysics. First, we have seen that Conway subscribes to a theory of spiritual monism, which is the claim that all things that exist are spirit. Such a view contradicts the prevailing theory of the time, substance dualism, which posits two essentially different types of things in the world, spirit and body, as well as materialism, which claims that all things are essentially material. Conway's main argument for spiritual monism is based on her concept of God and creation, and we will find this argumentative strategy repeated throughout the *Principia*. Given her assumptions concerning the attributes of God, and her Neoplatonic-inspired account of creation, it follows that it would not be possible for essentially material bodies (that are so ontologically different from God) to be created. As such, it follows that all things are essentially spirit. However, that does not mean that matter is an illusion; rather, matter is condensed spirit that can potentially become more spirit-like again.

We also saw that Conway bolsters her case by drawing upon a number of arguments against substance dualism, including appeals to scripture, the love and affinity that exists between all things in nature and contemporary scientific theories concerning the spontaneous generation of organic beings. Many of these arguments will perhaps not be persuasive to a modern audience, but Conway is clearly trying to draw upon as many sources as she can to offer the strongest overall case for her philosophy, with a contemporary audience in mind. In the next chapter, we will return to Conway's concept of God and consider in more detail what she thinks we can establish regarding the nature of time and creation.

3

Creation and the infinity of time

Conway's account of creation and time takes up much of the discussion in Chapters II–IV of the *Principia*. We are given many compressed arguments for a large number of potentially rather controversial claims. In this chapter, we will work systematically through the text as much as we are able, beginning with Chapter II, though with some necessary diversions as we go along.

After briefly summarizing, in Chapter I, her views concerning the nature of God, including some material on her recommendations concerning a more ecumenical account of the Trinity, in Chapter II Conway focuses on various arguments surrounding the infinity of time and what that means for our understanding of the created universe and God's creative action. We will begin this chapter by analysing these arguments and considering two of the most important influences on Conway's thought here, namely, Plotinus and Henry More. I argue that the main aim of Chapter II is to establish the claim that the universe has existed and will continue to exist for an infinite duration of time, based on arguments concerning the nature of God. Following this, I will consider the question of creatures and Christ, as a preamble to our more extended discussions of Christology and time in later chapters. We will see here that Conway treads a recognizably Christian line of attributing a role in creation to Christ as Logos, such that we can say both that creatures are created 'at the same time' and successively. Finally, I will discuss Conway's definition of time as 'nothing but the successive motion or operation of creatures' (2.6; 14). I argue that Conway's definition is stricter than this suggests at first glance and is in fact tied to the idea of creaturely motion towards perfection, which further reflects the influence of Plotinus and Neoplatonism more generally upon her philosophy.

Infinite time

From the extant correspondence, we know that questions concerning time and creation were of interest to Conway from a very early stage in her interactions with More (and very likely even before). In a letter from 2 November 1651, More states that he is willing to discuss whatever religious matters she wishes to examine in their correspondence:

> So soon as you please to send it, or impart your mind in any thing else, I am ready to serve you. Which willingness does not proceed from any confidence of my abilities in any grand points of Religion, as if my judgement were considerable: but as a friend I shall discuss with you what you shall be pleased to propound, but yourself must choose according to the present Light of your own mind.
>
> (L 54)

Though we do not have Conway's reply to this letter, we can infer from More's letter of 17 November of that year that one of the issues she raises concerns the possibility of eternal, uncreated matter, a notion that plays a prominent role in the Platonic tradition; yet, More rejects it as something 'that seems to me not so rational' (L 491).

The foundation of the theory of uncreated matter in the Platonic tradition lies in Plato's dialogue, *Timaeus*, in which the eponymous character suggests a possible account of how the world, as we know it, was created. Timaeus suggests that a Craftsman brought order to things by forming a world from disordered, pre-existing matter: 'God desired that all things should be good and nothing bad, so far as this was attainable. Wherefore also finding the whole visible sphere not at rest, but moving in an irregular and disorderly fashion, out of disorder he brought order, considering that this was in every way better than the other' (*Timaeus* 30a; Hamilton and Cairns (1961: 1162)). Though some have interpreted this story as metaphorical in various ways, the possibility of uncreated matter continued to have a hold on the Platonist imagination. From the perspective of recent Christian orthodoxy, the idea of uncreated matter is radical indeed, as it contradicts the tenet of creation *ex nihilo* (from nothing): nothing other than the Triune God is uncreated, for God is the sole creator of all things. The desire by Conway to discuss the issue of uncreated matter reveals her independence of thought from the restrictions of Christian orthodoxy, as well as a longstanding interest in the Platonic tradition.

Turning to Chapter II of the *Principia*, Conway states at the beginning that 'time is infinite from the moment of creation and has no quantity which the created intellect can conceive' (2.1; 12). So, the first question that faces us is: what does it mean for Conway to claim that time is infinite within the created universe? Conway is making both an epistemological and metaphysical point:

first, she is claiming that we are not able, with our finite minds, to comprehend the span of time since creation, and second, she is arguing that the universe exists for an infinite duration of time 'from the moment of creation'. Whilst the epistemological aspect of this is clear, the metaphysics is a little ambiguous. For reasons of mental limitation, we are not able to coherently formulate a statement of the form, 'the beginning of the universe was x years ago' – we simply cannot put a number on it. However, due to the reference to a 'moment of creation', Conway may be suggesting that there was a beginning of the created universe *in some sense*, but we cannot conceive of how long ago that beginning was. It could be that Conway believes that time is infinite in the sense that it will go on forever, but it did nevertheless begin at a specific moment in time (though so long ago that we cannot form a coherent thought about it). Such a position would be different from the claim that the universe has always existed in the sense that there was no first moment *and* the duration of the universe extends infinitely into both the past and the future. So, in which sense does Conway believe that the duration of the universe is infinite?

In Section 2 of Chapter II, Conway removes this ambiguity by offering an argument for the beginningless existence of the universe. In response to those who claim that time is finite, and thus that there is a 'first moment', she asks, 'If the world could have been created earlier or before this time?' (2.2; 13) Either way in which the finitist could answer this question, she argues, leads to difficulty: 'If they deny this, they restrict the power of God to a certain number of years. But if they affirm this, they admit that there was time before all times, which is a manifest contradiction' (2.2; 13). Here, Conway is offering a version of a longstanding argument (considered by Aristotle, Augustine, Aquinas and others) for a beginningless universe, which Sorabji calls the 'Why not sooner?' argument (see 1983: 232–40). If we say that God created the universe 6,000 years ago, that begs the question of why the universe was not created, say, 6,001 years ago instead. If the universe was not created 6,001 years ago, and there seems no logical reason why it could not have been (there is nothing obviously contradictory about the universe being created that many years ago), this potentially implies a limit to God's power. God surely would have wanted to create as soon as possible, and so there must be a reason (which could only be a limitation) why it was only 6,000 years ago that creation happened. However, we cannot accept any limitation of God (other than to do the logically impossible). Hence, we are unable to offer an explanation as to why the universe is only 6,000 years old, rather than 6,001 years old. The same reasoning applies to any possible picture of the universe that posits a first moment, and so we must conclude that the created universe exists for an infinite duration of time, without a beginning.

Of course, the Christian tradition has a number of answers to the problem posed by the 'why not sooner?' argument, in defence of creation at a definite point in time: for example, we could argue that Conway's very question does not make sense, insofar as it seems to boil down to 'Why did God act *when* he did (in creating the universe)'? Such a question can only be meaningfully asked if God is subject to time relations of later and sooner and there is a significant strand of monotheist thought that would say this is not the case: indeed, Conway herself is committed to God being outside of time (see 1.4; 9). So, this certainly is not a knockdown argument for a beginningless universe, but it nevertheless reveals the extent of Conway's claims concerning the infinite duration of the universe.

In arguing for a beginningless universe, Conway is following More's earlier view concerning the infinity of time. In his early work, *Philosophical Poems*, he posits that the universe has existed for all eternity, such that it makes no sense to speak of a beginning: 'A real infinite matter, distinct; And yet proceeding from the Deity; Although with different form as then untinct; Has ever been from all Eternity' (1647: 208). However, More later shifted his stance: there was a beginning of the universe, but it still exists for an infinite duration of time insofar as it will infinitely extend temporally into the future.[1] Beginning with the *Divine Dialogues*, More offers a number of arguments in later works against the notion of an infinitely existing universe without a beginning, arguing, 'What can be more contradictious, then that all things should have been really and essentially with God from all Eternity at once, and yet be born in time and succession?' (1668: 58) As such, Conway, in this regard, lies closer to the early (more Platonically inspired) More of the 1840s, rather than the More of later years.[2]

Though Chapter II of the *Principia* does contain a number of references to a 'beginning of time' (which gives rise to the possible interpretation that Conway in fact follows the later More in arguing for a universe with an infinite future, but a finite past), given Conway's use of the 'why not sooner?' argument, we must take such references as loosely referring to time's 'beginning' or foundation in the eternal creative activity of God, rather than as referring strictly to a beginning of time that took place x number of years ago (some 'first moment'). In this context, in speaking of the beginning of time, we are thinking of the origin of time in a logically and ontologically prior (as opposed to temporally prior) sense. In other words, we are seeking the *metaphysical ground* of time, rather than looking to identify one first moment as marking the beginning of time. Given this, we must not be misled by Conway's references to a 'beginning of time' and think that she is attempting to refer to a first moment of time.

The eternity of time

However, one worry that brings many theists to reject the notion of a universe of infinite duration is that it may bring the creation too ontologically close to the eternally existing God: in fact, it may even tempt some to the pantheist conclusion that the world simply is God. Conway shows that she is wary of this danger, stating that 'it cannot be said that creatures considered in themselves are coeternal with God because then eternity and time would be confused with each other' (2.1; 12). As such, in order to preserve the God–world distinction, the difference between an eternal God (outside of time) and an everlasting universe of infinite duration should be observed: if this is done, then God and the created universe cannot be equated, in contradiction to pantheism. In Section 3 of Chapter II, Conway indeed goes on to distinguish between the eternity of God and the infinite duration of the universe. God and creation can be kept securely apart, ontologically speaking, as long as we are clear that God's eternity is distinguishable from time and that the universe's eternity, if we are to use that term, consists of an infinite duration of time: 'If they understand by eternity and by time everlasting an infinite number of times, then, in this sense, creation was made from the beginning of time. If, however, they mean such eternity as God has – so it must be said that creatures are coeternal with God and lack a beginning – this is false' (2.3; 13). There are two potential senses of eternity, one of which is correctly applied to God (existing outside of time), and one of which is correctly applied to the created universe (which exists for an infinite duration of time), and we must be careful to not confuse the two.

Conway claims that God is timeless – 'In God there is no time, change, arrangement, or division of parts. For he is wholly and universally one himself and within himself ... And since there is no time in him nor any mutability, there can exist in him no new knowledge or will at all, but his will and knowledge are eternal and without time or beyond time' (1.4; 9) – and even goes as far as to deny that God has any passions, in order to maintain divine timelessness, '[for] every passion is temporal, having its beginning and end in time' (1.5; 9). God's timelessness, though, does not entail that he is utterly remote from his creatures, in the manner of a deistic God who created the world and leaves it to operate mechanistically, with no further divine intervention or interest. Conway states that God is 'present in everything most closely and intimately in the highest degree' (1.3; 9), through divine ongoing, sustaining creative action: 'All creatures simply are and exist only because God wishes them to, since his will is infinitely powerful and his command ... is alone capable of giving existence to creatures' (2.1; 12). The emphasis is put on God's sustaining activity (rather than on an initial creation) due to Conway's argument that time, within the context of creation, is infinite, and as such there is no beginning of time at which God 'began' creating, however we might like to understand that.

Conway argues that God has an essential timeless attribute of being a creator, and thus, as 'the infinite foundation and ocean of goodness, charity, and bounty ... it necessarily follows that he gave being to creatures from time everlasting or from time without number' (2.4; 13): in other words, a timeless creator leads to everlasting creative activity within time. As such, God's creative activity is understood primarily as a sustaining activity of infinite duration. It is through this activity of sustenance (taken broadly, including giving life to all things[3]) that we can understand a timeless, immutable God as nevertheless entirely present in creation. So, in Conway's system, we have both an infinite God and an infinite creation in terms of time, though with the term 'infinite' understood differently in each case:

> [The] eternity of creatures is nothing other than an infinity of times in which they were and always will be without end. Nevertheless, this infinity of time is not equal to the infinite eternity of God since the divine eternity has no times in it and nothing in it can be said to be past or future, but it is always and wholly present.
>
> (2.5; 13f.)

Thus, there is an everlasting created universe of infinite duration and an eternal God beyond duration.

The very question of a timeless God is one that is still very controversial, though there is evidence that key Christian theologians such as Augustine, Boethius, Anselm and Aquinas all affirmed the timelessness of God. As DeWeese has noted, it is clear that Neoplatonic influence may have had an impact here, particularly in relation to 'the concept of divine simplicity, immutability, and eternity' (2004: 158). Given that we can similarly discern Neoplatonic influence in the *Principia*, it is unsurprising that we also discover a timeless God here. As we saw earlier, Conway will have been introduced to Neoplatonic ideas early on in her philosophical development through her correspondence with Henry More, who, as Coudert notes, proposed 'his personal kind of Kabbalism, which had more in common with Neoplatonic thought than with the Kabbala proper' (1975: 645). It is clear that Conway adopted these Platonic ideas to the extent that More writes to her in 1660, 'your Ladiship is so good a Platonist as not to deny that famous maxim of their Schoole: *Animus cuiusque is est quisque* [The mind is the true self]' (L 144), which we find combined with Kabbalist notions in the *Principia*.

With regard to the development of Christian thought, one of the most influential Neoplatonists is Plotinus, who sees God's creative activity as an emanation, which, as Gerson notes, is to be understood as a sustaining principle beyond time: 'It is not intended to indicate either a temporal process or the unpacking of a potentially complex unity. Rather, the derivation [of the creative principle] was understood in terms of atemporal ontological dependence' (2014: section 2).[4] On the Neoplatonic emanationist model, the atemporality of the divine also involves the eternity of creation itself, that is, the created realm is understood to have existed for an infinite duration of time. It is a necessary aspect of the creative principle that it creates, insofar as its creative force cannot be contained within itself but emanates into different, inferior levels of being. As a corollary, creation has always been happening and will always happen: hence, we have a created universe of infinite duration. Again, we see this reflected in the *Principia*, where Conway affirms infinite time within the created universe.

A further salient aspect of Neoplatonic thought is related to the question of the sense in which God *can* be affirmed as being within time and the created universe. Though, as I have already mentioned, God's emanation results in inferior levels of being, nothing is lost in terms of the presence of the divine, even though that which is produced by the creative principle cannot be identical to it: as there can only be one perfect entity, any created thing cannot be perfect. As Whittaker in his discussion of Plotinus emphasizes, 'There is no disremption of the higher principle [through the process of emanation]. God and mind do not disperse themselves in individual souls and in natural things, though these are nowhere cut off from their causes' (1961: 55), and so the One (Plotinus's term for the ultimate ground of being) is both transcendent *and* entirely present through all things. In the Neoplatonic view of creation, then, we have two key ideas running alongside each other, namely, the emanation of being from the atemporally existing divine into differing, imperfect levels of being, as well as the absolute presence of the divine in all created beings. Such ideas are to be found in Conway's *Principia*, and due to the fact that they have had a major influence upon the development of Christian thought, they can be seen as largely consonant with a standard monotheist view regarding the creation of the universe and God's presence within it.

It must be noted, though, that whilst Conway does hold to the timelessness of God, at one point in Chapter II, Section 5, she seems to disown her previous position by stating, 'While [God] is in time, he is not bound by time' (2.5; 14). Loptson has accused Conway of contradiction here, arguing that she is claiming both that God is outside of time and that 'God is in time, but the nature of his temporal experience is such that ... God perceives all events, past, present, and future, as immediate' (1982: 32). Following Emily Thomas's reading of this passage (see 2017: 998f.), I argue that we should not read too much into this statement; Conway is simply affirming here that God is present in time, as we would want to do if we want to preserve a notion of a personal God that is present in his creation and who takes a providential interest in it. There is no contradiction in a timeless God being present in time in some sense and so Conway's position on this matter is consistent.

In addition, Thomas argues that Conway believes God to be holenmerically present in time, in the sense that God is *wholly present in each moment of time*, rather than his presence being spread through time, which is the case for creatures. Such a view of God's presence is analogous to the spiritual holenmerism that More claims concerning the presence of the soul in the body: as Thomas explains,

> On this view the entire spirit 'fully occupies and possesses' the whole body... and that it is entirely in every part or point of the body... We can make a parallel distinction for presence in time. Just as an immaterial substance may be holenmerically present in space, it may be holenmerically present in time, such that its being exists wholly at every successive moment in time. Similarly, just as an immaterial substance may be extendedly present in space, it may be extendedly present in time, such that its being is 'spread out' across the successive parts of time.
>
> (2017: 999)

I argue, in addition to this, that the holenmeric interpretation of God's presence in time gives us a way of understanding how a timeless, unchanging God can nevertheless have a presence within a world that has a temporal framework. We would expect that such a being would have a distinctive presence in the world that would point towards their fundamental timelessness, and having the unique feature of being holenmerically present in time, with absolutely no extension or division of divine presence, seems to meet our expectations in this regard.

So, part of Conway's view of God is of a timeless being who is holenmerically present in time.

In holding such a view of God, does Conway depart significantly from orthodox Christian thought? The philosopher of religion Richard Swinburne, in reviewing the history of the doctrine of the timelessness of God in the Christian tradition, admits that '[most] of the great Christian theologians from Augustine to Aquinas taught that God is timeless' (1993: 223), but argues that it is ultimately an unorthodox diversion brought about by the alien influence of Neoplatonism[5]: 'This doctrine of divine timelessness is very little in evidence before Augustine. The Old Testament certainly shows no sign of it ... The same applies in general for New Testament writers ... Like the doctrine of his total immutability, the doctrine of God's timelessness seems to have entered Christian theology from neo-Platonism' (1993: 224f.). If Swinburne is correct in his estimation of the tradition, and I think he broadly is, then by following the early More in arguing for the infinity of time in the created universe, Conway reveals her willingness to follow a Neoplatonic approach here.

Indeed, the Neoplatonic influence on Conway's account of creation becomes particularly prominent in Section 4 of Chapter II. Here, she argues for infinite time on the basis of the overflowing goodness of the divine:

> God is infinitely good, loving, and bountiful; indeed, he is goodness and charity itself, the infinite fountain and ocean of goodness, charity and bounty. In what way is it possible for that fountain not to flow perpetually and to send forth living waters? For will not that ocean overflow in its perpetual emanation and continual flux for the production of creatures?
>
> (2.4; 13)

The metaphor of overflowing can be found in Plotinus's *Enneads*[6]: 'Since [the One] is perfect, due to its neither seeking anything, nor having anything, nor needing anything, it in a way overflows and its superabundance has made something else' (2018: 549). The creation of the world is seen by Plotinus as an accidental by-product of the perfection of the One; insofar as its goodness is so great, it inevitably manifests itself externally as a generated universe. Though maintaining a personal element to God, such that we can still speak of the creative act as a choice, Conway holds that God does act of necessity in some sense (we will explore her account of divine freedom further in Chapter 6). Given that God is eternally unchanging and has a will to create, there will always be an operative divine will, everlastingly creating. Conway claims that 'creator' is 'the essential attribute of God', with the implication that 'God was always a creator and will always be a creator because otherwise he would change' (2.5; 13).

From the Neoplatonic-inspired view that perfection necessarily involves generation, Conway sets up another argument for a beginningless universe. As God, from eternity, always generates something, there must always be a created universe as a corollary of his eternal existence. God's power and overflowing goodness are infinite, and so the universe must be eternally generated also, existing over an infinite duration of time:

> Since he is not able to multiply himself because that would be the same as creating many Gods, which would be a contradiction, it necessarily follows that he gave being to creatures from time everlasting or from time without number, for otherwise the goodness communicated by God… would indeed be finite and could be then numbered in terms of years. Nothing is more absurd.
>
> (2.4; 13)

Conway ties the infinite duration of the universe to other claims about the infinite nature of the universe, including that there are an infinite number of worlds and an infinite number of creatures in those worlds (thus following the Platonist 'principle of plenitude', noted earlier, according to which the creation is as abundant with as many things as possible). The God of the *Principia* is not an impersonal, emanating principle; rather, Conway holds to the personal God of the major theist traditions who intentionally wills creation and its features. Being outside of time, the eternal will to create manifests itself, Conway argues, in a universe of infinite duration:

> God was not indifferent about whether or not to give being to creatures, but he made them from an inner impulse of his divine goodness and wisdom. And so he created worlds and creatures as quickly as he could, for it is the nature of a necessary agent to do as much as he can. Since he could have created worlds or creatures from time immemorial… it follows that he has done this.
>
> (3.3; 16)

So, from reflection upon the divine attributes (particularly omnipotence and omnibenevolence), we can come to know that the universe must be everlasting, not just in the sense that it will endure from now infinitely into the future, but that it has always existed and will exist for an infinite duration of time, both looking back into the past and forward to the future. Any other position on the question of infinite time, including the familiar Christian narrative of a finite universe that started a finite number of years ago and that will finish a finite number of years from now, is simply not doing justice to the perfect nature of God.

Creation of souls

Turning now from the creation of the universe as a whole to the question of the creation of creatures in particular, it is worth noting Conway's insistence that God has and continues to create an infinite number of creatures 'from time immemorial': 'He has multiplied and always multiplies and increases the essences of creatures to infinity' (3.4; 17). The creation of creatures is taken to be an ongoing, never-ending process that has always taken place and will always take place. In terms of comparison with general Christian thought on these matters, Conway seems to diverge from the tradition insofar as Christian eschatology takes the creation of creatures to be a finite process that began with a first moment *ex nihilo* and will end with the apocalypse: an end of history at which all creatures who have ever been and will ever be are finally judged. Conway rejects such eschatological notions, as the creative act of God will proceed as it has always proceeded for an infinite duration of time and will never come to an end in the manner envisaged in apocalyptic thought. As far as Conway is concerned, those who believe in a final apocalypse would need to explain why God would stop creating, and in answering that question, they would face an analogue of the 'why not sooner?' argument discussed above. Given the generally accepted theological commitments concerning creation and the apocalypse, the Christian tradition would also hold that there are a finite number of creatures, rather than an infinite amount, and this is another claim that Conway challenges.

In addition, Conway is firmly rejecting a major aspect of More's controversial theory concerning the pre-existence of the soul, which he holds throughout his philosophical works. According to More, all souls that there will ever be were created at the first moment of time. More suggests a number of philosophical and scriptural arguments for this theory (which could have caused great personal trouble for him, given its flirtation with heterodoxy). As an example, More agrees with Joseph Glanvill, who stated in his *Lux Orientalis* (1662) that the phenomenon of individuals having intellectual prejudices in philosophical debates can only be explained by their being readymade judgements from an earlier form of existence of the same soul.[7] More argues that such intellectual prejudices are not simply a matter of taste, as with the case of music, where the preference of an individual for one melody over another can reasonably be thought to be grounded in the bodily constitution of that individual in that life alone:

> If the Body can thus cause us to love and dislike *Sensibles*, why not as well to approve and dislike *Opinions* and *Theories*? But the reason is obvious why not; because the liking or disliking of these Sensibles depends upon the grateful or ungrateful motion of the Nerves of the Body, which may be otherwise constituted or qualified in some complexions than in other some. But for Philosophical Opinions and Theories, what have they to do with the motion of the Nerves? It is the Soul herself judges of those abstractedly from the Senses, or any use of the Nerves or corporeal Organ.
>
> (1682: 86f.)

Intellectual prejudices cannot be explained by bodily constitution, as it is the soul alone that determines the preference of the individual in such debates, apart from any bodily influence.

In addition, in order to rule out other possible sources for these prejudices, More notes that such partialities can be mistaken (indeed, the fact that people often have contradictory prejudices proves that they can be), and so they cannot be innate ideas that are implanted within us by God as a reliable guide to the way the world is. Also, it is argued that these prejudices could not be a result of sense-experience in the individual's current life, as they concern abstract questions that could not be determined one way or the other through empirical means, and they cannot be the result of pure intellectual thought in that lifetime either, as sometimes individuals are immediately inclined to one side of an abstract debate upon being introduced to the issues involved. Having ruled out these various sources of intellectual prejudices (the constitution of the body, divinely given innate ideas, sensory experience and intellectual contemplation in this life), the only possible explanation for our intellectual prejudices is that they are judgements formed in previous phases of our soul's existence. In this way, More argues, we are given good reason to believe in the pre-existence of the soul.

However, even if we accept More's arguments for pre-existence of the soul, why should we think that God has stopped creating new souls? More holds that his view on this matter has impeccable scriptural authority, based on the claim from the Book of Genesis that on the 'seventh day', God rests from his creative work:

> *That God on the seventh day rested from all his works.* This one would think were an Argument clear enough that he creates nothing since the celebration of the first seventh day's rest. For if all his works are rested from, then the creation of

Souls (which is a work, nay a Master-piece amongst his works scarce inferior to any) is rested from also.

(1682: 16f.)

More interprets Genesis 2:1–3 as a very broad claim that God's creative act with regard to the creation of individuals is complete for the rest of the eternity:

> Thus the heavens and the earth were finished, and all the host of them. And on the seventh day God ended his work which he had made; and he rested on the seventh day from all his work which he had made. And God blessed the seventh day, and sanctified it: because that in it he had rested from all his work which God created and made.

However, as we see from this Biblical passage, it must be admitted that Genesis is certainly not decisive on the question in hand, so More needs to offer some kind of explanation as to just why God would stop creating individuals. Surely, we might think, God would want to keep creating as many individuals as possible, so that as many created beings can come to know and love him. God certainly has the power to create more individuals, so there must have been a positive decision to no longer create individuals. More argues that the reason for this decision ultimately lies in God's goodness, which would bring God to create individuals as soon as he can, namely, at the first moment of the created universe. Any attempt to claim of a particular creature that they could have been created sooner, but God declined to, does not do justice to divine goodness, and so we are brought to the conclusion that God's nature guarantees that no other creatures will be created after the initial creation of souls.[8]

So, whilst Conway agrees in broad terms with More's narrative of the journey of souls from one phase of existence to another (an aspect of her philosophy that we will go on to consider in more detail), such that we can claim that there is pre-existence of the soul in some sense, she firmly rejects the details of her mentor's claims concerning the creation of the soul. There is no sense in Conway's system of God 'resting' from creation; rather, the creation of new individuals is an ongoing, never-ending process, involving an infinite number of creatures. You cannot blame Conway's God for not creating any particular individual sooner than they were created, for God could hardly do any more in creating an infinite number of creatures for an infinite duration of time. In this way, Conway undercuts More's philosophical argument for holding that God creates no further souls. We can see that, on this point at least, Conway and More really could not be further apart.

Creation of creatures through/with Christ

At the beginning of Chapter IV, Conway makes further noteworthy remarks on the question of the creation of creatures and of Christ, which illustrate the varying perspectives we can have upon creation in the context of her system. In answer to the question of whether all creatures were created at the same time, Conway unequivocally answers in the negative, 'if "to create" refers to the creatures, then [creation] occurred successively over time' (4.1; 21), whereas Henry More, as we have seen, would have answered affirmatively. However, Conway's reason for her answer is a little obscure: 'For just as it is the nature and essential attribute of God to be immutable and eternal, so it is the nature of his creatures to be mutable and temporal' (4.1; 21). Whilst we may grant that it is the nature of creature to be within time and changeable, this does not seem to settle the question of whether or not all creatures were created at the same time, insofar as their being both in time and mutable seems consistent with all creatures being created at the first moment of time.

Nevertheless, Conway goes on to claim that we can think about creation in two other ways. First, from the perspective of God and the eternal will to create, we can indeed say that all things are created at the same time. Presumably, given the illegitimate designation of temporal attributes to God and the divine will, Conway is referring to something like the metaphorical 'eternal now' that any eternal being inhabits. As temporal beings with limited understanding, perhaps the only way we conceive of eternal existence is as a single moment, and so when we attempt to think of creation from this perspective, we think of it as happening all 'at the same time'. From our limited perspective, then, given the juxtaposition of an eternal, timeless God and a universe of infinite duration, we can think of creation in two different ways: either as happening successively or 'all at once', in a metaphorical sense that tries to capture the timeless standpoint of God.

However, Conway goes on to offer another perspective upon creation, which leads into discussion of her Christology. She states that we can take 'create' to refer to 'universal seeds and principles, which are like springs and fountains from which creatures flow forth in an orderly succession determined by God (who is the greatest and first principle of all things)' (4.1; 21). Whilst this reference to 'universal seeds and principles' may seem rather puzzling, a clue for understanding what Conway means by this is to be found in her reversion here to Neoplatonic imagery, as we saw her using when she explains the link between God's creative act, his goodness and omnipotence. These principles of creation that she refers to are likened to flowing fountains, though they are said to be directed by God as 'first principle'. Again, we can see the influence of Plotinus, who has a multi-layered metaphysical system that goes beyond a simple God–world dichotomy. In the *Enneads*, Plotinus offers a hierarchical system of the main intelligible principles (or hypostases) that begins with One, which generates Intellect, which in turn is expressed in Soul. Plotinus characterizes the One as 'the productive power of all things' (2018: 541), a simple, sheer unity that grounds all plurality. The One has an internal activity which overspills into the generation of the Intellect, which is the first step in plurality on the way to the world of our everyday experience.[9] The internal activity of Intellect is itself thought: in a state of lacking self-sufficiency and perfect unity, the Intellect attempts the impossible task of thinking the One.

For Plotinus, thinking is necessarily plural, and so this activity only results in more plurality, namely, the Ideas or Forms familiar to the Platonic tradition. As Emilsson explains, the Intellect thereby acts as an archetype for the material universe and all the beings that dwell within it:

> Since the sensible universe 'is a living being containing all living beings'…, the whole archetype of this universe must be in Intellect. This archetype is the intelligible universe itself which Plotinus identifies with the absolute being Plato speaks of in *Timeaeus*… Everything that exists by nature in the world of sense is derived from the intelligible world and none of the things that exist in the intelligible world are against nature.
>
> (2017: 114f.)

With the Plotinian notion that these Forms or Ideas, as part of the attempt of the Intellect to think One, give an image or reflection of One (though this reflection will necessarily be imperfect), it is a short step to conceiving of them as eternal divine thoughts underlying the creative activity that results in the created universe.

Returning to Conway, we can take her reference to 'universal seeds and principles' as akin to these Plotinian ideas: 'divine thoughts' that are generated by the necessary activity of God, and act as archetypes for divine creative activity. As in the case where we consider creation from the perspective of the eternal will to create, if we take 'create' as referring to these creative principles, then again we can say that all creatures were created at the same time, reflecting their eternal status as expressions of necessary divine thoughts. However, this picture is soon complicated by the role of Christ in the production of creatures: 'It can also be said that all creatures were created at the same time, especially if one considers the Messiah or Christ, who is the first born of all creatures, through whom all things are said to have been made' (4.1; 21). In this way, Conway signals her adherence to the view of Christ as 'logos', the Word that has a distinctive role to play in God's creative activity. In the following section, she writes: 'Jesus Christ signifies the whole Christ, who is God and man. As God, he is called *logos ousios*, or the essential word of the father' (4.2; 21).

The main Biblical authority for the notion of Christ as Logos having a role in creation comes from the Platonically inspired Gospel of John,[10] which famously begins with a retelling of the creation narrative in Genesis,[11] but from a Christological perspective: 'In the beginning was the Word, and the Word was with God, and the Word was God. The same was in the beginning with God. All things were made by him; and without him was not any thing made that was made. In him was life' (John 1:1–4). As Kieffer notes, the Johannine Gospel begins with a striking revaluation of Christ as having a distinctive multi-faceted role in creation: '[John] now describes the Word's function in creation, as either the instrument by which God created, or as the fountainhead which made creation possible. The whole creation is marked by God's Word and reveals God … The Word in John is both an instrument and a model' (2010: 189).

The Logos theology of the Johannine Gospel also has a clear forebear in the thought of Philo of Alexandria, a Jewish theologian who lived from around 20 BC to AD 40. As we have already noted, Conway and More were both deeply impressed by what they believed to be ancient Jewish literature, such as the Kabbalah, and this included the extant works of Philo. Two aspects of Philo's thought that particularly drew Conway and More were the clear impact of Platonism on his work and his Logos theology, which could be construed as having a nascent Christology and as even pointing towards a full-blooded Trinitarianism. In a parallel with the Prologue to John's Gospel, Philo reinterprets the opening chapter of the Book of Genesis in Platonic terms, taking references to the creation of Adam in Gen 1:26 as referring to the Platonic Form of humankind, as opposed to the single human individual, Adam, who is the subject of the creation narrative in Genesis from 2:7 onwards. Philo also distinguishes the creation of the intelligible realm from that of the sensible (see Wedderburn (1973: 305) [*et passim*]). Such a Platonic Form of humankind is taken to be the Logos, identified in the creation narrative as the first created being, which also acts as an archetype, along the lines of the Johannine Logos. Sarah Hutton argues that, for More, it is the dual nature of Philo's Logos that particularly marks it out as anticipating Christological and Trinitarian reflection upon Christ, the Logos and creation within the Christian tradition: 'The putative compatibility between Philo's concept of the *logos* and Trinitarian doctrine rested, in large measure, on his understanding of the *logos* as being dual-faceted. Philo differentiates between the *logos* as eternal archetype and the *logos* as first created being, between the *logos* as only begotten son and as first-born son of God' (2004: 159).

More points to Philo, in *Explanation of the Grand Mystery of Godliness*, as demonstrating that the source of the doctrine of the Trinity lies in ancient Jewish wisdom, before the historical establishment of the Christian Church.[12] In fact, he argues, the influence of the ancient Trinitarianism of the Jews can even be seen in ancient Greek philosophy:

> For my own part I make no question but that the Greek philosophers, as *Pythagoras* and *Plato*, had not only their [Word], but *the whole Mystery of their Trinity* from the Divine Traditions amongst the Jews. *Philo* the Jew speaks often of this Principle in the Godhead, calling it [the Word of God] or [the Divine Word], or sometimes [God], othersometimes [the First-born Son of God] and attributes unto it *the Creation of the World*... insomuch that this Author might be a good Commentator upon this first chapter of [the Gospel of] S. *John*.
>
> (1660: 12)

More believes that apparent evidence of Trinitarianism in both ancient Jewish and Greek thought both adds to the plausibility of the doctrine of the Trinity, on the basis of the principle that agreement of different ancient traditions adds to the probability of something being true, and shows that Christianity and Judaism, in terms of doctrinal commitments, are not necessarily as far apart as they are often taken to be.

In granting Christ a role in creation, Conway is therefore following a familiar Christian line of thought, as well as echoing More's interest in attempting to excavate distinctively Christian doctrines from Jewish and ancient Greek texts. Given his status as a created being, the Logos is strictly within time, but his creative activity is everlasting (continuing and unchanging throughout all time). As the 'universal seeds and principles', reflecting the immutable nature of God, are embedded within the creative activity taking place through the Logos, then from this perspective it can indeed be said that 'all creatures are created at the same time'. The nature of things, in the form of archetypes, that are to be created for an infinite duration of time is already set ontologically (but not temporally) prior to the creation of the material universe. There was no temporal process by which these 'universal seeds and principles' were brought into being, and so in the same analogous way by which we can say that all things were created 'at the same time' from the perspective of God, we can claim the same from the perspective of Logos.[13]

Conway further expands her Christological claims in relation to creation in the following section (Section 3 of Chapter IV), in which she states that 'all things are contained in [Christ] and have their existence in him, because they arise from him just like branches from a root, so that *they remain forever in him* in a certain way' (4.3; 22 – my emphasis). In having the archetypes for the created universe residing immutably and everlastingly in the Logos, all creatures have a pre-existing bond with Christ as Logos, apart from any moral or spiritual status that an individual creature might have. The forms of things are fixed for the infinite duration of the created universe, and so, in this sense, we can say that 'all things are created at the same time', though in a loose sense. As we shall see (in Chapter 5), there is an opportunity in Conway's metaphysical system for creatures to come even closer to Christ through a process of moral development and potential salvation, and it is this fundamental ontological root in the Logos which acts as a necessary (but not sufficient) condition for this soteriological progress.

So, Conway draws upon the logocentric Christology of the Christian tradition, as well as ideas from Jewish sources, to grant a distinctive role to Christ in divine creation. Christ as Logos acts as an everlasting conduit for creation, containing the universal seeds and principles that inform the kinds of things that are created throughout the universe. Given the eternal status of these principles (in the sense of 'everlasting'), we can from the perspective of the Logos claim that creation happened 'at the same time', but this does not hold for creatures themselves, who are continually created at each moment in time. Though we have so far in this chapter talked a great about time, we have yet to explore Conway's account of its nature. We will consider her suggested definition of time in the following section.

Time and motion

Conway considers time to be infinite in the sense of a created universe of infinite duration. However, what does this time consist of? What *is* time? Fortunately, Conway offers us a seemingly clear answer to this question: 'Time is nothing but the successive motion or operation of creatures' (2.6; 14). Such a definition of time suggests another reason why Conway holds that God is entirely outside of time, insofar as she takes motion or operation as implying a kind of imperfection that could not be imputed to the absolutely perfect divine being: 'Since in God there is no successive motion or operation toward further perfection because he is absolutely perfect, there are no times in God or his eternity' (2.6; 14). Further to this, such a statement by Conway suggests that she actually means something more limited by 'time' than what her original basic definition holds. God must be outside of time, Conway argues, because he is not able to participate in movement or operation *towards perfection*, and so this suggests that her definition of time is not simply as the motion of creatures *simpliciter*; rather, her more exact definition of time would be something like, 'nothing but the successive motion or operation of creatures *towards or away from perfection*', in the sense of engaging in moral development and becoming more (or less[14]) like God. As such, we can think of Conway as proposing a kind of moral-ontological definition of time, in which questions of being and virtue are interlinked.

This definition of time has important consequences for our understanding of other aspects of her philosophy, such as her Christology, theory of moral development and eschatology, and I will explore these implications in later chapters. By defining time in this way, Conway is rejecting an absolutist approach, according to which it has a separate existence apart from the being or operation of material things: it is the sphere in which things happen, rather than being an aspect of things or events themselves. In opposition to this view, Conway is arguing that time simply consists in a certain kind of motion. If there were no such motion, then there would be no time. This non-absolutist approach, in which morality and ontology are connected, is captured in Conway's claims that 'the ordinary sense of the word ["time" is] a successive increase or decrease of things during which they grow for a certain period and then decline until they die or change into another state' (5.6; 26). Time is not the framework in which things happen; rather, it is *simply things happening*.

Furthermore, this passage also links time to both ontology and morality. Neither God nor Christ is subject to time as they stand outside of a process in creation that involves both growth and decay, in a moral and ontological sense (for as we shall see, neither can deteriorate morally or in terms of their mode of being). Creatures who are still caught in this process, on the other hand, are subject to time. Thus, this later passage also points to Conway's holistic approach to time that views it as both involving questions of morality and ontology.

This account of time offered in the *Principia* has brought some scholars to interpret Conway as at least approaching a process philosophy. As Carol Wayne White explains, process thought sees the universe as fundamentally a state of becoming, of constant change or motion: 'Process metaphysics diametrically opposes the general view that subordinates processes to substantial things, or denies them altogether. In a process conceptual framework, events, and relationships – rather than separate substances or separate particles – constitute reality' (2009: 82). Conway's theory of time as a kind of motion of creatures certainly seems to metaphysically prioritize process as the fundamental structure of the material universe, rather than material substance per se. White goes on to argue that Conway's emphasis in her metaphysical system on the soteriological journey of creatures towards perfection finds echoes in the twentieth-century process philosopher, Arthur Whitehead: 'Conway's depiction of all creatures perfecting themselves in the participation of goodness resembles one of Whitehead's earliest views that all living things are characterized by a threefold urge: to live, to live well, and to live better' (2009: 84). Conway certainly sees the universe as a whole as engaged in an ontological and moral process, though whether she does subordinate substantial things to processes is not entirely clear at this point. We will return to the question of Conway's relation to process philosophy later (in Chapter 7), when we consider her account of the constitution of creatures.

So, as we have seen, Conway's definition of time should not simply be taken as 'the successive motion or operation of creatures', but more specifically as 'successive motion or operation of creatures *towards or away from perfection*'. There would be good reason for Conway to nuance her definition in this way because the suggested definition of time as motion *simpliciter* had long been roundly considered and rejected in the philosophical tradition. In particular, given Conway's familiarity with Plotinus, it is probable that she is aware of the famous discussion in the *Enneads* of definitions of time linked to motion. To begin with, Plotinus rejects any definition of time as motion *simpliciter*, for the reason that motion *is in time*, and not time itself: as support for this view, he argues that they must be distinct as 'motion can both cease permanently or be in abeyance for a while whereas time cannot' (2018: 342). We are seemingly able to conceive of all motion coming to a stop, but time as still flowing, and so our intuitions point to their metaphysical distinction. Plotinus then goes on to reject the Aristotelian definition of time as equated to the number or measure of motion, on the basis that questions concerning the number of something are separate from questions regarding their nature. Due to this, he claims that, 'it is one thing to talk of time, another to talk of a particular quantity of time. For before speaking of the quantity one must say what that is which is of a particular quantity' (2018: 346).

However, Plotinus does not wish to entirely dissociate the definition of time from questions of motion; rather, like Conway, he attempts to equate time with a particular kind of motion. He begins the argument for his positive account of time by approaching the question from the standpoint of the intelligible realm, apart from the world of our everyday experience. In the same way that Intellect proceeds from the external activity of One, Soul proceeds from the external activity of Intellect. On the next step of plurality, Soul introduces successive activity, whereas the activity of Intellect is always complete. As Lloyd Gerson explains, Plotinus understands Intellect as having a peculiarly timeless 'life':

> Such a life is nothing but the primary activity of Intellect, the cognitive identification with the totality of intelligible reality. The denial of temporal predicates to that life… depends on the key concepts of completeness and partlessness… The activity of Intellect is to be conceived of so that that activity does not have a beginning, a middle, and an end.
> (1994: 117)

Soul introduces succession into the intelligible realm, with activity that can be thought of as incomplete, moving from a beginning to an end. It is in this life of the Soul, then, that we find the origin of time. Plotinus asks,

> Would it, then, make any sense to say that time is the life of the soul in its changing motion from one way of living to another?… [Instead] of identity, sameness, and remaining in itself [which characterises the life of Intellect], there is not remaining in itself but exercising different actions, instead of the unextended and unity, the image of unity, the unity found in continuity; instead of being unlimited from the start and whole, there is the progression to infinity leading to continuous succession, and instead of the whole being gathered together, the whole which will and will forever be is going to exist, part by part.
> (2018: 348)

So, on the Plotinian view, time comes into being as a part of the procession of Soul from Intellect, and it is simply successive activity of the Soul.[15] Its external activity, in turn, results in the changeable world, inhabited by individuated souls, that is the object of our everyday experience.

It is notable, remembering Conway's definition of time, that we can understand Plotinus's account of time as itself tied to a kind of motion, insofar as the life of Soul can be taken as motion[16]: he states, 'Intellect just is as it is; always the same and established in a steady state of activity. By contrast, motion toward and around Intellect is already Soul's work' (2018: 209). Due to the different kinds of life enjoyed by Intellect and Soul, the activity of the latter can be said to be characterized by an incompleteness that results in desire (see Gerson 1994: 62). The motion of Soul in turns acts as an archetype by which our individual souls have motion towards ends that we lack (a feature that characterizes Soul's motion, but not that of the Intellect, which is complete). Insofar as our souls participate in the intelligible realm, the motion that is the life of our soul is *itself* time in a manner which would not apply to any material object, such as our physical body. As Emilsson notes, there is a distinction to be made between 'time as the life of soul, and being *in* time. The latter is the lot of the sensible world and the things in it. He even equates this with being "a slave to time"' (2017: 172). The motion of the soul can, then, be said to be part of the *constitution* of time, whereas the motion of material objects is merely *subject* to time, or constrained by it.

With this brief foray into Plotinus's account of the origin of time, we can see that there are parallels with Conway's own definition that have not been explored in the past and reveal another influence of Neoplatonism on her thought. Both Conway and Plotinus wish to tie the notions of time and motion together, but not in the straightforward Aristotelian sense of 'time=motion' *simpliciter*. Rather, time is taken as a particular kind of motion, namely, the activity of a life that is changeable and incomplete, seeking to move towards a desired end. Though Conway does not have the metaphysical baggage of One, Intellect, and Soul (though really, considering her Trinitarian views, she is not at a great distance from Plotinus here), we can nevertheless see clear parallels in the idea of time grounded in the development of the soul. As has already been mentioned, Conway holds that all things are essentially spirit and involved in movement towards perfection, and so in her system, time becomes the development of soul, writ large, towards the goal of approaching and becoming one with God. Of course, this overall movement in Conway's philosophy is merely an abstraction and not metaphysically grounded in a separate hypostasis, Soul, as is the case in Plotinus's system. However, given the Christianized context of Conway's thought, it is not surprising that such a shift would be made due to the fact that Christianity has a greater emphasis on the direct individual creation of souls by God, rather than by some sort of lower level of reality below perfect being.

With this comparison of Conway and Plotinus, however, we can also reveal a distinctive aspect of the account of time found in the *Principia*, as opposed to that found in the *Enneads*. As we saw, Plotinus strikes a distinction between souls, which are more directly connected to the life of Soul, whose motion forms the metaphysical ground of time, and mere material objects. Such an account suggests a familiar Platonic separation in the individual between the body, which is inextricably tied to an imperfect, changeable world, and soul, which can in some sense participate in the perfect intelligible realm. However, in the context of Conway's system, no such distinction can be made (or at least not made in quite the same way), as all things are essentially spirit. Given her definition of time, then, there is nothing that is merely subject to time, or constrained by it, in the manner that Plotinus argues applies to material objects. In the *Principia*, all things are equally able to engage positively with the motion towards perfection that characterizes time and so nothing is constrained by time. We can therefore glimpse the all-encompassing aspect of Conway's picture of all things moving towards the same goal, regardless of natural classification (a notion that we will develop and explore throughout the rest of this work). However, if we think of Conway as retaining something of the notion of materiality being linked to being merely subject to time, we can see those beings which are more material, due to their moral backsliding, as *making themselves* more constrained and at the whim of events as they occur: a kind of giving up of one's own freedom, perhaps. However, this is not a suggestion that I will consider further here.

For a possible influence upon Conway with regard to the connection between time and the perfection of things, we can look to Origen. In various works, he suggests a soteriological approach that views time as the process by which humans grow in perfection and reach heaven. As noted by Tzamalikos (1991: 544), Origen views the extension of time in the universe as a road which can either be walked well (through carrying out virtuous actions) or badly (acting against the will of God). This moral perspective upon time is exemplified in his *Commentary on the Book of John*, where he considers the first phrase, 'In the beginning was the Word' (John 1:1). Origen points out that 'beginning' does not necessarily refer to coming into existence, but rather 'a commencement, as in the beginning of a road or distance' (Trigg 1998: 120). He points to a passage from the Septuagint version of Proverbs, which refers to a beginning as the start of a virtuous course of action: 'The beginning of a good way is to do righteous things' (LXX Prov. 16: 7)[17]. When read in this way, the beginning of time as referred to at the start of the Gospel of John is construed as the start of the progress of a creature towards 'God's way', conforming themselves to the divine will through virtuous action and contemplation. The end of time will therefore come with the moral 'restoration' [*apokatastasis*] of all things, when, as Origen puts it, 'no enemy [to God] will remain' (Trigg 1998: 120). Though by no means entirely rejecting a more physicalist viewpoint upon the nature of time,

Origen emphasizes a moral, soteriological perspective upon time that takes into account God's purpose for creation, namely, its moral restoration. In this way, time, morality and soteriology are fundamentally intertwined. It is just this kind of approach, I argue, that we find explored in Conway's *Principia* and is likely inspired by her discussions concerning Origen with Henry More and others.

Once we see that Conway's definition of time is tied specifically to the movement of creatures towards perfection, it becomes clear that in the context of her system, questions concerning the history of the universe are inextricably intertwined with questions of salvation and moral perfectibility. As such, time is not to be taken as a straightforward, metaphysical notion; rather, her definition is infused with the familiar Abrahamic tradition of viewing the history of the universe from the perspective of fall and restoration. I will return to these themes in Chapter 5, where we will consider further the implications of this definition of time for our wider understanding of Conway's philosophy, including the role of Christ and the possibility of our continuing moral perfectibility.

Conclusion

To sum up the discussion of the chapter, I have claimed the following:

1. Conway argues for the infinite duration of the universe (extending into both the past and the future), in contrast to the usual Christian view that creation happened x number of years ago.
2. Whilst much of the discussion in Chapter II suggests that she may follow the later More in arguing for a universe that stretches infinitely into the future, but nevertheless has a beginning, Conway's use of the 'why not sooner?' argument reveals that her sympathies are in fact with a beginningless universe. In this, as well as through such references as to creation as an 'overflowing' and 'emanation', the influence of Neoplatonism upon her thought is revealed.
3. Conway's strict definition of time is best understood as something along the lines of 'nothing but the successive motion or operation of creatures towards perfection'. In tying time to the motion of the soul towards some ultimate end (namely, perfection and increasing unity with God), we see further parallels with the Neoplatonist Plotinus and the Christian theologian Origen, though this is not to say that there are no important differences there either.

4. There are three different perspectives that we can take upon the activity of creation in Conway's system: namely, from the point of view of the eternal will of God, from that of the Logos and that of creatures. Depending on the perspective we take, we can both claim that all creatures are created successively and 'at the same time' (though with the latter phrase taken metaphorically or analogically).
5. Conway follows the familiar Christian doctrine of Logos as having a distinctive role in creation (grounded in the scriptural authority of the Gospel of John).

In the following chapter, we will continue our review of the fundamentals of Conway's metaphysical system by considering in more detail her key distinction between God, Christ and creature. We will explore their distinctive capacities with regard to the notion of change, which we have already seen as fundamental to Conway's notion of time. This will lead us on to looking at Conway's Christology in more detail, with particular regard to the Quaker and Neoplatonist-inspired idea of the Christ Within.

4

God, Christ and Creature

As we have seen, Anne Conway had fully adopted Quakerism by her death in 1679.[1] Not only did her epitaph simply state, 'Quaker Lady', she brought many prominent Quaker figures, such as George Fox, Robert Barclay and George Keith, into her intellectual circle at her residence, Ragley Hall, and employed a number of Quaker women as servants, praising them in her correspondence as a palliative against her severe health issues (see L 421f.). In the *Principia*, Conway reveals deep engagement with Quaker ideas in currency at the time. However, this aspect of her thought has not been widely recognized, and even where potential Quaker influence upon Conway's philosophy, as presented in the *Principia*, has been noted, it has not always been deeply explored.[2]

The main aim of this chapter is to delve more deeply into Conway's Christology, one of the most mysterious aspects of her philosophy, through the lens of her engagement with Quaker thought. There are two main questions that we need to consider: (1) what is Christ, and (2) what role does Christ play in Conway's metaphysical system? I believe that it is instructive to look to the Quaker milieu in which Conway is operating at the time of the writing of the *Principia* in order to help us answer these questions. In particular, I argue that it is instructive to look at the theology of the early Quaker thinker, George Keith, with whom Conway had extensive contact, through both correspondence and meetings at Ragley Hall. So, in what follows, in order to explicate Conway's Christology, I will explore the parallels between her thought and that of George Keith on the question of the Christ Within and of Christ as an extended, distinct metaphysical principle.

To begin with, though, we need to consider Conway's claim that there is a distinct metaphysical principle, 'Christ', that acts as a mediator between two other kinds of thing, God and Creature. We shall see that these kinds of things (God, Christ and Creature) can be distinguished by the kind of change they can undergo, which will have consequences for our later discussion of Christ and the possibility of salvation. I will also introduce the current interpretive debate concerning the nature of Conway's monism, which we will revisit in Chapter 7.

Following this, I will further explore Conway's rejection of the dualist aspects of the ontology of her philosophical mentor, Henry More, grounded in her views regarding the implications of God's goodness for the nature of creation. I will also introduce the early theology of George Keith, with a particular focus upon his religious epistemology and Christology. I will argue that the notion of the Christ Within, found in Quaker thought, provides a distinctive Christology for Conway's philosophy, centred on the question of change and the intermingling of spirits. Finally, I will conclude the chapter with reflections upon future potential avenues of research regarding the interplay between Anne Conway's philosophy and early Quaker theology, as well as the impact that Conway's philosophy may have had upon George Keith, leading to his schism with Quakerism in the 1690s.

Three types of substance?

We have so far skirted around one of the major claims of Conway's philosophy, but it cannot be ignored any longer given our interest in this chapter in her Christology. The claim is this: there are three types of thing (what I will call quiddities)[3] that exhaust reality, and we can label these types, 'God', 'Christ' and 'Creature'.[4] In making such a claim, Conway is seemingly rejecting two major metaphysical traditions: monism, which is committed to there being one kind of thing in the world (e.g. materialism, which claims that there is only matter), and substance dualism, which is usually the claim that reality is exhausted by matter and some kind of spirit. Earlier, I argued that Conway is a spiritual monist, in the sense that all things are spirit. However, this picture is complicated by the claim that there are three types of quiddity. We thus need to carefully distinguish some claims:

1. Conway is a monist in the sense that she claims that all created beings are made out of the same kind of stuff;
2. Conway is a monist in the sense that she claims that all things (created and uncreated) are essentially spirit;
3. Conway claims that there are three distinguishable types of spirit.

Claim (1) is undoubtedly true, but given that Conway claims (3), is it right to call her a monist in the sense captured by (2)? Does she not end up diluting monism so much that she essentially ends up with an ontological trialism, according to which there are actually three types of substance? If it seems that Conway is ultimately committed to there being three types of thing, then perhaps she cannot be understood as a monist in the sense of (2). However, her Neoplatonist-inspired account of creation, explored earlier, seems to commit Conway to a more thoroughgoing monism than this, on the basis that all levels of reality must be fundamentally alike, with the lower levels merely imperfect reflections of God. It seems that Conway's system is ultimately left with a degree of tension between a potential commitment to all things being spirit and there being three distinguishable types of quiddity that make up reality. We will return to this potential problem at the end of this section.

First, we must review what precisely Conway claims, and how she seeks to establish this ontology. Conway offers a metaphysical system of three quiddities: God, Christ and Creature. God is described as immediately present in all of creation, but also as using a mediator, Christ, which is 'generated', rather than created. The necessity of this intermediate principle is due to the radical difference between God and his creatures:

> [God] is immediately present in all things and immediately fills all things. In fact, he works immediately in everything in his own way. But this must be understood in respect to that union and communication which creatures have with God so that although God works immediately in everything, yet he nevertheless uses this same mediator as an instrument through which he works together with creatures, since that instrument is by its own nature closer to them.
>
> (5.4; 25)

However, despite a trichotomy of quiddities, Conway argues that there is only one kind of substance (see 7.1; 41f.). As such, there are, in Conway's ontology, three types of being or quiddity – God, Christ and Creature – all of which are kinds of one fundamental type of substance.

Given that all things are spirit, Conway argues that all that allows us to distinguish between the different kinds of being is the kind of change that they can undergo. As is common in philosophical reflection upon divine immutability, Conway states that God is already perfect, cannot become less or more perfect and so cannot undergo change: '[There] is no greater being than God, and he cannot improve or be made better in any way, much less decrease, which would imply his imperfection. Therefore it is clear that God, or the highest being, is wholly unchangeable' (5.3; 24). Christ can change, but only towards perfection, whilst Creature can both change towards and away from perfection: 'The creatures could not be equal to Christ nor of the same nature because his nature could never degenerate like theirs and change from good into bad. For this reason they have a far inferior nature in comparison to the first born' (4.4; 22). Summing up her view, Conway states:

> [There] are three kinds of being. The first [God] is altogether immutable. The second [Christ] can only change toward the good, so that which is good is by its very nature can become better. The third kind [creatures] is that which, although it was good by its very nature, is nevertheless able to change from good to good and as well as from good to evil.
>
> (5.3; 24)

Due to this, Conway posits two different kinds of change, or more specifically, two different kinds of power that a being potentially has to bring about change in themselves: 'One has the intrinsic power of changing itself either for good or bad, and this common to all creatures, but not the first born of all creatures. The other kind of change is the power of moving only from one good to another' (5.3; 24). It is the power of change that different things enjoy that, for Conway, allows us to distinguish between the three quiddities that we find.

The journey towards perfection is characterized by Conway as becoming more spirit (and less materially condensed) and approaching God on an infinite path that can never be completed: 'No creature can become more and more a body to infinity, although it can become more and more a spirit to infinity … [A] body is always able to become more and more spiritual to infinity since God, who is the first and highest spirit, is infinite and does not and cannot partake of the least corporeality' (7.1; 42). Depending on the relative perfection of a creature, they can become either more spirit or more materially condensed, with the ideal journey towards divine perfection being understood as an infinite journey that approaches the perfect spiritual nature of God: 'All God's creatures, which have previously fallen and degenerated from their original goodness, must be changed and restored after a certain time to a condition which is not simply as good as that in which they were created, but better … [The] spirit imprisoned in such grossness or crassness is set free and becomes more spiritual' (7.1; 42f.). Thus, Conway's ontology has something of a soteriological slant, in that creatures are able to engage in a salvific transformation from body to spirit.

Conway does retain matter in her metaphysical system, but it is understood negatively as being less spirit and hence falling away from perfection. As such, spirit is conceived of by Conway as the fundamental substance, stemming from the infinite spirit, God, and as something that can become increasingly corporeal or gross as the being in question moves away from the divine perfection. Further to this, as we saw in the previous chapter, all creatures, regardless of where they stand on the continuum[5] between infinitely perfect spirit and gross matter, contain within them an intermingling, infinite number of spirits, themselves on their own infinite journey to perfection. Conway takes it as an implication of God's overwhelming goodness that he would wish to share this goodness to the greatest extent possible, with the effect of an everlasting, ongoing creation involving an infinite number of creatures.

The main argument that Conway employs to establish these metaphysical claims is based upon her understanding of the possibility of change and immutability. As we have seen, Conway distinguishes between communicable and incommunicable divine attributes: namely, those which can be shared with created beings and those that cannot be. Immutability (the state of being unchanging) is an incommunicable attribute, and so one of the distinguishing features of creatures is that they are changeable (see 6.1; 28f.). On this basis, given the immutability of God and the mutability of creatures, Conway concludes that they must be different kinds of things. A further claim to recall is that God creates as much as he can, and this extends to the kinds of things he creates. Conway invites us to consider what types of being are conceivable, in terms of the possibility of change. In Section 4 of Chapter VI (30), Conway states that we can conceive of substances that are wholly immutable, wholly mutable and partly mutable. In what way can a creature be only partly mutable? As we saw, Conway links physical change with the good, such that one changes by becoming either more good or less good. Given this, we can divide mutable creatures into those that can change in either direction (can become more or less good) and those that can only change in one direction (can only become more good or can only become less good): the former kind of creatures can be thought of as wholly mutable, and the latter partly mutable, in that they can only change in one direction on the spirit–matter continuum. So, on the assumption that God creates as much as he can, we can expect that God would create wholly mutable beings and partly mutable beings of both types, given their apparent conceivability and possibility.

Given that God, Christ and Creature are distinguishable on the basis of their respective powers of change, we can return to the question of the unresolved tension between the monistic and trialist aspects of Conway's system. The easiest way to resolve the tension, I argue, is to emphasize Conway's monism, the claim all things are spirit, whilst allowing that spirit will appear in different guises or quiddities at different levels of reality (following the Platonic model of creation we considered earlier). The three quiddities – God, Christ and Creature – are the forms in which spirit is found at different levels of reality, so the appearance of trialism is in fact illusory: all things are spirit, albeit in different forms depending on their order in creation, composed of the ground of all things (God), the mediator (Christ) and creation (Creature). We can therefore claim that Conway is a 'spiritual monist' and therefore rejects the dualism of her mentor, Henry, which we will discuss in the following section.

Rejecting Henry More's dualism

As noted in the Introduction, the extensive correspondence between Henry More and Anne Conway appears to have begun in 1650, at the prompting of her brother, John Finch, who had studied under More at Christ's College, Cambridge, and led to a longstanding intellectual engagement that continued until her death. In the very briefest of terms, More's own philosophy combined his reading of the Neoplatonists with the Cartesianism prevalent at the time, in order to bring about his own idiosyncratic mixture of the two traditions.

As we have seen, Descartes (1968: 150–69) argues that there are two fundamental types of substance, mind or spirit (which has thought or thinking as its primary attribute) and body or matter (which has extension as its primary attribute). The mechanical sciences, which were making great advances at the time, were taken to be concerned solely with the province of matter, whilst philosophy and theology could help us in some way to understand spiritual substances, exemplified in Descartes's use of the method of systematic doubt to demonstrate the existence of the self as a thinking thing. However, it soon became clear that this dualist ontology faces some significant difficulties: for example, in her correspondence with Descartes, Princess Elizabeth of Bohemia questions how we can make sense of any kind of interaction between two entirely different kinds of substance, which would be required in any Cartesian account of bodily action tied to intention[6]: 'For it seems that every determination of movement happens from the impulsion of a thing moved, according to the manner in which it is pushed by that which moves it ... You entirely exclude extension from your notion of the soul, and contact seems to me incompatible with an immaterial thing' (Descartes 1971: 661).

In addition to the interaction problem (which we discussed in Chapter 2), as Duran points out, Descartes's dualism also strikes a distinction between God and the physical universe in a manner that some theists may be uncomfortable with: given the sharp separation between spirit and matter, we may not be able to 'derive any notion of what, necessarily, God creates from Descartes' account, since there is a complete ontological break between the substance that is God and any other substance' (1989: 76). In other words, how can a spirit, such as God, create something that is so entirely different from it, namely, matter? Both More and Conway would move away from strict Cartesian dualism, in different degrees, in order to avoid positing such a sharp distinction between God and his creation, which could potentially lead to a system where the role of God in creation is increasingly undermined.

Henry More, for his part, attempts to meet such worries through reconceiving the ontological status of spirit and arguing that mechanical causes alone could not be sufficient to account for the motion of all matter in the universe. Relying upon Neoplatonic assumptions, More posits an active principle, the 'Spirit of Nature', which plays the role of a secondary immaterial cause, acting upon material substance: he describes it as 'the vicarious power of God upon this great automaton, the world' (1712: 46). In order to avoid worries concerning interaction between two fundamentally different kinds of substance, More allows this principle to have extension, unlike Descartes's extensionless 'thinking thing'. In his *Explanation of the Grand Mystery of Godliness*, he contrasts this Spirit of Nature with the Holy Spirit:

> [It] is evident, that though the *Holy Spirit of God* and the *Spirit of Nature* be everywhere present in the world, and lie in the very same points of space; yet their actions, applications or engagings with things are very distinct. For the Spirit of Nature takes hold only of matter, remanding gross bodies towards the centre of the Earth, shaping vegetables into all that various beauty we find in them.
>
> (1660: 458)

Unlike the Holy Spirit, the Spirit of Nature is taken to interact directly with matter, forming creatures and governing their interactions,[7] having extension but not being itself material: as Henry puts it, it is an 'immaterial, universal hylarchic principle which was invoked as a moving, ordering, and animating principle in all physical phenomena' (1990: 57).

Further to this, More assigns an important theological role to the Spirit of Nature, insofar as it reveals the circumscription of divine powers in line with the moral necessities that follow from God's absolute goodness. The operations of the Spirit of Nature are taken to be one effect of God's understanding of the essential nature of things and thus how things *must be*, leading to the achievement of the best possible creation. As Henry explains, More is committed to a view of God's will shaped by a prior understanding of the fundamental nature of things: 'God used intellectual powers, even before the Creation, to arrive at an understanding of certain essential features inherent in the very nature of things … [including] moral concepts like good and evil, justice and injustice, as well as natural concepts such as the categorical distinction … between body and soul' (1990: 63). It is simply part of the essential nature of things that there is a fundamental distinction between matter and immaterial spirit, and as More understands it, there would be a dead world of inert matter were it not for the spirit of nature as an active principle, enlivening creatures and making them part of the divine providential plan.

Despite More's attempts to remedy some of the perceived defects of Cartesianism, which went some way towards distancing him from Descartes, Conway is still dissatisfied with the aspects of Cartesian dualism that her mentor retained in his thought, including the very possibility of there being dead matter in a created universe (which More seems to leave open). As we saw earlier, Conway believes that there is something inconceivable in the notion of God, the source of life and goodness, creating 'dead' matter. Rather, all things, in some sense, are living, even if at a given moment in time they have taken a more material form. Later in this chapter, I will discuss how Conway's ontology of spirit, which is formulated as a reaction to the Cartesian postulation of dead matter, leads to a distinctive Christology that shows the potential influence of George Keith. First, in the following section, we will consider the early theology of George Keith and the manner in which he responds to Henry More's dualism.

The Christ Within and the extended spirit

Conway's convincement in the very last years of her life is perhaps best characterized as the culmination of a long religious and intellectual journey, for which the groundwork is laid in her very early years through her correspondence with her mentor, Henry More (despite the latter's often-stated antipathy towards the Quakers[8]). In the 1670s, during the last decade of her life, one frequent visitor to Ragley Hall was the prominent Quaker, George Keith.

Keith, in a similar manner to Conway, had received his philosophical education via an early introduction to Cartesianism and Henry More's Neoplatonism. According to Kirby's biography of Keith, as a young student in Aberdeen, he had been taken with Cartesian claims regarding reason and intuition as a source of religious truths apart from any authority or tradition, which 'prepared the way for a faith which would depend not upon shibboleths and priesthood but upon the eager receptiveness of the individual' (1942: 7). Around the same time, Keith began reading the work of the Cambridge Platonists and was particularly struck by More's *Explanation of the Grand Mystery of Godliness*, which had been published in 1660. It seems to have been the approach to religious epistemology that Keith found agreeable in this work, in particular the notion that the righteous individual, apart from scripture and church authority, can themselves come to theological truths:

> [If] the soul receives no impresse from God, it discovers nothing of God. For it is most certainly true, *that like is known by like*; and therefore unless the *image of God* be in us, which is *righteousness* and *true holiness*, we know nothing of *the nature of God*, and so consequently can conclude nothing concerning him to any purpose. For we have no measure to apply to him, because we are not possessed of anything homogeneal or of a like nature with him… But when we are arrived to that righteousness or rectitude of spirit or uprightness of mind, by this, as by the geometrical quadrate, we also comprehend with all saints what is that spiritual breadth and length and depth and height, as the apostle speaks. What the rectitude of an angle does in mathematical measurings, the same will this uprightness of Spirit do in theological conclusions.
>
> (More 1660: 403)[9]

In this way, More places emphasis upon the dogma of humankind as created in the image of God, arguing that one of the implications of this idea is that all human beings, apart from the historical circumstances in which they may be placed, have the ability to achieve righteousness and thereby genuine wisdom concerning God and other theological matters. Indeed, if the individual is truly righteous, such knowledge will attain similar status as that of mathematical knowledge, which was often taken as the standard of infallible, foundational knowledge at the time, including by the Cartesians.[10]

Following his convincement, Keith decided to begin writing his own works of Quaker theology, in addition to the usual apologetic pamphlets in response to the sect's many vociferous critics. Two of the most important works of this early period, written just prior to Keith's first meeting with Conway, are *Immediate Revelation* (first published in 1668) and *The Way to the City of God Described* (written during Keith's imprisonment from 1667 to 1668, but not published until 1678). An important question which Keith, amongst many other Quaker writers of the period, feels required to answer in these works is that of the necessity of belief in the historical Christ. Such an account is felt to be essential due to the epistemological considerations, deriving from Descartes and More, that underlie Keith's understanding of faith and righteousness.

More's religious epistemology, centred on the notion of a righteous individual being possessed of theological truths, naturally lends itself, for Keith, to traditional Quaker imagery concerning 'the inner light' or 'the light within'. By the time that Keith came to write his first treatises, the inner light had long been associated with the figure of Christ, the Christ Within. As Rosemary Moore states, such an association can be primarily traced back to George Fox, who holds that the believer can be mystically united with Christ, though his use of such phrases as 'the light of Christ' perhaps lacks some precision: 'Fox was mainly concerned with the unity between Christ and the believer ... When he spoke of the "light," sometimes he used the phrase as equivalent to Christ and sometimes he meant the way Christ made himself known ... "The light" was an overwhelming invasive force, not a vague mental illumination' (2000: 81). Given Keith's immersion in both Quakerism and More's Neoplatonism, it is natural for him to also associate Christ with the kind of individual revelation proposed by More.

However, if the Christ Within allows us to grow both morally and intellectually, what role is left for the historical Christ? Robert Gordon, one of the most vociferous critics of Quakerism at the time, argues that a focus upon redemption through the Christ Within inevitably leads to a heretical undermining of the importance of redemption through the life, death and resurrection of the historical Christ. Addressing George Keith in print, he writes: 'I take notice of thy slighting that great work of man's redemption as already purchased by Christ for sinners, by that one sacrifice of his crucified body once offered for sins ... Speaking first of a redemption wrought in us by the Spirit, as if that were the cause and foundation thereof' (1671: 7f.). To remain within the bounds of Christian orthodoxy, Gordon argues, one must emphasize the primacy of salvation through the historical Christ, and the Quaker notion of the Christ Within gives an unfortunate temptation to depart from this essential part of the Christian tradition. More, for his part, also attacks the notion of Christ Within in his *Explanation of the Grand Mystery of Godliness*, claiming that it implied either that believers unified with Christ are themselves divine, or that Christ is not divine: '[A] subversion of the Christian religion ... that fanatical piece of magnificency of some enthusiasts, who would make *their union with God the same with that of Christ's*. For then were they truly God, and divine adoration would belong to them; or if not, it is a sign that they are not God, and that therefore Christ is not' (1660: 14). Given such attacks, and the desire on the part of Keith to stress Quakerism's compatibility with Christian orthodoxy, he feels it incumbent upon him to offer a theology that accords a substantial role to the historical Christ.

As Hutton explains (see 2004: 189–99), Keith is preoccupied throughout the 1670s with questions of Christology, and one of his major innovations at this time, in his theology, is the notion of Christ as an extended soul throughout the universe, with two manifestations, as Logos and as the Incarnated Christ. As such, the Christ Within, which as Logos illuminates the believer with religious insight, is merely the other side of the coin from the historical Christ. The notion of Christ as an extended soul is introduced in *Immediate Revelation* in the context of a discussion regarding the Logos as immediately present in all beings in the created universe:

> God made… this whole fabric of the creation by his Word, his immediate Word; and he upholds all things thereby… He had no other means but the word of his Mouth, the word of his eternal power, which was in the beginning, whereby all things are made, and without it was nothing made… [The] Word worketh in all things immediately which God ever made, means are but ciphers without this, means operate but mediately, but the Word immediately; and this Word is Christ.
>
> (1668: 56)

In this manner, Keith conceived of Christ as an immediately present principle within the created universe, extended throughout all things. The historical Christ is the pre-eminent manifestation of this principle, alongside the feeling of the Word working within the individual.

Elsewhere, in his correspondence, Keith argues that this connection between the historical Christ and the inner light, which is available in principle to followers of other religions, could encourage conversion to the Gospel message: 'If the Jews can be led to believe that they are divinely illuminated through God by virtue of those human-like rays flowing from the Great Man [i.e. Logos] … then they may love that divine illumination and obey the same. And in this way they may feel Christ, that is, the divine soul live and move in them' (Letter to von Rosenroth, November 1675, quoted in Hutton 2004: 192). For those who have yet to accept Christ, Keith states, bringing them to realize the workings of Christ within them could act as a powerful tool in bringing them into the Christian Church and accepting the message of the historical Jesus. In this manner, Keith sought to place the historical figure of Christ in the centre of Quaker theology, alongside the familiar notion of the Christ Within, in that Jesus of Nazareth was simply a manifestation of the very principle through which believers are granted the kind of insight characterized as the 'inner light'.[11]

In a letter to Henry More from November 1675, Conway evinces great interest in Keith's Christology, and indeed defends it, on the basis that it emphasizes the historical Christ in a manner that is lacking in the Familists, another sect from the time that also spoke of the inner light: 'I am sure this new notion of G. Keith's about Christ seems far removed from Familisme, he attributing by that more to the external Person of our Saviour, that I think any ever hath done' (L 408). Indeed, Conway claims that this Christology may even have Scriptural and Kabbalist authority: '[His] opinion, if true, would facilitate the understanding of many places in Scripture, as well as it would make better sense of the Kabbalists'' (L 408). Though Conway states that she awaits her mentor's opinion on the matter, Keith's Christology has clearly impressed her and this is noteworthy as this letter falls just before the period in which we presume the notes that would make up the *Principia* were taken down. The question we will consider in the following section is the way Keith's theology may have had an impact upon her Christology.

Salvation, monism and Christ

Let's now consider the notion of Christ and the Christ Within in the context of Conway's philosophy, for there is a sense in which Christ is present in all human beings in a manner which has interesting soteriological consequences. We must first note that, for Conway, Christ is extended throughout the universe. As we saw earlier, Christ is construed as a generated instrument of God that is immediately present in all things. Christ's role is to facilitate divine cooperation with creatures throughout creation, given his lower ontological status: 'Although God works immediately in everything, yet he nevertheless uses this same mediator as an instrument through which he works together with creatures, since that instrument is by its own nature closer to them' (5.4; 25). However, Christ's being is close enough to God, in fact 'his most exact and perfect image' (5.4; 26), that he can share some of the divine attributes that cannot be had by creatures: so, the sphere of communicable attributes is wider for Christ than it is for creatures. In particular, Conway emphasizes that Christ is omnipresent[12] and indeed has to be in order to fulfil his mediating role between God and creation. In this way, Conway reflects Keith's view that Christ is extended throughout the universe and present in all things in a manner that God is not, in virtue of his status as something that has been generated (though not created).

Given the manner in which Christ is extended, he is seen as intermingling with all creatures: as Conway states, 'all things are contained in him' (4.3; 22) and he is 'intimately present in them, yet is not to be confounded with them' (7.4; 50). In particular, as Hutton points out (2004: 201), Christ plays an essential role in the occurrence of vital action through his intimate presence in all things. As Conway explains, all creatures have both a material and virtual extension, the difference between the two depending on the sphere of influence the creature in question has through its action: 'Material extension is that which matter, body, or substance itself has, but without any motion or action ... Virtual extension is the motion or action which a creature has whether given immediately from God or received immediately from some fellow creature' (9.9; 69). As the virtual extension of a creature can be wider than its material extension, Conway allows for the possibility of action at a distance, though a medium is required to facilitate this: 'Vital action can proceed together with local motion from one thing to another when a fitting medium exists to transmit it, and this even at a great distance' (9.9; 68). One important kind of vital action, Conway argues, is the 'internal motion' that proceeds from a creature's 'inner being ... the proper life and will of a creature' (9.9; 69), including our conscious actions. As such, the notion of vital action through an intimately present medium is giving additional detail to Conway's explanation of how the soul can have an impact upon matter: the soul has a vital extension through which it can act upon matter, even at a distance, and this capability is guaranteed through the omnipresent mediator, Christ.

At the very end of the *Principia*, Conway uses the notion of vital action to explain all motion concerning creatures. Noting the philosophical problem of how to explain the transmission of motion from one body to another, she states that local motion, defined as 'the carrying of the body from one place to another' (9.9; 67), cannot be responsible as motion itself is not a thing that is moved in space; rather, it 'moves the body in which it exists' (9.9; 70) as a mode or property of a particular thing. Thus, vital action must be used to explain how the apparent transmission of motion is possible: through the vital extension of a creature, it is able to, in a sense, create the motion of another being as a *sui generis* property of it. Of course, divine action is really the only way that something can be created, and so vital action requires the kind of intercession provided by the presence of Christ. Without Christ acting as a mediating principle in this way, any transmission of motion from one creature to another would not be possible.

As Hutton notes (2004: 201), this attempted explanation of the transmission of motion would not strike the seventeenth-century reader as particularly unusual, as it is at least superficially similar to the occasionalism of Nicolas Malebranche (1638–1715), who attempted to explain causation through God's creative action at each individual moment in time. According to the occasionalist theory, motion was not really transmitted from one body to another; rather, God continually creates objects in different places in a manner that gives the illusion of genuine causation. So, as the snooker ball 'moves' across the table, it is continually created at different points on that table as it follows a particularly trajectory, until it 'hits' another ball, at which the two balls are created at different places on their own trajectories.[13] Conway's own theory reflects occasionalism to some extent, insofar as motion is created through divine intercession, though the role of God is very much indirect here, as the medium is in fact directly provided by Christ. It was seen by many at the time as rather beneath God to be so involved in the causal workings of nature and Conway is able to avoid this objection by positing the middle nature of Christ as the immediate facilitator of the motion of bodies.

Thus, Christ has a crucial omnipresent role throughout all of creation by facilitating the motion of all things. Conway brings about the important soteriological implications of this in the last paragraph of the *Principia*: she writes that, given her theory of vital action, 'it can be easily shown how the body gradually attains that perfection, so that it is not only capable of such perception and knowledge as brutes have, but of whatever perfection can befall any human being or angel' (9.9; 70). Through vital action, we are able to live in a manner which helps bring about perfection, but this can only happen with the mediating role of Christ. In this manner, Conway states, we can understand the saying of Christ: 'God is able of these stones to raise up children unto Abraham' (Matthew 3:9). By providing the medium of Christ for our vital action, God ensures that we have the ability to engage with the world in a manner that allows us to conform ourselves to the divine will and thereby become closer to him, both morally and ontologically (on the spirit–matter continuum, as discussed earlier). In this way, Christ has a fundamental role in allowing not only for motion between creatures, but for creatures to undertake actions such that they can better themselves and eventually attain salvation.

As discussed already, in addition to this, the distinguishing feature of Christ is that this substance can only move towards perfection, whilst creatures are able to move both away and towards perfection, glossed as becoming more or less spiritual. However, a question we might consider is how we distinguish Christ and creature at the moment that the latter, at some point in their infinite journey towards God, has joined with the spiritual level of Christ and moves together with the intermediary towards perfect spirituality. At that moment in time, there will be nothing to distinguish them in terms of change and level of spirituality, and thus, although one would not have become numerically identical with Christ at this point (an impossibility due to the difference in quiddity), we nevertheless will have become qualitatively identical with the intermediary. Conway seeks to strike a balance between the possibility of joining with Christ on the path to perfection and maintaining the necessary ontological distance between these two different types of being: '[Creatures] can never strictly speaking become him, just as he can never become the Father. Moreover, the highest point they can reach is this, to be like him, as Scripture says. Consequently, inasmuch as we are only creatures, our relation to him is only one of adoption' (4.4; 22). I suggest that it is through this notion of 'adoption' that Conway is attempting to capture the manner in which creatures are able to become at one with Christ in one sense, and thus have the Christ Within, whilst nevertheless maintaining an ontological distance between creature and Christ. As we grow towards perfection, with Christ intermingled with us (and also changing towards perfection), we in a sense are 'adopted' by Christ – becoming a child of Christ in analogy with the relation between God the Father and Christ. We cannot *become* Christ, but we can *be at one with him*.

We must also note that, for Conway, a growth in perfection entails a growth in wisdom or knowledge concerning God. Conway speaks of the 'more excellent attributes' attained by the being who developed in such a manner: '[They] are the following: spirit or life and light, by which I mean the capacity for every kind of feeling, perception, or knowledge, even love, all power and virtue, joy and fruition, which the noblest creatures have or can have' (9.6; 66). As such, we have clear parallels with the early Quaker notion of the Christ Within bound up with the inner light. In the same manner in which the inner light, construed as the Christ Within, brings a growth of theological wisdom, correlated with the moral development of the individual, Conway's process of becoming more spiritual, having joined with Christ in the change towards perfection, brings us closer to God and to the kind of eschatological realization where we may be able to 'see' the face of God.

Unfortunately, as discussed in Chapter I, the details of Conway's religious epistemology are somewhat sketchy, so it is difficult to expand upon this thought further. However, it is noteworthy that Conway links the Quaker way of life with a growth in religious knowledge, as White points out: 'Conway recognized among the Friends a type of profound faith that was not mere common intellectual assent to propositional truths; in their lives, she grasped and appreciated a modality or a way of being in the world, namely, a full (embodied) commitment to illuminating goodness that confronted one, awakening one to transformative action in the world' (2008: 30). Conway sees, in the example of the Quakers around her, the manner in which a way of being connects ineluctably with a deepening faith, grounded in the influence of the Christ Within or the 'inner light'.

Finally, it is worth returning to the question of the historical Christ, this time in the context of Conway's philosophy. Conway seems to follow Keith in positing the historical Christ as a manifestation of a metaphysical principle, here designated as 'Christ', a kind of being that can only change towards the good: 'Jesus Christ signifies the whole Christ, who is God and man. As God, he is called *logos ousios*, or the essential word of the father. As man, he is the *logos proforikos*, or the word which is uttered and revealed, the perfect and substantial image of God's word' (4.2: 21). However, although there may be a substantial sense in which Christ, as an extended substance, plays a direct soteriological role in creation (and the historical Christ can be recognized as a manifestation of this principle), this is some way removed from traditional Christian notions of the importance of the historical Jesus of Nazareth. There is seemingly little role in the system presented in the *Principia* for the Incarnation, the Gospel message, the Resurrection and so forth – all key Christian doctrines associated with a specific historical figure.

For one thing, Conway claims that soteriological development occurs due to the imperfections of creation, which inevitably brings about pain and suffering that ultimately has a palliative effect: 'Just as all the punishments inflicted by God on his creatures are in proportion to their sins, so they tend, even to the worst, to their good and to their restoration and they are so medicinal as to cure these sickly creatures and restore them to a better condition than they previously enjoyed' (6.10; 38). In this manner, redemption becomes akin to a naturally occurring process, in which inevitable suffering leads to overall progress towards the good for all things: '[Nature] always works toward the greater perfection of subtlety and spirituality since this is the most natural property of every operation and notion. For all motion wears away and divides a thing and thus makes it subtle and spiritual' (8.5; 61). We will discuss this idea in more detail in Chapter 7, but for now we can note that within Conway's theology there is no space for a definitive Christ-event which has a fundamental soteriological impact upon all human beings[14]: in an infinite creation, an infinite number of beings have always been and always will be on an infinite journey towards spiritual perfection, and events concerning the historical figure of Jesus of Nazareth seemingly have no essential impact on this process, even if the historical Christ is taken as a manifestation of the metaphysical principle, Christ.

Such a position will not be surprising for us when we consider: (1) Conway's approach to the Trinity, another distinctive Christian doctrine, and (2) her universalizing agenda, which she shares with van Helmont. In the *Principia*, Conway seems happy to undertake a fundamental re-conception of the Trinity, away from traditional understandings of the doctrine: in the following chapter, I will argue that Conway presents us with a Trinitarian theology that contains aspects of both subordinationism (subordinating one Person of the Trinity to another) and modalism (undermining the distinction between Persons of the Trinity by construing them as mere modes of a single substance), which have been held, since the early Church, as unacceptable from a strictly orthodox perspective. At points in the *Principia*, Christ is apparently given the subordinate role as an ontological middle ground between God and creation, whilst elsewhere, Christ is equated with God's wisdom, which certainly appears a clear-cut case of modalism. Given Conway's openness to reshaping the Trinity in such a manner, it is not surprising that she would also be willing to jettison any substantial role for the historical figure of Jesus of Nazareth, which is another departure from strict Christian orthodoxy.

Such an approach is consonant with her universalizing agenda, in which she seeks to bring together all believers into the same fold, which may not necessarily involve all of the aspects of traditional Christian orthodoxy, including the Trinity and doctrine of atonement. As part of this, Conway uses Kabbalist theology in order to emphasize the similarities that already exist between religious traditions. As an example, Conway claims that the Kabbalist notion of 'Adam Kadmon' should be identified with the 'Son of God' preached by Christianity: '[The] first born of all creatures, whom we Christians call Jesus Christ ... The ancient Kabbalists have written many things about this ... whom they call in their writings the celestial Adam, or the first man Adam Kadmon, the great priest, the husband or betrothed of the church, or as Philo Judaeus called him, the first-born son of God' (5.1; 23).

It is here also that we potentially come to a point where George Keith, in turn, is influenced by Anne Conway. As is well known, Keith would eventually come into conflict with established Quakers, largely due to the growing role he accords to the historical figure of Jesus in his theology. After Keith moved to Philadelphia in 1689, he increasingly complained of the focus on the inner light in the Quaker community there at the expense of the historical Christ.

Though it lies far beyond the scope of this chapter to examine Keith's schism from Quakerism,[15] it is entirely possible that, in reflecting upon Conway's ideas, which incorporated at least some sense of his notion of the Christ Within, he was able to see the manner in which his own theology naturally leads away from a substantial soteriological role for the historical Jesus. As such, it may be that his time at Ragley Hall, conversing with Conway and others, laid some of the foundations for the schism in Philadelphia around fifteen years later.

It is unlikely that Keith's interactions with Conway were the primary motivating factor in his break from Quakerism (it is more likely that there were a multitude of interconnecting factors[16]), but it is possible that they nevertheless had an impact upon his developing views. If Conway, taking in part her cue from early Quaker theology, is only too happy to leave behind any such Christology, there may be something worrying for the Quaker who wishes to preserve at least some aspect of this traditional Christian approach, which Keith certainly intends: in a work from 1692, he complains of the Quaker community that 'they exclude the man Christ Jesus from having any part in our salvation, placing it wholly and only upon the light within' (1692: 2). So, while it is most likely that a large number of factors led to Keith's break with Quakerism, it is possible that viewing some aspects of his theology through the prism of Conway's system helped to reveal for him the difficulty that he would have in incorporating a substantial role for the historical Christ in his thought. Needless to say, such a suggestion is rather speculative for now, but could offer an interesting future avenue of research in this area.

Conclusion

In this chapter, I have argued that the influence of George Keith can be discerned in the manner in which Conway's philosophy reacts to Cartesianism and the thought of her mentor, Henry More. Conway is distinctly uncomfortable with the notion of an all-good, all-powerful God creating dead matter and thus desires to avoid such a notion in her metaphysics, which necessitates her moving beyond More's invocation of a 'spirit of nature' which can enliven matter. George Keith also constructs his theology in reaction to his early reading of More: positively, in relation to his adoption of the inner light and its connection with the familiar early Quaker tradition of the Christ Within, and negatively, with regard to the requirement he feels, in the face of More's criticism, to incorporate a substantial role for the historical Christ in his theology. I have argued that

Conway's system involves a Christology and religious epistemology that reveals the influence of George Keith's early theology, and explored the sense in which a being may become at one with Christ, hence embodying the Christ Within, on their soteriological, infinite journey to greater spirituality.

From a more general viewpoint, we can see that Anne Conway's philosophy perhaps reveals a deeper impact of early Quaker theology than has been hitherto recognized. Indeed, we may need to reconceive Conway's place in history, insofar as we could potentially regard her as an early Quaker theologian, like George Keith, in addition to her well-known label as a rationalist metaphysician of the late seventeenth century. We have also had cause to question whether Conway may have in turn had an impact upon the theology of Keith, potentially helping to lead to his separation from Quakerism later in his life. Certainly, it is to be hoped that further research will be undertaken on the interconnections between Conway's philosophy and Quaker thought of the time: such work could serve as mutually illuminating for both scholars of Conway and of early Quaker theology, as well as opening up interactions between philosophy and theology in this area. In the next chapter, we will build on our discussion to this point by considering Conway's conception of time, the Trinity and salvation in more detail.

5

Christ, salvation and the end of time

In this chapter, we are going to continue considering Conway's conception of the Triune God (particularly the role of Christ), soteriology and eschatology (theory of the 'final things').[1] I will argue that her understanding of the Trinity offers a distinctive role for Christ and the Holy Spirit to play in her philosophical system. In addition, I will propose an interpretation of Conway's eschatology in which time is understood as grounded in a never-ending soteriological process of the overall movement of creatures towards perfection and a state of spirituality, crucially involving the activity of Christ.

In the first major section of the chapter, after reviewing some of the most salient elements of Conway's system with regard to the discussion here, I will focus upon the nature of God and the role of Christ as a mediating metaphysical principle. I will consider the potential problem that Conway's conception of the Triune God is caught between subordinationism and modalism, due to the desire to mediate both Neoplatonic and Kabbalist influences, as well as to offer a universalist message in the *Principia*. In order to defuse this tension, I will argue that we can look to the different senses in which Conway speaks of Christ as the Word or Logos.

Given the metaphysical standing accorded to God and Christ in Conway's system, I will then, in the following section of the chapter, consider what this might mean for her metaphysics of time, which I introduced in Chapter 3. Building upon my previous discussion, I argue that in the context of Conway's system, time and cognate notions such as change need to be interpreted with reference to God's sustaining activity and his wider soteriological plan with regards to creation. We also need to bear in mind Conway's theory of substances: as we have seen already, spirit and matter are to be understood as a single kind of substance. There are also three types of quiddity, which are distinct due to the kind of change they can go through: whilst God is unchangeable, Christ can change but only towards perfection, and creatures can change both towards and away from perfection. Although creatures can become less perfect, ultimately all things tend towards perfection and thus all eventually become more spiritual over the course of eternity. With these metaphysical assumptions on the part of Conway, I argue that we can understand time as grounded in the soteriological process of the overall movement of creatures towards perfection and the divine.

In addition, going back to the original identification of time with the successive motion or operation of creatures, we can understand what it would be for time to cease for Conway. It would be the end not only of change on the level of created beings, but also of the soteriological process in the created universe. However, due to Conway's assertion that the soteriological progress never ends, the only kind of timelessness that a being can accede to is a 'relative timelessness', where one has become united with the moral development of Christ. It is only in this sense, I argue, that we can speak of Conway having an eschatology. Finally, I will conclude the chapter with some brief reflections on Conway's theory of universal salvation, returning the question of the influence of Origen and Henry More.

The Triune God

At first glance, Conway may appear to be firmly anti-Trinitarian in her theology. In Chapter I, she targets the idea of Father, Son and Spirit understood as three distinct persons, complaining that it is an unscriptural, irrational idea that hinders efforts to persuade those of other faiths of the truth of Christianity: 'It is a stumbling block and offense to Jews, Turks, and other people, has truly no reasonable sense in itself, and is found nowhere in Scripture' (1.7; 10). It is indeed a crucial part of the orthodox understanding of the Trinity that the three components of the Godhead are understood as three persons, set authoritatively by early Church councils in the fourth century AD and developed in the later theological tradition. Any rejection of the personhood of God, Son and Spirit thus constitutes a major departure from the orthodox understanding of the Trinity.

Furthermore, returning to the emanationist model of creation that we considered in Chapter 2, we can see it having a further impact upon Trinitarian thought. There are two general perspectives upon the Trinity, through which, amongst other things, we can attempt to understand the relation between the Persons of the Trinity, namely, the immanent and economic models. Speaking generally, the immanent Trinity is the Trinity viewed from a purely ontological perspective, whilst the economic Trinity is understood as the way in which the Triune God is revealed to us through revelation (so it has more of an epistemological aspect than the former).[2] The Neoplatonic model of the divine emanating into lower, more imperfect degrees of being can be seen as suggesting a potentially problematic view (from the perspective of Christian orthodoxy) of the immanent Trinity, namely subordinationism.

Christian orthodoxy maintains that the Persons of the Trinity are consubstantial (of the same substance), and thus from the ontological perspective of the immanent Trinity, one Person cannot be understood as subordinate to another. If we were approaching the question of the Trinity from a Neoplatonic perspective, though, it would perhaps seem natural to adopt a subordinationist view, with the Father being the ultimate atemporal ground of being, and the Son and Spirit emanating from this supreme creative principle, with the implication that these two Persons are ontologically subordinate (in fact, they would be lacking in perfection). Yandell describes this way of 'applying Plotinian philosophy to Christian theology' as beginning with 'The One [who] is the highest being of all which is the source of the Intellect. The Father, as the One, begetting the Son (the Intellect) would require that the Father be, by nature, the cause of the Son, and the Son be the second highest being' (2009: 157). Yandell makes clear that this approach to the Trinity fundamentally strays from the orthodox understanding of this doctrine: 'Whatever begetting is, [from an orthodox perspective] the Son being begotten is not the Son's being "made" or "created" or having a lesser nature than that of the Father. Ontological Subordination is no account of the Christian Trinity. For a Christian, there aren't degrees of being God' (2009: 157). Thus, if the Neoplatonic influence on the *Principia* extends to Conway's understanding of the Trinity, this would make it likely that it is on this question that she begins to step away from the standard Christian approach, and this is in fact what we find.

What does Conway say about the Trinity in the *Principia*? To begin explicating this, we need to return to her understanding of time and change. As we saw earlier, for Conway, change takes place on two parallel levels, spirit/matter and perfection/imperfection, and the kind of change you can go through depends on the kind of quiddity you have. Conway argues against a strict ontological separation between spirit/mind and matter/body by stating that spirit and body lie on a continuum, with inverse degrees of corporeality and spirituality. God lies at one end of this infinite continuum, with all the beings of creation towards the other end, all of whom are able to change their mode of existence such that they can become more spirit or more matter (see 7.1; 42).

In addition, as we have seen, there are three types of quiddities according to this view, namely, God, Christ and Creature. To explicate the essential difference between them, Conway begins by reiterating the immutability of God, 'as sacred Scripture and our understanding, which has been placed in our minds by God, shows us' (5.3; 24). If further proof of God's immutability is required, she argues that God, as the highest good, could neither change away or towards perfection: if he became less perfect, he would no longer be the highest good, and he could only become more perfect by sharing in the 'virtue and influence' (5.3; 24) of an even higher being, which there could not be. Given that God is essentially immutable, then, the way in which we can distinguish that substance from other kinds is through the question of whether or not they can change, and our everyday experience indeed shows us that all things in creation can change. As such, change is not only key to Conway in terms of being able to characterize time, but also insofar as it is the way in which we can distinguish different kinds of things, between God and creation.

In addition, the change that creatures can undergo is linked by Conway to a scheme of divine justice that encompasses all beings in the created universe. Conway discusses the divine punishment meted out to a human being 'who has so greatly degraded himself by his own willful wrongdoing' of being compelled by God 'to bear the same image in his body as in that spirit into which he has internally transformed himself' (6.8; 36). So, the potential change that a creature can undergo is construed not just as a possible transfer from more ethereal spirit to more condensed matter (or vice versa), but also as a function of divine reward and punishment, reflecting the moral inner progress of the being concerned. However, Conway is also committed to the view that there is an overall progress of creatures towards perfection, even though some backsliding does occur, and this forms part of her understanding of the scheme of divine justice: 'Just as all the punishments inflicted by God on his creatures are in proportion to their sins, so they tend, even the worse, to their good and to their restoration and they are so medicinal as to cure these sickly creatures and restore them to a better condition that they previous enjoyed' (6.10; 38), and '[at] this time every sin will have its own punishment and every creature will feel pain and chastisement, which will return that creature to the pristine state of goodness in which it was created and from which it can never fall again because, through its great punishment, it has acquired a greater perfection and strength' (7.1; 42). The system of divine punishment and reward, Conway argues, is set up such that it guarantees an overall movement towards spirit and perfection.[3]

Due to God's perfect wisdom and goodness, divine punishments are carried out with a view to their cleansing properties, helping to bring about a more perfect state for the creature in the long term. Conway particularly focuses upon the restorative power of pain and suffering through which 'whatever grossness or crassness is contracted by the spirit or body is diminished; and so the spirit imprisoned in such grossness or crassness is set free and becomes more spiritual' (7.1; 43).[4] We are, therefore, left with an optimistic view of divine justice and moral development, insofar as all creatures will eventually tend towards perfection and union with the divine, even though they may fall short and may have to suffer (even considerably) along the way.[5]

If we then wish to distinguish between Christ and creatures, we need to go back to the two directions of change, towards matter and imperfection, and towards spirit and perfection. Conway argues that whilst creatures have 'the intrinsic power of changing [themselves] either for good or bad', Christ has 'the power of moving only from one good to another' (5.3; 24), that is, Christ can undergo change, but only in the direction of spirit and perfection. In order to distinguish Christ from creatures thoroughly, Conway points towards Christ's nature as being unable to 'degenerate' like those of creatures and 'change from good into bad', which ensures that 'creatures could not be equal to Christ nor of the same nature', in the same way that, due to his mutability, Christ 'can never become the Father' (4.4; 22). It is due to the fact that Christ can only become more perfect that he is 'of a greater and more excellent nature than all remaining creatures. On account of his excellence he is rightly called the son of God' (5.2; 24). The most we, as creatures, can hope for is to 'be like him' (4.4; 22), but we are ultimately not able to *become* him.

So, in Conway's metaphysical system, we have three types of quiddities, distinguishable by the kind of change they can undergo: (1) the atemporal God, who undergoes no change, (2) Christ, who can change but only ever towards perfection and (3) creatures, which can change both towards and away from perfection, but have an overall tendency towards perfection. The question of mutability, or not, in the case of God, is key to the distinction between atemporal God and creation in time, with Christ in the middle, both '[sharing] in the immutability of God and the mutability of the creatures ... [thus sharing] eternity (which belongs to God) and time (which belongs to creatures)' (5.5; 26). It is in this metaphysical context that we must approach the Trinity in Conway's system.

It is clear from very early in the text of the *Principia* that the interpretation of the doctrine of the Trinity is very important for Conway and plays into a wider ecumenical project that she shares with van Helmont. A first important aspect of Conway's construal of the Trinity is revealed when she states that her interpretation is intended so that 'Jews, Turks, or other peoples would not be offended, if these words, "three distinct persons," which are not in Scripture and have no reasonable sense are omitted' (1.7; 10). We see that Conway is not afraid to challenge core Christian teaching in light of her desire to pursue a universalist agenda, in which the similarities between different religious belief systems (given the historical context, Conway had only monotheist belief systems in mind) are the focus, rather than the differences. Indeed, it seems Conway is happy to challenge Christian teaching in order to make it more palatable to Jews and pagans, who may happily convert to Christianity if some of the more controversial elements of the religion (and this would certainly include the traditional understanding of the doctrine of the Trinity) are jettisoned. As Coudert (1975: 636) notes, this universalist project is part of the reason for the interest that Conway and van Helmont had in the texts of the Jewish Kabbala, which they hoped could simultaneously confirm what they saw as the fundamental truths of Christianity whilst opening up a way in for believers of other traditions. Therefore, we should not be surprised if we find, in the *Principia*, such a construal of the Trinity.[6]

Conway goes on to explicate her understanding of the Trinity through the Kabbalist notion of the *Adam Kadmon*, which she links with the Christian notion of Christ. Conway speaks of this metaphysical principle as

> the natural medium between [God and creature], through which the extremes are united. It is therefore the most fitting and appropriate mediator, for it partakes of one extreme because it is mutable in respect to going from good to a greater degree of good and of the other extreme because it is entirely incapable of changing from good to bad.
>
> (5.3; 24f.)

Christ is clearly intended here, then, to act as a kind of ontological and moral middle ground between God and creatures (a being of 'a lesser nature than God and yet of a greater and more excellent nature than all remaining creatures' (5.2; 24)), though the specific status as 'mediator' that Christ (or *Adam Kadmon*) is supposed to undertake in Conway's system is not immediately clear. Conway states that he 'comes into existence by generation or emanation from God rather than by creation strictly speaking, although according to a broader meaning and use of this word he can be said to have been created or formed' (5.4; 25) and that he is 'immediately present in all … creatures so that he may bless and benefit them' (5.4; 26).

However, Conway's conception of the Trinity is further complicated by a passage in which she focuses on the Logos as 'the image or the word [of God,] existing within himself, which in substance or essence is one and the same with him' (1.6; 10). Instead of Christ as mediator between God and the world, indeed as an intermediate substance between God and the world, we have moved to the notion of Christ as the Word, an archetype in line with which creatures are created, and of one substance with God.[7] In addition to the Logos, we also have the notion of a Holy Spirit, 'which comes from him and which is in terms of substance or essence nevertheless one with him, through which creatures receive their essence and activity' (1.7; 10). In contrast to the apparent subordinationist view connected with the *Adam Kadmon*, Conway is now pursuing a seemingly opposed view of the Trinity, where the Son and Spirit are equated with God's wisdom and will, respectively. Indeed, Conway seems to have moved from a subordinationist Trinity to a form of modalism, in which some of the Persons are understood merely as aspects of the Father, rather than as distinct individuals in their own right, which is confirmed when she states, 'Wisdom and will in God are not entities or substances distinct from him but, in fact, distinct modes or properties of one and the same substance' (1.7; 10). Going back to Conway's universalism, it is clear that she envisages such a view as making the Trinity more amenable to followers of other religions, particularly the monotheisms of Judaism and Islam, partly by advocating the end of any commitment to the existence of three distinct Persons in the Godhead (1.7; 10).

We can look to the same discussion towards the end of Chapter I of the *Principia* for hints of Conway's Christology. First, with regard to the Word, she writes, 'In God there is an idea which is his image or the word existing within himself ... through which he knows himself as well as all other things and indeed, all creatures were made or created according to this very idea or word' (1.6; 10). In referring to an image within God that acts as an internal vessel for creation, it certainly seems that Conway is referring to the Word as envisaged in Johannine theology (as noted in Chapter 3). However, what complicates matters here is that Conway is not referring to the kind of Christ, the middle nature, as a separate substance that she discusses later, for she is clear that this Word of which she speaks is 'in substance or essence is one and the same with [God]' (1.6; 10). It would appear that we must carefully distinguish, then, between the Word or Logos and Christ as middle nature in the context of Conway's philosophy. This reading is confirmed in the following section, when it becomes clear that Conway is referring to features of God (as infinite spirit), rather than to a middle nature. Section 7 begins, '*For the same reason* there is spirit or will in God, which comes from him and which is in terms of substance or essence nevertheless one with him' (1.7; 10). Conway makes it clear, then, that she is discussing divine properties or modes in this section, not beings distinct from God such as the mediating substance.

Conway goes on, in the same section, to discuss her recommended ecumenical recasting of the doctrine of the Trinity. The notion of the Trinity as three distinct persons is her specific target here, on the basis that it hinders conversion efforts, is nonsensical and has no scriptural basis. Such an understanding of the Trinity can be traced back to the Athanasian Creed, which grew out of the Western Christian orthodoxy set by the Council of Nicaea in the fourth century AD. According to the Creed, the one God worshipped by Christians is composed of three distinct eternal, uncreated Persons. However, the Son and the Holy Spirit can be less controversially understood as modes of God: the former standing for God's knowledge within himself (including the essence of all things created) and the latter being God's will, which creates beings in accordance with the ideas he has. Together, the divine word and will bring about creation. However, it is not necessary that these things be understood as distinct persons; if they are rather conceptualized as modes of God, then widespread religious agreement could be found. Conway therefore argues here for a modalist understanding of the Trinity, according to which Father, Son and Holy Spirit are taken as different expressions, manifestations or aspects of God, rather than as distinct persons. What Conway is *not* arguing for is the Christology we find later, revolving around the notion of Adam Kadmon and a middle substance that acts as a bridge between God and creation.

Why might we think that Conway is referring to Christ as middle nature here? The one major piece of evidence comes from the 'Annotations to the First Chapter', which is presented as a gloss of 1.7 according to the 'ancient hypothesis of the Hebrews' (10) and refers to a first created being, Adam Kadmon, that fits the role assigned to the middle nature by Conway. However, we must tread carefully, because it is most likely that these Annotations are editorial additions by van Helmont.[8] As such, we cannot take any mention of Adam Kadmon here as evidence that Conway is referring to the middle nature in the latter part of Chapter I. The first main reason for taking these comments as editorial is that it is not clear why they are not incorporated into the main text if they were indeed written by Conway. There is no other section like this in the entire text of the *Principia* and so there is at least a strong suggestion that these annotations should be read differently to the rest of the text. As Reid has also pointed out (in correspondence), the full title of the *Principia* also suggests that these annotations have been appended to Conway's notes: the text is designated as 'A Short Posthumous Work translated from English into Latin, with annotations taken from the ancient philosophy of the Hebrews' (1). Again, this is not definitive proof, but nevertheless a strong suggestion that the annotations have been inserted by the editor.

Furthermore, it could be that even if the annotations were written by Conway, they are not intended to be taken as her own claims, but merely the Kabbalist version of what she had been saying in 1.7. The section begins, 'The ancient hypothesis of the Hebrews in respect to the last part of this chapter is as follows ... ', which suggests that the annotations are reporting what Kabbalists have said, rather than expressing Conway's own views. However, given the other reasons I have offered (and particularly what I argue is the mismatch between the Kabbalist ideas found in the Annotations and the approach to the Trinity in 1.7), my conclusion is that the preponderance of evidence points towards the Annotations being an editorial addition, probably by van Helmont, and not the work of Conway herself. Admittedly, there is no definitive evidence that the Annotations are editorial, but there is at least some textual evidence such that we have a good cumulative case for reading them in this way.

Conway returns to the topic of the Word in Chapter IV, where she distinguishes between the *logos ousios* and the *logos proforikos* as two aspects of Christ, as both God and man. Whilst the logos ousios is 'the essential word of the father', logos proforikos is 'the word which is uttered and revealed, the perfect and substantial image of God's word, which is eternally in God and perpetually united to him so that it is his vehicle and organ' (4.2; 21). Christia Mercer has glossed logos ousios as the overall plan set for creation in the being of Christ (as second substance), whilst logos proforikos is how the logos appears to us as it is progressively manifested in time: 'Think of Christ, the *logos*, as the detailed blueprint of the world, statically conceived by God .... *Logos proforikos* is the blueprint being instantiated in the world and unfolding through time' (2019a: 62f.). For Mercer, the two logoi are two aspects of the second substance as viewed from two perspectives: from the timeless perspective, we see the fixed blueprint of creation in the logos ousios, and from the time-bound perspective, we see this plan playing out over history as the logos proforikos (including the historical manifestation of this logos in the figure of Jesus of Nazareth). Mercer's two-aspect account gains credence if we consult the original Latin translation, which does not refer to a 'logos ousios' or 'logos proforikos' per se; rather, it is clear that Conway is referring to one thing, the 'logos' which is thought of in two ways, 'ousios' and 'proforikos' (see 4.2; P2 79). The logos ousios is the actualized word, existing as a separate substance from God and willed into being by him, whilst the logos proforikos is how the logos ousios is revealed to us over time.

In bringing together these Christological reflections, it has been suggested by Hutton that the *Principia* shows some internal tension arising from Conway's Trinitarian and anti-Trinitarian remarks (see 2005: 216–23). Despite the subordinate position given to Christ as the 'second substance', Conway nevertheless speaks of Jesus Christ as 'God and man'. Though the Latin at 4.2 is not entirely clear, I argue that Conway is speaking here of what Christ *represents to us*, in other words, what his appearance *signifies*, rather than making an ontological statement about the nature of the second substance (which we find explained elsewhere). Conway refers to Christ 'quatenus Deus' and 'quatenus autem homo' (4.2; P2 79), which a less elegant (but perhaps more accurate) translation would render as 'insofar as he is God' or 'to the extent that he is God', and 'insofar as he is also man' or 'to the extent that he is also man'. Given that Conway's metaphysics rule out the possibility of something being substantially both God and man, we must read her here as referring (even more inelegantly) to Christ 'insofar as he is called God' or 'insofar as we think of him as God (or God-like)', and 'insofar as he is called man' or 'insofar as we think of him as man'. So, the tension between Christ as middle substance and Christ as God is only apparent, insofar as here Conway is only referring to how Christ appears to us, that is, in a God-like manner given his higher status as the second substance. The tension is further dissolved when we recall that Conway distinguishes between the Word in God, logically prior to its actualization through the divine will, and the Logos as second substance. Such a distinction allows her to use Trinitarian-style language with regard to God in Chapter I, whilst postulating a 'second substance', called Christ, later on in the *Principia*, without falling into obvious contradiction.

Hutton points to the influence of Philo as constructing this dual role for Christ in Conway's metaphysical system: she explains that 'Philo differentiates between the logos as eternal archetype and the logos as first created being, between the logos as only begotten son and as first-born son of God. In this way the logos, as both bridge between and separator of God and creation, is the mediator between God and the world' (2004: 160). Whilst it is not wholly clear, it seems that Hutton views the logos proforikos as the mediating second substance, whilst the logos ousios is the eternal archetype residing within God (see 2004: 200). One benefit of this reading is that it accords with Conway's account of the Word in Chapter I, which she claims is 'in substance or essence … one and the same with [God]' (1.6; 10). We can now identify the Word that

Conway is writing of here as the logos ousios, a mode of the first substance, and not Conway's mediating second substance. The reading also gains support when we note that Conway speaks of Christ 'as God' (4.2; 21), which seems to strongly suggest that at this point she is referring to the first substance, God, and not the second. In addition, the use of the term 'logos ousios', I suggest, points towards Hutton's reading. Philo distinguishes between the logos proforikos and the *logos endiathetos* (the word within), which Conway changes to logos ousios. Why does she make this change? One possibility is that logos ousios more definitively points to the logos as a mode of God. Speaking of the 'word within' does not uniquely mark anything out, insofar as all beings are within God in some sense as far as Conway is concerned. Logos ousios, on the other hand, does grant a special status to the Word, insofar as it is of the same substance as God. The main use of the Greek term ousios within the Christian theological tradition is in terms of Trinitarian theology, where it is claimed that the three Persons of the Trinity are 'homousious' or of the same substance. Origen also used 'ousia' to speak of the unified being of God. Therefore, by speaking of logos ousios, Conway is perhaps indicating to us that she is speaking of the Word that is of the same substance with God and not the second mediating substance that can be equated to Adam Kadmon.

Further support for Hutton's reading follows from the Biblical references Conway provides that supposedly mention the logos proforikos. Whilst most references provided are general references to the word or wisdom or God, Proverbs 8:22 is a specific reference to the first-born creature, 'The Lord created me at the beginning of his work, the first of his acts of long ago', and Ephesians 3:9 speaks of the appearance of the historical Christ as making 'everyone see what is the plan of the mystery hidden for ages in God.' The logos proforikos, then, is perhaps intended to be the first-born second substance that is manifested in Jesus of Nazareth, whilst the logos ousios is something else entirely.

There are clearly good interpretive points in favour of both positions offered by Mercer and Hutton. Either way, the difference between them has little substantial impact upon our overall understanding of Conway's philosophy. Regardless of the specific interpretation we follow, Conway's Christology is rather complex, perhaps reflecting the different influences that shaped her thought about Christ. We essentially find Christ in three guises in Conway's metaphysical system: (1) the logos ousios, (2) the logos proforikos and (3) the historical manifestation of Christ in Jesus of Nazareth. Given that the logos ousios and historical Christ only get passing mentions in the *Principia*, it is clear that she sees the mediating role of the logos proforikos as the most significant aspect of her Christology. With regard to the historical manifestation of Christ, Conway is clear that one need not recognize Jesus Christ as Messiah in order to have true belief in him; rather, a belief in the mediating substance is sufficient. However, once one does accept the existence of the mediator, then she claims that 'they will indubitably come to acknowledge also, even if they are unwilling, that Christ is that mediator' (6.5; 32).

Nevertheless, Conway is left with the claim that belief in Jesus Christ is not necessary for true faith or salvation, and thus she significantly departs from Christian orthodoxy here. In addition, in emphasizing the salvific achievements of the individual apart from any divine assistance, Conway undermines the atonement granted through the suffering and death of Christ. Conway argues that it is up to each created being's own efforts to achieve the salvation that is open to them:

> This wisdom of God sees that it is more fitting for all things to proceed in their natural course and order, so that in this way they may achieve that maturity which he bestows on each and every being and so that creatures may have the opportunity to attain, through their own efforts, ever greater perfection as instruments of divine wisdom, goodness, and power.
>
> (9.6; 66)

The place of the historical Jesus in the scheme of salvation is therefore greatly reduced; rather, it is the mediating substance, the logos proforikos, that as a metaphysical principle has a key role to play in the divine moral scheme.

A further possible tension within Conway's Christology, particularly with regard to the question of salvation, has been noted by Allison Coudert. In Chapter V, Conway does attribute some role to both the inner and outer Christ in salvation. Whilst the historical Christ's suffering was able to 'heal, preserve, and restore creatures from corruption and death', the work of the inner Christ 'saves, preserves, and restores their souls' (5.6; 27). However, as Coudert notes, 'these references fit uncomfortably within the overall scheme of a kabbalistic work that presents an optimistic philosophy of universal salvation predicated on an individual's own actions' (1999: 207). Conway is ultimately stuck between two rival intellectual movements that nevertheless both influence her: on the one hand, we have the Kabbalist and heterodox Christian view of salvation achieved by the individual alone, and on the other, the Quaker apologist standpoint that is keen to preserve a substantive role for Christ in salvation. However, perhaps the tension goes even further, for we in fact have three different narratives concerning salvation that have made an appearance in the *Principia*:

(1) salvation is at least partially accomplished by the suffering and death of Jesus Christ, (2) salvation is a matter of the individual's own efforts alone and (3) salvation is an inevitable result of the purifying action of pain and suffering upon the individual, beyond their control. Coudert collapses (2) and (3) by shaping Conway's argument concerning the role of suffering into one about the importance of the individual's reaction to suffering: 'salvation is the result of an individual's positive response to suffering' (1999: 207), and so it is not suffering per se that brings about one's salvation but one's own active response to it that is important. This interpretive option is not open to us, though, because Conway does not explicitly highlight our reaction to suffering in this regard. Rather, she states that the salvific effect of the experience of suffering upon the creature in question necessarily occurs, regardless of their response to it (see 7.1; 43). So, there are at least three different narratives concerning salvation to be found within the *Principia*, and whilst it is possible that (1) and (3) could form part of a coherent system, there are still Conway's comments concerning salvation being achieved through the efforts of individual creatures that cause tension within the soteriology she presents.

A further perspective upon Conway's approach to the historical Christ is offered by Parageau, who explores the feminist nature of the Christology presented in the *Principia*. Parageau notes a prominent medieval Christian tradition of women mystics who identified themselves with the experience of the suffering Christ, on the basis that they are more sympathetic to the pain of others (see 2018: 261). Conway herself tended to be viewed by others through this perspective due to her health issues. For example, in a letter from 1677, Quaker preacher and writer Lillias Skene uses Christological language to express her hope that Conway's pain may be for her benefit: 'My desires are that more and more that eye may be opened in thee that looks beyond the things seen … [and] that by all thy present sufferings thin iniquities may be perched away and sensitive nature be crucified' (L 439). By imitating Christ through her suffering, it was hoped that Conway could be brought closer to him and thereby closer to the salvation that he offers. Parageau points out, though, that the Christology found in the *Principia* does not follow this approach; rather, Conway seeks to undermine the importance of the masculine historical figure of Christ at the expense of a genderless metaphysicalized figure that is equally accessible to men and women alike: 'The metaphysical Christ of Conway's philosophy, who is present in each creature, whether male or female, is himself neither male nor female. Gender differences are thus neutralized, and an egalitarian theology of redemption is put forward by Conway' (2018: 263). Therefore, instead of settling into a highly gendered Christological debate, with women seen as especially sensitive to the example of the suffering masculine Christ, Conway seeks to move beyond a gendered account. We can undoubtedly see this as part of Conway's overall universalizing project, which seeks to present a philosophical and religious system that is open and accessible to all (whilst remaining within touching distance of a theist Christian framework) and offers equal access to the scheme of salvation for all beings.

In this section, I have been exploring Conway's conception of the Triune God. We have seen that Conway offers a complex Trinitarian theology, in which Christ is given a multi-faceted role as both logos ousios and logos proforikos. We have also explored potential tensions within this account, related to both modalist and subordinationist tendencies in her view. In the following section, I will argue that Conway's challenge to the Christian tradition is not limited to her conception of the Triune God, as we proceed to examine more thoroughly her soteriology (including the soteriological role played by Christ) and eschatology.

Time, soteriology and eschatology

In the *Principia*, Conway provides an account of the soteriological role played by Christ that in turn sheds light upon her eschatology and understanding of time. We have already seen that Christ, in the context of Conway's metaphysical system, acts as a mediator between the atemporal God and created beings within the universe, and this extends to time, insofar as 'he can be said to share eternity (which belongs to God) and time (which belongs to creatures)' (5.5; 26). The idea that Christ both partakes of atemporal eternity and of time is certainly a potentially difficult one to understand: whilst Christ exists in time in the sense that all created things are in time, the soteriological role played by Christ means that this is not the end of the story.

Conway states that we can consider the soteriological movement of Christ and creatures towards spirit from a new perspective, leaving the more metaphysically focused notion of time we have been operating with, and instead adopting the 'ordinary sense of the word, [namely] a successive increase or decrease of things during which they grow for a certain period and then decline until they die or change into another state' (5.6; 26). According to this different sense of time, 'one can say that neither this mediating being nor any creature perfectly united to God is subject to time and its laws' (5.6; 26). Such a state, I argue, is perhaps best understood as a kind of relative timelessness, in contrast to the strict timelessness of God, in that Christ and creatures still undergo change, even when united with each other in the process of becoming more spirit:

> [Christ] is like a most powerful and efficacious balm, through which all things are preserved from decline and death, and whatever is joined and united with him is always new, lively, and growing… [He] may raise the souls of men above time and corruption up to himself, in whom they receive blessing and in whom they grow by degrees in goodness, virtue, and holiness forever.
>
> (5.6; 26f.)

We can, therefore, find in Conway's system a kind of eschatology, in which creatures can become 'united' with Christ to the extent that they can achieve a kind of relative timelessness, though they are still strictly subject to time and the mutability that is the essence of their quiddity.

To further explicate this state, Conway writes that 'those who achieve a perfect union with Christ are raised to a region of perfect tranquillity, where nothing is seen or felt to move or be moved' (5.7; 27).[9] However, this is not to say that such creatures are no longer moving or changing, '[for] although the strongest and swiftest motions exist there, nevertheless because they move so uniformly, equally, and harmoniously, without any resistance or disturbance they appear completely at rest' (5.7; 27.). Thus, Conway seems to envisage a possible state where creatures, though still potentially capable of becoming less perfect and more material, can nevertheless become like Christ and other, more purified, creatures in joining a sustained movement towards perfection. Conway argues that 'Christ and the soul can be united without any other medium because of their great affinity and likeness' (8.3; 60), so it is natural to see the notion of 'adoption' as linked to the point where Christ and creature reach a measure of likeness such that we can think of the latter as saved.

If we were then to consider the possible way in which a creature can become like Christ, then given that what distinguishes Christ is that he only changes towards the good, we can think of saved creatures as having reached a position in their moral development where they also only move towards the good. However, there is no end to such a process and so this is the limit of soteriology and eschatology that we can discover in the *Principia*. Whilst we, as creatures, can unite with Christ and attain a kind of relative timelessness, strictly speaking, time and the history of the universe, characterized by an ongoing process of change overall towards perfection, will never cease.

As I argued in Chapter 3, Conway's understanding of time, as one of the fundamental building blocks of the created universe, is not a merely secular metaphysical account; crucially, to be fully understood, it must be viewed in the context of a wider soteriological scheme. As such, Conway's metaphysics is imbued with religious significance, with philosophy and theology intrinsically intertwined. Key metaphysical components of her system, such as her tripartite view of fundamental substances and the possibility of change, are configured so as to reveal a foundational providential plan for creation: a world of created beings, guided by an intermediary substance, 'Christ', who is immune to the possibility of sin at an imperfect level of being, slowly but inexorably moving towards a morally perfected world of spirits, which is the eschatological endpoint of Conway's system. Time, for Conway, is precisely this soteriological process, and not merely the space in which events occur. In line with her syncretic approach, then, philosophy and theology form the completed whole of Conway's philosophy, both disciplines pointing towards the wider picture of the infinite development of the universe, correlatives in terms of both spirit and moral development.

As before, Conway's blending of time with soteriological considerations has a further impact upon her relation to traditional Christian thought. We noted earlier that Conway holds that time is infinite in the sense that the created universe has existed and will continue to exist for an infinite duration of time. Relating back to soteriology, this has the implication that the soteriological process of creatures inexorably perfecting themselves, transitioning from a more material state to a more spiritual one, also has infinite duration. The narrative of creatures becoming more spirit and thus closer to God in perfection is one that is never-ending, insofar as 'this progression and ascension cannot reach God, who is the supreme Being and whose nature infinitely surpasses every creature, even one brought to the highest level' (9.5; 65). As such, there is no sense, in Conway's system, of an eschatological endpoint, a final event of history in which all are judged and the Kingdom of God is established for all eternity, in whatever way you wish to understand that. The *Principia* proposes a picture of the universe in which history never ends, with creatures slowly becoming closer to God and yet never truly becoming at one with the divine. The goodness of God is boundless, so history and the soteriological process itself will never end, with God eternally creating more, so that more beings can become close to the divine. Such a view, again, shows Conway willing to decisively move away from a traditional Christian view of soteriology and eschatology.

Universal salvation and Origen

Further to this, the process of increasing in perfection is available to all creatures, insofar as they are all fundamentally constituted by the same substance. Moral growth, then, unlike the traditional Christian view, is not restricted to human beings alone; rather, all creation, in whatever form, is able to grow in perfection, become more spirit and thus closer to God.[10] Such anti-anthropomorphic tendencies in Conway are intensified by her claim that 'an infinity of worlds or creatures was made by God ... Thus it clearly follows that his creatures are infinite and created in an infinite number of ways' (3.4; 16). Not only is salvation not restricted to human beings, it is available to an infinite number of kinds of creature, all of whom have equal standing and access to the process of becoming closer to God. Such a universalist eschatology is in keeping with Conway's willingness to open up Christianity to all, not only desiring to accommodate those of other belief systems through a reinterpretation of key Christian doctrine, but even allowing salvation for all of creation.

Conway argues that all things can and will be saved; that is, they will become adopted by Christ in the manner described above. Such a theory of universal salvation is anathema to Christian orthodoxy, which is not only committed to the view that only human beings can be saved, but also restricts that salvation to a certain section of human beings (determined either by pre-election, by faith, or by the works of the individual). However, the idea of a human being damned for all eternity declined throughout the seventeenth century, as it became increasingly seen as fundamentally unjust and contrary to the loving nature of God. At the time of the writing of the *Principia*, the ideas of the Church Father Origen had found a new popularity, even though much of his theology had long been held to be heretical. Henry More, for his part, had praised Origen highly and adopted some of his rather controversial views, such as the claim that the human aspect of Christ had existed for all eternity alongside the Logos (see Crocker 2003: 100f.). Another contentious part of Origen's theology was his doctrine of universal salvation, and as Hutton points out (see 2004: 69f.), it is probable that Conway's own understanding of salvation is shaped by this influence, either by reading the original texts by Origen or through works by admirers of Origen, such as George Rust (who was a friend of both More and Conway).

Origen's notion of the *apocatastasis* is particularly noteworthy for our purposes. It is a wider notion than simply the salvation of the individual; rather, it is a final state in which all things are not only saved, but *restored* to their beginning, rightful position. Rabinowitz describes this picture of salvation as

> a restoration of all things to a previous existing and perfect state... [that] occurs for all beings at the same time. It begins with the incarnation and is followed by the subjection of the individual to the appropriate punishment for sins leading

to willing submission to Christ. The soul begins an ascent throughout which it gains knowledge about the workings of the universe. When the soul reaches the highest levels of understanding its return is completed and it retains its intelligible qualities.

(1984: 321)

We see, in Origen, a vision of the salvation of the entire creation, achieved with Christ, involving ascent back to God and the gaining of knowledge concerning the universe. We have seen all these features in Conway's soteriology, apart from any emphasis on the gaining of knowledge as one ascends on the spirit–matter continuum. However, we shall see in the next chapter that Conway attributes misuse of the freedom of the will by creatures to some kind of ignorance or misunderstanding on their part. It would seem that moral development will at least partially involve a growth in knowledge, such that the creature in question will no longer be led astray in the courses of action they undertake. As such, we can see that Conway offers a vision of moral redemption that follows Origen in at least broad strokes. However, we will have to complicate Conway's soteriology slightly in Chapter 7, when we turn to the question of the identity of creatures and the possibility of movement from one kind of life to another.

Conclusion

We have seen in this chapter that Conway offers a distinctive view of the nature of God, Christ and salvation. Conway's eschatology reveals a picture of the universe that is universalist and optimistic, insofar as all created beings will ultimately be able to unite with Christ on the infinite journey towards moral perfection. The approach to the Trinity and the question of salvation, grounded in her theory of substance and change, found in the *Principia* will always be problematic for the Christian believer, and almost certainly would have always been a major barrier to widespread influence in the realm of Christian thought, even if the *Principia* had garnered more intellectual attention in the centuries following its original publication. However, it may be amenable to later thinkers, such as John Hick, who seek to find an eschatological account which is more universalist, less anthropocentric and transcends one particular religious belief system. In the following chapter, we will continue exploring Conway's account of the nature of God, Christ and creatures by focusing on the topic of freedom.

6

Freedom

The main aim of this chapter is to examine Conway's often-overlooked account[1] of freedom.[2] As an aid for reconstructing the brief account found in the *Principia*, I explore the manner and extent to which Conway adopts the account of freedom of her philosophical mentor, Henry More, who had presented his theory of freedom in *Enchiridion Ethicum* (1667). I argue that Conway's treatment of human and divine freedom provides further evidence for her willingness to decisively depart from the views of her mentor, whilst also retaining some elements of his ethical theory.

I start the discussion proper with a consideration of the account of freedom presented by More in *Enchiridion Ethicum*. We will see that, with regard to divine freedom, More claims that there is no indifference to the divine will and that it is constrained by its own nature in a manner that is logically prior to divine creative action. Furthermore, in his account of human freedom, More distinguishes between those individuals who have indifference of the will (in the sense that a will is able to spontaneously act upon one intention rather than another in a given situation) and those who have attained a good nature such that they are constrained to do the right thing, in a manner analogous to the moral constraints upon divine action. I will then seek to reconstruct Conway's account of divine and human freedom from the hints she gives in the *Principia*.

I argue that, given evidence from correspondence regarding Conway's familiarity with More's work, and the timing of the writing of the notes that would be compiled in the *Principia*, it is highly likely that Conway had the account of freedom in More's *Enchiridion Ethicum* in mind when she offers her own theory of divine and human freedom. We will see that Conway posits a stark distinction between human and divine freedom by claiming that God does not have the kind of indifference of will that is granted to us. When we come to compare Conway and More, I argue that whilst they both agree in attributing substantive freedom to both God and human beings, the *Principia* departs from

More's philosophy in refraining from limiting freedom to human beings alone (as far as created beings are concerned), but extending it to all creatures.

More on divine and human freedom

We first consider More's account of divine freedom.[3] More argues for constraints upon divine freedom (construed in a broadly libertarian sense[4]) with regard to creation. In reflecting upon the divine attribute of omnipotence in his *Divine Dialogues* (undertaken through the guise of the character, Philotheus), he argues that he 'could yet never understand that the most omnipotent power that is imaginable can ever have a right to do what is wrong' (1668: 23f.). More construes omnipotence as morally constrained, in that even an omnipotent being could not act against what is good, in addition to the usual caveats regarding logical possibility (such as God famously not being able to create a stone so heavy that God cannot lift it). Due to divine wisdom and goodness, God cannot, of necessity, act in any way other than doing that which is best, which fundamentally shapes all divine action with regard to the created universe (see More 1668: 24). More argues that there is no indifference to the divine will, as God's goodness is 'so perfect, immutable and permanent', that he cannot be in a state of 'supine indifferency, to be carried otherwise than to what is the best' (1668: 24f.).

More's account of divine freedom emphasizes a logically prior moral order to things that shapes God's creative action. As John Henry notes, More had a 'belief in the inherent order in the nature of things which dictated to God the essential nature of the world that must be created' (1990: 65). A fundamental part of the constraints upon divine freedom lies in essential truths regarding the nature of things that (at least conceptually) hold prior to God's creative act, which fellow Cambridge Platonist, George Rust, glosses as 'mutual respects and relations eternal and immutable, and in order of nature antecedent to any understanding created or uncreated' (1682: 166). God grasps these essential truths and undertakes creative activity on that basis to bring about that which is the best. What would be best for God to do, then, is set prior to any exercise of divine will: given such truths, and the nature of the divine attributes, there is only one way in which God could have acted. Hence, a kind of necessity attaches to divine freedom, stemming from the interplay of essential truths and the divine attributes of omnipotence, wisdom and perfect benevolence. However, that is not to say that More denies that there is divine freedom (e.g.

More writes of God acting 'freely, wise, and benign' (1679: 101 – quoted in Reid 2012: 341)); God is still free, even though there is, by necessity, only one way in which he can act.

Having considered More's account of divine freedom, we can now move to examine his theory of human freedom. Before his more extended treatment of human freedom in the *Enchiridion*, More had briefly characterized this notion in *The Immortality of the Soul* as part of a critique of Hobbes, whose philosophy had been taken to have troubling consequences for the possibility of human freedom. In *Leviathan*, Hobbes argues for a strict materialism concerning human beings, speaking of the notion of incorporeal substances, such as the individual soul, as 'insignificant sounds' that 'signify nothing at all' (1985: 4.20-1; 108). More's worry is that without an immaterial soul, a human being would be a mere mechanical being, subject to the necessarily operating mechanical laws of nature alone, and so could not be held to be genuinely free (see 1662: *The Immortality of the Soul*, 65–70). It seems to be an intrinsic part of the notion of free action (at least for human beings) that we could have acted otherwise[5]: for example, I can be said to be freely typing this sentence partly (or maybe entirely) because I could have been doing something else right now, such as drinking the coffee sat by my computer. However, if I am entirely subject to the operation of the laws of nature, then it seems that none of my actions could have been otherwise: given the total state of the universe at a particular moment, plus the operation of the laws of nature, the next total state of the universe necessarily follows. Having an individual soul was supposed to safeguard our freedom,[6] insofar as there is a part of the human individual that lies outside of the necessary workings of the laws of nature, and is somehow able to have an effect upon the material universe such that we can genuinely claim that our actions within it could have been otherwise.

Hobbes's refusal to countenance immaterial souls, or any kind of incorporeal substance, indeed formed part of his denial of free will, in the sense of a libertarian freedom described by Robert Kane as 'the power of agents to be the ultimate creators (or originators) and sustainers of their own ends or purposes' (1996: 4). Hobbes argues instead for a weaker form of freedom as self-determination, construed as not being hindered from doing what we will (see Hobbes 1962: 51f.).[7] In defence of his views concerning freedom, Hobbes had claimed that future events must be determined in advance, as it is necessary that either outcome A or not-A come to pass.[8]

In opposition to Hobbes's challenge to the notion of freedom of will, More argues that we do indeed have a power to determine ourselves to freely act in a particular way: 'We are conscious to ourselves of that Faculty which the Greeks call *autexousion*, or *a Power in our selves*, notwithstanding any outward assaults or importunate temptations, *to cleave to that which is virtuous and honest, or to yield to pleasures or other vile advantages*' (1662: *The Immortality of the Soul*, 69f.). More sees human beings as torn between virtue as 'an intellectual Power of the Soul' and 'the animal Impressions of bodily Passions' (1690: 11). Such a view, as Aaron Garrett notes, reflects the shared vision of the Cambridge Platonists, who wish to argue for freedom of will (against Hobbes), whilst holding to 'an intellectualist tradition stressing control of the passions by the intellect and that knowing the good to be necessary means doing the good' (2013: 35). The control of the passions is necessary as we are subject to both the animal and intellectual sides of our nature. As Jasper Reid argues (see 2012: 369), More is more concerned with striking the right balance between the animal and the divine within us, rather than castigating our animal nature as inherently sinful.[9] In *An Explanation of the Grand Mystery of Godliness*, More states that the animal life, and anything arising out of it, such as the animal passions, is without sin in itself (see 1708: 32). Nevertheless, we feel ourselves caught between the two sets of motivations that we are presented with by these two aspects of us: on the one hand, the self-love of the animal passions, and on the other, the virtues of the life lived in obedience to God (see More 1708: 37). The very possibility of our having *autexousion* is grounded in the fact that we have these two sets of motivations to choose between, and further, by freely choosing those motivations from the intellectual side of our nature, we are able to perfect ourselves. Animals, on the other hand, do not have such a freedom as they only have the animal passions motivating them to action.

As evidence for the claim that we have a faculty of *autexousion*, More appeals to the fact that we have a sense of morality through our conscience, which he claims is 'an evident and undeniable witness of [our free will]' (1662: *The Immortality of the Soul*, 70). In *An Antidote against Atheism*, he characterizes such feelings of conscience as 'a fear and confusion of mind arising from the presage of some mischief that may befall a man beside the ordinary course of nature, or the usual occurrences of affairs, because he has done thus or thus' (1662: 29). More claims that our feelings of conscience are a truthful reflection regarding our capabilities, insofar as we would not have such a feeling if we did not have a genuinely free power to seek after good or evil in our actions: 'As we feel the check of conscience after doing some things which were doubtingly acted, and without mature deliberation: even from hence it is manifest, that we sometimes act so, as that to have willed and acted otherwise, was in our power.

And this power, of abstaining from ill, is that very thing, which is truly called free-will' (1690: 179f.).

Moving to More's discussion in the *Enchiridion*, he begins by marking a parallel between divine and human freedom. More remarks that some would be 'extremely scandalized' by the question as to whether 'virtue gets into men by custom, or by nature, or by some divine fate (which is the same as good fortune?)', on the basis that 'they judge a thing voluntarily done, to be of far different merit from what happens by compulsion' (1690: 173). More argues, in contrast to this view, that we can be held to have freely done an action even under this kind of constraint (thus we could potentially distinguish between the unrestrained freedom originally granted by our capacity of *autexousion* and the morally constrained freedom of the virtuous). He points out that we do not see God's actions as less free due to the moral constraints set by his nature (see More 1690: 173), and the analogy can be extended to humans also.

Once an individual has acquired virtue (in whatever manner), More states that they become akin to God insofar as they become unable to act against their good nature: 'whoever is good, either by nature or the divine fate, is also endowed with so true and efficacious a sense of honesty, that he can no more go against this sense, than that a sober man should stab himself with a dagger' (1690: 173). In a sense, such people are constrained by their virtue to act in a certain way, but this does not mean that they have thereby lost their freedom. Virtuous individuals are esteemed by More as a kind of moral hero, someone who is at least analogous to God insofar as they have reached a state in which they are unable to act in an unethical manner. How strong the analogy is supposed to be is not entirely clear, but at the very least it seems that we can attain a state in which we are constrained by own nature to always do the right thing.[10]

More's position in this regard relies upon his underlying conception of virtue as a power, rather than an acquired habit (as might be claimed by an Aristotelian). He argues that virtue is not something that is necessarily brought about by the kind of process of habituation emphasized by the Aristotelian tradition: 'A *habit* is not essential to virtue ... For it is not the external causes, but the internal, which makes the essence of a thing' (1690: 12). Elsewhere, he writes in a similar vein,

> Tho *habit* be a sort of *power*, arising from exercise and custom; yet this very way and circumstance of acquiring virtue, is nothing material, as to the true nature of it. For if this *power* or *energy* be got within us, and operates in our souls as by a native spring or elasticity, what matter is it, whether it came by repeated actions, or by inspiration?
>
> (1690: 174)

With a conception of virtue that disregards the influence of habit by focusing only on the power we have to self-determine (i.e. to spontaneously determine the will through one motivation rather than another, regardless of the source of the motivation in question), More removes any doubts concerning moral luck and whether we can be held responsible for our virtuous nature gained through habituation: our will is free, regardless of how our virtuous nature came to be. Such a view seems to posit an analogy between divine freedom and that enjoyed by the virtuous individual, in that humans can (at least in principle) have an intrinsic virtuous nature such that their actions are morally constrained, and yet also still be genuinely free (and be held morally responsible for what they do).

However, despite the possibility of some people attaining virtue, More goes on to claim that most of us remain in a state that falls significantly short of such a goal. It is therefore required that such people be persuaded to adopt virtuous ways of living: 'While they may exercise the liberty of their wills to either side, [they] should be urged and excited by all that can be said, to incline their wills to that side, where right reason, and a sense of their duty, calls them' (1690: 174). If they can be exhorted in such a direction, then they 'are enabled by a liberty in their wills, to shake off, and gradually destroy those ill desires, with which they are beset; and, by the help of heaven to assert that liberty, which is most suitable to a creature made by God's image, and a partaker of divine sense' (1690: 175). More expands upon his notion of free will, 'the *having a power to act or not act within our selves*', by contrasting that power with mere spontaneity or voluntariness, 'a principle of acting within one's self … what the Greeks call hecousion' (1690: 176). Spontaneity itself is to be contrasted with acting from ignorance or some kind of external compulsion: 'In the one case (that of *force*) the agent does not act from his own principles, but is compelled from without: In the other case (that of *ignorance*) though he act from his own principle, yet he has no notice of the moral circumstances of the action, which if he had known, he would not have done that action' (1690: 178).

So, to act from spontaneity is to act from a sufficient comprehension of the morally salient details of the situation, and to be acting without some form of overwhelming external compulsion forcing you to act in the way in which you act: in other words, a voluntary or spontaneous agent is an individual 'whose principle of action is in himself, and who understands and takes cognizance of his own actions that the circumstances that relate to them' (More 1690: 178*).* More argues that freedom of the will is a subset of voluntariness or spontaneity:

> When we say that a man has *liberum arbitrium* or *free-will*, we add a particular difference to the general notion of *voluntariness*, that is to say we suppose he is such a voluntary agent, as can act and not act as he pleases: whereas to the being a voluntary agent, simply or generally speaking, there is no such difference required.
>
> (1690: 177)

Whilst a merely voluntary agent can act as they please, an agent with free will is in a position such that if they were to will the opposite course of action, they could do so. Returning to the question of those who have not attained virtue, such that it is possible that they could do either the right or wrong action in any particular situation, they can be said to have freedom of the will in the sense of *liberum arbitrium*: not only are they able to act as they please, but they have a capacity to undertake differing courses of action, depending on what they will at that moment.

As a further part of his critique of Hobbes, More adds that even our determination of events through our free actions does not confer necessity on those events. As Reid notes:

> When A (or, as it might be, not-A) was a freely chosen action, More felt that it would indeed be true that it would happen, and even true that it would be *made* to happen by something, but he believed that this 'something' was to be found in the spontaneous volitions of the agent. Since the agent *could* have chosen otherwise, his choice would not confer any genuine necessity onto the resulting event.
>
> (2012: 180)

It would be wrong, on this account, to hold that determination of events through our free actions confers any sort of necessity on the world (such events are still contingent and genuinely could have been otherwise), and so we have freedom of the will, with no suggestion that events surrounding our free actions are necessitated.

Given our previous discussion, we can take the implication that those beings who have a good nature, such that they are morally constrained to do the right thing, do not have freedom of the will; however, their actions are still to be taken as voluntary, free and the possible subject of moral judgement. It seems that our freedom of the will is both analogous to, and distinguishable from, that enjoyed by God: we undertake voluntary or spontaneous action, and in that sense we are free, but I have a free will in a sense not enjoyed by God, by which I am able to choose between that which is the right and the wrong thing to do. There is a significant sense, according to More, in which human and divine freedom can be distinguished: for those humans who have not achieved virtue, they have the capacity for an arbitrary will, which is not possible for a being, such as God, who is morally constrained by their good nature to always aim for that which is best in their actions. As More argues, the capacity of an arbitrary will cannot be a perfection, insofar as it can be used for both good and evil: 'Now this power of not acting, when it regards those things which are base and dishonest, is a great perfection; But when it has respect to things that are noble and honest, 'tis a great imperfection' (1690: 179). As God, or the idealized virtuous human individual, perhaps, has a good nature such that they are morally constrained in their action, they do not have an arbitrary will, and this is simply part of their moral perfection. In fact, it is good that they do not have such a choice. However, such beings are still free, as they are acting voluntarily or spontaneously.

So, we can sum up More's view concerning divine and human freedom in this way:

1. God, as a divinely omnipotent being, is both logically and morally constrained, and thus does not have indifference of the will.
2. Humans have a faculty of *autexousion*, which allows us to freely determine ourselves to particular courses of action.
3. This freedom of the will allows us to act spontaneously, without some form of overwhelming external compulsion.
4. Virtuous humans and God analogously have a state of morally constrained freedom, without an arbitrary will.

With all this in mind, we can now go on to consider Conway's own account of the freedom of God and creatures.

Comparing More and Conway on freedom

In this section, I explore the account of human and divine freedom offered in the *Principia*, before comparing and contrasting this with More's account. Conway almost certainly read *Enchiridion Ethicum* soon after publication, in the late 1660s. More clearly implies, in a letter from 27 March 1668, that he had already sent an early copy of the work for Conway's perusal: 'I am solicitous that neither [the *Divine Dialogues*] nor the *Enchiridion* [*Ethicum*] I sent you before may give occasion of intending your mind more then will consist with so much ease of your body as your pains will permit you' (L 293). Given that the notes that would later be compiled into the *Principia* were composed within the next decade, it is highly likely that the *Enchiridion*, including its account of freedom, would have been close to the forefront of Conway's mind during that period. In addition, we know from the correspondence between More and Conway that she was familiar with all of More's writings and often discussed them in detail with him.

In a similar manner to More, alongside outlining her views concerning human freedom, Conway offers reflections concerning divine freedom, which can be contrasted with that autonomy which is granted to us. She introduces the topic of divine freedom in the *Principia* through a presentation of her account of creation, which is clearly influenced by Neoplatonist sources, as discussed in Chapter 3. It may seem at first as if Conway is willing to sacrifice the freedom of God, due to her views concerning divine creation. Though she states that '[all] creatures simply are and exist only because God wishes them to' (2.1; 12), she nevertheless uses Neoplatonic imagery regarding the process of divine creation that may seem to imply a lack of freedom:

> God is infinitely good, loving, and bountiful; indeed, he is goodness and charity itself, the infinite fountain and ocean of goodness, charity, and bounty. In what way is it possible for that fountain not to flow perpetually and to send forth living waters? For will not that ocean overflow in its perpetual emanation and continual flux for the production of creatures?
>
> (2.4; 13)

Such a use of emanationist imagery, in which the creative act is characterized as an overflowing of divine goodness, suggests a necessary, inescapable process, as opposed to the intentional act presupposed by the major theist traditions of the day. We could say that, under this view, God has voluntary agency in the sense that he has the capacity to act spontaneously, but does not enjoy indifference of the will, such that it is possible that he would be able to do anything other than what he does.

However, it becomes clear that the use of such imagery should not be taken too strictly, in that its talk of necessity should not be understood as implying a denial of divine freedom: 'God is a most free agent and yet most necessary' (3.1; 15). Conway reveals her main target to be the voluntarist theological tradition that attributes indifference of will to God, in the manner of Descartes, who had claimed a certain arbitrariness attaching to the divine will, which was unconstrained by any kind of prior framework of rationality and morality.[11] In the *Sixth Replies*,

Descartes claims that God's will makes things true or false, and so there is no logically prior scheme of goodness or truth to which God's will must conform (see 1984: 291). This view of God's creative action is a radical rejection of any sense of necessity applied to divine action. Though Descartes's voluntarism is a matter of ongoing scholarly debate,[12] the traditional interpretation of Descartes on this matter is reflected by Frankfurt, who argues that the Cartesian view holds that God's freedom consists in absolute indifference of the will:

> Since there *are* no truths prior to God's creation of them, His creative will cannot be determined or even moved by any considerations of value or of rationality whatever... The divine will is, in other words, entirely arbitrary. There are no prior conditions of right or reason to which it must conform; indeed, there are none to which it might choose to conform.
>
> (1977: 41)

Conway's main argument against a voluntarist account of divine freedom centres on her view that indifference of the will is the sort of freedom that can only be imputed to creatures and not the Creator. Indeed, an indifferent will, for Conway, is a sign of a being's imperfection and thus a perfect being such as God could not have such a freedom:

> Although the will of God is most free so that whatever he does in regard to his creatures is done without any external force or compulsion or without any cause coming from the creatures (since he is free and acts spontaneously in whatever he does), nevertheless, that indifference of acting or not acting can in no way be said to be in God, for this would be an imperfection and would make God like his corruptible creatures.
>
> (3.1; 15)

Freedom of the will, in the sense of an indifferent will, implies the possibility of a kind of change for that being that could potentially lead that creature away from perfection. For a being with an indifferent will, which has a capacity to choose between morally good and bad options for any morally salient action, there is an ongoing possibility that any of their volitions could result in a morally impermissible action and a decrease in perfection. Such a being (as ourselves) is in contrast to one whose nature is such that these types of volitions are not possible for them: these potential bad options for action do not even occur to them. There is only one way they can act (and that is to always do the right thing) so there is no indifferency in their will and no possibility of moral backsliding or a decrease in perfection. For this reason, an indifferent will is the mark of an imperfect being. God, a perfect, immutable being, could never decrease in perfection and so cannot have this sort of freedom.

Further on, Conway expands upon her understanding of God's freedom as lacking indifference of the will:

> True justice or goodness has no latitude or indifference in itself but is like a straight line drawn from one point to another, where it is impossible to have two or more equally straight lines between two points, because only one line can be straight and all others must be more or less curved to the extent that they depart from that straight line.
>
> (3.2; 16)

As God is uniquely perfect, there is no question of him acting in any other way than how he chooses to act, and in that sense the divine will is not indifferent and divine actions are necessary: '[God] must do whatever he does to and for his creatures since his infinite wisdom, goodness, and justice are a law to him which cannot be superseded' (3.2; 16). Divine action is necessary, as it will always follow in line with the perfection of God's wisdom, and yet free insofar as he is a transcendent self-mover, unaffected by any external compulsion. So, God's perfect goodness, for Conway, has the implication that there can be no such thing as divine indifference of the will, contradicting the traditional understanding of Descartes's account of divine freedom and the creation of necessary truths. In light of the preceding discussion, we can readily see that there is apparently little substantive difference between More and Conway on the question of divine freedom, insofar as they posit that God has no indifference of the will and thus seems to have (due to the divine perfect nature) a kind of freedom not enjoyed by human beings. As such, I argue that it is on questions of human and creaturely freedom that Conway begins to decisively depart from the account proposed by her mentor.

Turning to creatures, Conway claims that they have an entirely different sort of freedom than that enjoyed by God, in that they have indifference of will and he does not. In fact, it is our indifferent wills that allow us to engage in moral development and corruption, in a manner that would not be possible for a perfect being. As Lascano rightly points out, for Conway, God grants creatures indifference of the will as part of his creative project to communicate his goodness as much as he can (see 2017: 170). By giving creatures indifference of the will, we are able to morally develop ourselves and thereby also communicate goodness to others. There seems to be some inevitability, however, that an indifferent will may be used for evil, in that we are led to 'often [act] from pure will but without any true and solid reason or the guidance of wisdom' (3.1; 15). Conway is therefore claiming that it is possible that the indifferent will is able to act in one way or another. However, epistemic factors, including lack of understanding of the salient facts of the situation or an incorrect assessment of what possible course of action best promotes the good, sometimes lead the indifferent will astray.

Conway adds that any view that would attribute such a will to God would make him potentially like 'those cruel tyrants in the world who do most things from their own pure will, relying on their power, so that they are unable to give any explanation for their actions other than their own pure will' (3.1; 15). The faculty of an indifferent will allows the being that has it to potentially act on the basis of a bad reason, something that is in some sense false, not 'solid' or wise. It seems that a reason could be bad in the sense of confused or unclear for Conway, as she states that a 'good man is able to give a suitable explanation for what he does or will do because he understands that true goodness and wisdom require that he do so' (3.1; 15f.). The individual who acts well will be acting upon a clear, good reason that they can at least potentially communicate to others, and we could therefore perhaps use the ability to communicate one's reasons for action as a test for whether one is acting rightly or not. Doing the right thing involves being able to disclose and explain oneself, showing that you are acting upon a reason that is clear to you as the right thing to do (in this way, being in an epistemically sound position is complementary to acting well).

On this basis, we can see the reason why Conway holds that having indifference of will, a faculty that God does not have, nevertheless makes us less free, because in a sense we are inhibited from doing the right thing by being presented with bad or confused reasons for action. In this regard, Conway seems to be following a generally Platonic–Socratic view that wrongdoing is due to ignorance or confusion (see, for example, Plato's *Meno* (2005: 77b6–78b2)). As all beings naturally desire that which is good, the only explanation for their doing wrong will be confusion or ignorance about what is truly good: in other words, cognitive error is the basis of moral error. As Conway is following such a view, it is clear why indifference of the will, which allows us to be confronted with bad or confused reasons, inhibits our freedom, insofar as it gets in the way of our always choosing the good.

However, this explanation of immoral action, based on ignorance or confusion, does pose a potential problem for Conway. If a creature is to morally develop over different lifetimes, then it will also need to gain the kind of knowledge over these different forms of existence that allow it to avoid acting on bad or confused reasons for action. Conway, though, asserts that memory is tied to a particular body (see 6.11; 39), so that memories are lost when a spirit moves from one body to another. So, all memories are lost when a particular spirit ends one life and starts another. In that case, it is hard to envisage how a creature could gain in knowledge over many lifetimes in the manner that seems to be implied by Conway's soteriology.

The only way of avoiding this problem, as far as I see it, is to allow that each creature cannot retain their memories from one lifetime to the next, but due to their more refined form of existence as they develop ontologically, they are able to gain more morally salient knowledge than they could in their former lives. In this way, they are able to more reliably avoid bad or confused reasons for action and work towards the good more successfully, and thus the loss of memory is not a major hindrance to moral development across lifetimes. We can also recall Conway's likely adherence to a Platonic-inspired epistemological framework of divine illumination: as we become more like God, we come to reflect his being to a higher degree in ourselves and this will naturally involve a growth in knowledge (given that God is an omnipotent being). It is also probable that, as we become more spiritual, our epistemic capacities are less limited and so we are able to more easily gain knowledge about God and creation. For these reasons, again, the loss of memory across lifetimes does not necessarily mean that we are unable to grow in knowledge overall as we morally develop.

Returning to the question of divine freedom, in contrast to his creatures, God is metaphysically constrained by his nature to always do that which is best, although in a manner which is not incompatible with a distinctively divine kind of freedom. As Lascano notes, for Conway, God's freedom is safeguarded by the fact that he is not under any kind of external compulsion to act in the way he does; rather, his will 'is always completely determined by his perfect reason, wisdom, and goodness' (2017: 165) and so perhaps we could say that the divine will is internally compelled in this manner. On the other hand, human beings are not constrained in such a manner and so have indifference of the will. We are thus able to act upon both good and bad or confused reasons. Being presented with bad or confused reasons inhibits our freedom, though, as we are offered a distorted view of how to achieve that which is best for us. Conway's emphasis upon ethical disclosure on the part of good human beings, however, does not necessarily imply that God could (and should) disclose his purposes to us, even though he would always act upon true, 'solid' and wise intentions. Whilst human beings need to be tested for right reasons, faith in God's goodness would negate any such need with regard to the divine, and it would be hubristic anyway to expect God to disclose himself in such a manner.

Having now reviewed the respective accounts of human and divine freedom offered by Conway and More, we can see that (at least at first glance) there is remarkable agreement between the two, as befitting their collaborative relationship and the increasing recognition of Conway as an important part of the Cambridge Platonist school. Both affirm that God and humans are free in significant ways. In fact, they can be said to have an analogous freedom in the sense of voluntariness or self-moving spontaneity (though, admittedly, this parallel is not something that is explored by Conway). More and Conway both point to external compulsion and ignorance as salient characteristics of an unfree action. Conway, as we have seen, does talk about unwise or confused reasons hindering our freedom in some sense, which would perhaps involve reasons forced upon us by external compulsion and ignorance, and so it seems that she is quite close to More on this point.

However, there is at least one major difference between More and Conway on the question of divine and human freedom. More's account of creaturely freedom is explicitly tied to that of human beings, whilst Conway offers an account of creaturely freedom which is not limited to human beings, but rather applies to all created beings. In order to see why she is compelled to do this, and why she may want to hold such a position, we need to recall that questions of freedom, morality and salvation are, for Conway, not limited to human beings, but are extended to all creatures, who are all equally mutable in terms of the spirit–body continuum and have the possibility of approaching perfection through becoming less crass and more spiritual.

As an example of this process in action, Conway writes of 'a human being [who] has so greatly degraded himself by his own wilful wrongdoing and has brought his nature, which had been so noble, to a lower state', being punished by God by being compelled 'to bear the same image in his body as in that spirit into which he has internally transformed himself' (6.8; 36). In other words, through our wrongdoing as human beings, it is possible that we could (in a future life) be put into the body of a beast, though with the possibility of later continuing our moral development: indeed, Conway is committed to this possibility due to her universalist theory of salvation. Confirming her retreat from an anthropocentric approach, Conway triumphantly proclaims that salvation will ultimately be achieved for all creatures: '[The] grace of God will prevail over judgement and judgement turn into victory for the salvation and restoration of [all] creatures' (6.8; 37). As we saw earlier, More holds that animals do not have freedom in the sense enjoyed by humans, insofar as they are only presented with one set of motivations grounded in their brutish nature. As such, animals do not have indifference of will and cannot engage in self-perfection through acting on the right motivations. In this way, we have an important aspect in which Conway departs from More, insofar as she brings all creatures into the sphere of freedom and the possibility, through action on good or confused reasons, of moral development.[13]

One major point of comparison between More and Conway on this topic revolves around the possibility of the moral development of humans to the point where they have a good nature, such that they can no longer be said to have the metaphysical capacity of an indifferent will. As we have seen, More allows the possibility for a free human being to morally develop in such a manner. Whilst Conway, for her part, allows for the possibility of moral backsliding, understood as moving away from spirit to body, she also incorporates an account of perpetual virtue into her ethical theory: one could achieve a good nature in the sense that a substantial change in the individual, such as losing the capacity of an indifferent will, might come about. Conway is clear that the development of the creature towards perfection is an infinite process – 'a body is always able to become more and more spiritual to infinity since God, who is the first and highest spirit, is infinite and does not and cannot partake of the least corporeality' (7.1; 42) – but there still is space for what we may call a creaturely good nature or character within her ethical theory. Conway describes the state of perpetual virtue as a 'pristine state of goodness', from which a creature 'can never fall again' (7.1; 42). In a comment reminiscent of More in *Enchiridion Ethicum*, she states that a perpetually virtuous creature has used their indifferent will to '[rise] until it only wishes to be good and is incapable of wishing any evil' (7.1;42). In terms of postulating a point in the moral and spiritual development of the creature at which perpetual virtue is achieved, Conway states that they become like Christ, though 'inasmuch as we are only creatures, our relation to him is only one of adoption' (4.4; 22).

As I suggested in Chapter 5, a straightforward way of construing how creatures can become like Christ, who can only move towards perfection, would be that they join with him on the development towards divine perfection and reach such a scale on that infinite journey that they are no longer prey to the kind of moral backsliding we discussed earlier. As Conway puts it, 'Those who achieve a perfect union with Christ are raised to a region of perfect tranquillity, where nothing is seen or felt to move or be moved. For although the strongest and swiftest motions exist there, nevertheless because they move so uniformly, equally, and harmoniously, without any resistance or disturbance, they appear completely at rest' (5.7; 27). Such creatures, who have achieved this point in the development towards perfection, become at one with Christ in the sense that they join with him on the spiritual journey towards God without any moral backsliding. Given this, we could potentially construe such creatures as themselves losing indifference of the will in a manner analogous to those human beings, as postulated by More, who have achieved a good nature and are compelled to follow it. In this regard, then, we can say that there is in fact a hidden similarity between More and Conway on this point.

However, I do not believe we should read Conway in this manner, as she is clear that our power of change is what distinguishes us as the kind of being we are. As such, it would be implausible to read Conway as allowing for creatures to undergo such a substantive change that they undergo a loss of the indifference of the will. Using the language of 'adoption', regarding our possible enhanced relation to Christ, suggests a loose connection to him, insofar as we only change for the good, but does not imply anything more radical than that in terms of our freedom. Thus, even those creatures who have grown in virtue and spirituality such that they become 'adopted' by Christ still retain indifference of the will.

Christ's freedom

Whilst we have explored the freedom of God and creatures to this point, there is another important being in Conway's philosophical system whose freedom we have not yet considered, namely, Christ. With regard to specific details concerning the freedom of Christ, though, Conway leaves us in the dark, and so we have to reconstruct her view on the basis of what we have already considered. Christ is mutable which, as we have seen, would suggest that he has the kind of indifference of will that is imputed to all creatures. However, the situation is more complicated than that, insofar as it would appear that Christ only ever acts upon good reasons, such that he only progresses towards the good. Indeed, Conway argues that it is the fact that Christ can only progress towards the good that definitively distinguishes this mode of being from that of all creatures: 'The creatures could not be equal to Christ nor of the same nature because his nature could never degenerate like theirs and change from good into bad. For this reason they have a far inferior nature in comparison to the first born, so that they can never strictly speaking become him' (4.4; 22). Given that Conway imputes an entirely different power of change to Christ than that which is imputed to creatures, this raises the question about whether Christ shares their indifference of will. It could be that Christ does indeed have indifference of will and has cause to select between good and bad reasons for action, in a manner which ensures that Christ is not equated to God, or perhaps Christ does not strictly have indifference of will at all, in that he is only presented with good reasons for action: bad or confused reasons for action never occur to him, perhaps due to some aspect of his nature that distinguishes him from creatures. It could be that Christ's being is such that he can gather the kind of knowledge required to ensure that he is never led astray by bad or confused reasons for action, and so he always acts for the good, despite having indifference of the will. Conway ultimately seems to leave both interpretive options for understanding Christ's freedom open, and thus we are unable to fully reconstruct her theory of freedom here. Perhaps further work on Christ in Conway's philosophy may shed further light on this, but until then, we have to leave this point of interpretation open.

Conclusion

We have seen that Conway offers an account of freedom that marks a departure from that suggested by More in the *Enchiridion Ethicum*, but nevertheless still shows signs of the influence of her philosophical mentor. More and Conway are both concerned with rejecting what they see as unacceptable aspects of some of the most influential traditions of thought concerning freedom at the time, including materialism and Cartesianism. More attacks materialist views as undermining the reality of human freedom, whilst Conway wishes to avoid theories of divine freedom that do not do justice to the perfect goodness of God, as she sees it.

In exploring both Conway's and More's theories, I have attempted to take a balanced approach to the question of More's influence on Conway, taking into account both the importance of his mentorship and the radical nature of the philosophical system that is suggested in the *Principia*. Unlike More, Conway seeks to shape her account of freedom around the ontological framework she establishes to capture the distinction between an immutable God and a corrupted, constantly changing creation that can nevertheless begin to approach unchanging perfection. Conway and More both distinguish divine freedom from human/creaturely freedom, on the basis of the capacity of an indifferent will. The universalist scheme of salvation proposed by Conway in the *Principia*, however, marks decisive differences between them on questions concerning freedom and morality, particularly with regard to the moral development and salvation of all creatures. The question of the attainment of perpetual virtue is also an interesting point of comparison between them: Conway clearly states that we can achieve such a state, and it is likely that she thinks that this can be done whilst retaining indifference of the will, whilst More hints at such a possibility but does not expand upon this in great detail. As such, it may be that there is ultimately little difference between them on this question.

We therefore see Conway offering a distinctive account of divine and creaturely freedom that marks another aspect of her rejection of Cartesianism, as well as the influence of the Cambridge Platonist philosophy of Henry More. Though her philosophy is shaped by her Cartesian education and her interactions with More, she nevertheless constructs her own system that departs from that of her mentor and other philosophical influences, and we can particularly see that here in her extension of freedom to all creatures. As our understanding of both Conway's and More's philosophies grows, we will be able to engage in even deeper comparative research on these two figures, which will mutually shed further light on their fascinating works.

7

The constitution of creatures

We have now considered many of the aspects of Conway's philosophy in detail, but there is one topic remaining that we left earlier and need to return to, namely, her vitalism and theory concerning the constitution of creatures. I will begin by discussing the notion of life in Conway's philosophy. I will argue that, by considering Conway's tripartite metaphysical structure of God, Christ and creatures, we can approach her notion of 'life' as not tied to a kind of activity, but rather a particular ontological state, namely, a unity or system that can be either atemporal or successive.[1] I will also suggest that this interpretation can aid us in understanding how life can be a communicable divine attribute.

Following this, I will consider some of the key aspects of the vitalism propounded by Conway's physician and friend, Francis van Helmont, and his father, Jan Baptist. I will argue that the Helmontian notion of the archeus provided for Conway a model for describing the generation and structure of living beings that could also be applied to the question of divine creation, and thereby helped to shape her understanding of life as a communicable attribute.

I will also return to the current debate concerning the nature of Conway's monism, as consideration of Conway's vitalism and her account of the nature of life may help us in answering the open question whether she subscribes to an existence-monism, according to which there is only one existent creaturely substance, or a type-monism, which postulates an infinite number of creaturely substances, all of which share the same quiddity. Using the results of the discussion, I will offer some points in favour of a type-monist interpretation of Conway's philosophy.

Furthermore, I will consider the question of creaturely identity in the *Principia*, following claims regarding the constitution of creatures as systems of spirits, as well as Conway's theory of the original equality of creatures. These discussions will help illuminate Conway's unified account of nature. The points under consideration here will also be used to evaluate the extent to which Conway can be viewed as offering a process philosophy. I will argue that though there is some overlap, such that we might call Conway a 'moral process philosopher', the parallels between modern process thought and the metaphysics found in the *Principia* should not be overemphasized.

Finally, I will consider Conway's account of the role of pain and suffering in the purification of creatures. Whilst the specific details of this account are not altogether clear in the text, I argue that the revivifying effect of pain stems from the reminder it offers of the deep universal sympathy between all things. I also explore how this account is perhaps inspired by Helmontian ideas concerning the cause of disease and the use of models from alchemy in treating illness.

Defining life

Conway paints a picture of a world teeming with life. As we saw earlier, Conway argues that God creates an infinite number of living creatures for an infinite amount of time, in a never-ending process that has always taken place and will always take place. However, one question we may wish to consider is precisely what Conway might mean by 'life'. One potentially straightforward answer to that question would be to equate life with 'activity', broadly understood. Conway states that it is through divine creativity that each creature receives its 'essence and activity' (1.7; 10) and so it would be a natural reading, given that life is a communicable attribute of God, to conclude that it is the capacity for activity that suffices for life as far as she is concerned.

However, this would leave open the question as to what kind of activity Conway has in mind in respect to the life of creatures. Again, a natural answer comes to mind, namely, the activity that she points to that allows us to make a fundamental distinction between the different kinds of beings there are: the change from spirit to matter, or vice versa. As we know, Conway posits three types of quiddity, which we can label as God, Christ and Creature that are distinguishable by the kind of change they can undergo: 'The first is altogether immutable. The second can only change toward the good, so that which is good by its very nature can become better. The third kind is that which, although it was good by its very nature, is nevertheless able to change from good to good as well as from good to evil' (5.3; 24). Such change is manifested in ontological terms by movement on a spirit–matter continuum, in that a being who changes to the good becomes more spiritual and closer to God, whilst a being who moves towards evil becomes more bodily (in this manner, body or matter is construed as condensed spirit). So, is this kind of movement on the spirit–matter continuum, from good to bad or vice versa, what life consists of for Conway?

I argue that this would be a misreading for two reasons. The first is that God does not engage in this kind of activity, insofar as he sits at the top of the spirit–matter continuum as the infinite spirit. As Conway states, God 'is the first and highest spirit, is infinite and does not and cannot partake of the least corporeality' (7.1; 42), and so there is no movement on the spirit–matter continuum possible for him. However, Conway clearly sees God as having a kind of life of his own, and so life per se cannot be linked to movement towards either matter or purified spirit. One might reply to this that my interpretation only holds if Conway is committed to a strong immutability, such that God could not engage of necessity in such activity. It may be that Conway is in fact committed to a weaker form of immutability, such that God could *in principle* engage in such motion, but never in fact does so. If that is the case, then at least the possibility of such motion could be sufficient for God to be said to have life.

However, given various statements in the *Principia* concerning divine immutability, it would seem that Conway does prefer strong immutability. As we have seen, Conway states that 'there is no time in [God] nor any mutability' (1.1; 9) and that we cannot conceive of God as having the kind of indifference of will that would leave him open to change, at least in principle (see 3.1; 15). A further reason for avoiding such an interpretation of the notion of life would be that this activity is linked by Conway to the motion necessary for time, rather than being connected to the life of beings. Such a definition of time suggests a reason for holding that God is entirely outside of time, insofar as she takes motion or operation as implying a kind of imperfection that could not be imputed to the absolutely perfect divine being: 'Since in God there is no successive motion or operation toward further perfection because he is absolutely perfect, there are no times in God or his eternity' (2.6; 14).

In addition, as I argued in Chapter 3, this statement by Conway suggests that she actually means something more limited by 'time' than what her original basic definition holds. God must be outside of time, Conway argues, because he is not able to participate in movement or operation *towards perfection*, and so this suggests that her definition of time is not simply as the motion of creatures *simpliciter*; rather, her more exact definition of time would be something like, 'nothing but the successive motion or operation of creatures *towards or away from perfection*', in the sense of engaging in moral development and becoming more (or less) like God. So, given that time is to be taken as the activity of creatures insofar as they move up and down the spirit–matter continuum, this gives us another reason to not take such activity as indicative of life for Conway.

Another possibility for the kind of activity Conway might have in mind would be engaging in causal activity. Broadly construed, God, Christ and creatures all engage in such activity, though admittedly of quite different kinds. Whilst God's causal agency consists of communicating his perfect being and goodness through creative action, Christ undertakes a mediating role between God and creatures that is rather difficult to discern from the text, but seems to involve an omnipresence that allows creatures to morally develop to the point that they can achieve 'a perfect union' (7.5; 27) with him,[2] and creatures themselves stand in sympathetic relations of vital action, grounded in 'subtler mediating parts, which come between them and which are emanations from one creature to another' (3.10; 20). Given the very different types of causal activity that distinct types of substance can engage with, I argue that it would be strange for Conway to claim that it is this type of broad activity that marks all things out as having life. Such an interpretation would have the upside of explaining why it is that even inanimate objects such as rocks can be said to have a form of life (insofar as they also stand in causal relations to other things), but Conway does not mark out being in causal relations as having any special significance with regard to the attributes shared between God and creatures, and this is presumably something that would have been emphasized in the *Principia* if this was the intended reading.

There must be something else, then, that links all three types of quiddity in Conway's system and suffices for life but is not linked to spirit–matter activity. To answer that question, it might serve us to reverse our direction and focus on the kind of life that God can be said to have. The question becomes particularly potent when we recall that Conway's God is outside of time, existing in an eternal, unchanging state (and not merely enjoying a kind of everlasting existence inside of time). A particularly well-known example of a discussion of the life of an atemporal being can be found in Boethius, who is strongly influenced by both Augustine and Neoplatonism. In his *The Consolation of Philosophy*, Boethius defines eternity as the 'total and perfect possession of life without end' (2000: 110). Clearly, Boethius cannot be thinking of life along purely biological terms, nor as something that will persist over time (as God is not subject to time[3]). We are thus drawn to think about the notion of life rather differently, as a kind of ontological state that can be either successive or atemporal. Despite creatures being composite beings, and God being perfectly simple (in the sense of having no parts), their similarity lies in their status as unified beings. Of course, God and his creatures form very different kinds of unities, but nevertheless it is their being as a unified system that allows us to identify them as the thing they are: God is the perfect unity that has all of the mutually entailing divine perfections, whilst creatures, for Conway, are a unified system of spirits[4] (a claim that I will consider in more detail in the next section).

The importance of systematic unity for ongoing life, as far as Conway is concerned, can be seen in an argument she offers regarding the possibility of the division of matter to its smallest part: though maintaining an agnosticism regarding the question of whether or not God could do this, she argues that he would not do so even if he could. Conway writes,

> [God] never reduces creatures into their smallest parts because all motion and operation would then cease in those creatures... To do this would be contrary to the wisdom and goodness of God. For if every motion or operation would cease in some creature, that creature would be entirely useless in creation and would be no better than if it were pure nothingness and utter non-being.
>
> (3.9; 20)

Conway's argument is not entirely clear, but at the very least, it seems that she believes that if a particular spirit were entirely isolated from others, which would be the case if God were to reduce something to its smallest part, that spirit would functionally cease to be (if not actually go out of existence) because it would not be able to play a part in any kind of activity. Thus, a spirit cannot be entirely isolated from others if it is to enjoy anything that is recognizably life. In this way, Conway shows the importance of systematic unity of spirits as a prerequisite for creaturely life.

The significance of this understanding of life for our interpretation of Conway is multi-faceted. For one thing, I will argue later that it can help decide the question of the precise nature of Conway's monism. Another advantage is that it makes clearer how life can be a communicable divine attribute. God, as a timeless, transcendent being, clearly cannot have life in any kind of natural sense, biological or otherwise. So, there must be some feature of divine existence that we can identify as God's 'life' and can be replicated at the level of creatures. It also must not be strictly identical to anything else that features on Conway's list of divine attributes that begins the *Principia* (otherwise, why mention it?): 'God is spirit, light, and life, infinitely wise, good, just, strong, all-knowing, all-present, all-powerful, the creator and maker of all things visible and invisible' (1.1; 9). One aspect of the being of God that meets these criteria is precisely his unified nature. God has created beings who form a unity, albeit a more limited unity in comparison with that which he possesses, that can persist over time.

This interpretation can also help us understand Conway's claim that all created beings are fundamentally alive (she states that all body 'not only has quantity and shape but also life' (9.9; 70)), including such things that certainly do not have 'life' in the usual, biological sense of the word, such as rocks. As Conway explains, such parts of inorganic nature are themselves alive insofar as they are systems of spirits, and reflective of a hierarchy that has fallen into a coarse state that is further from humans and other animals on the moral/ontological scale of the spirit–matter continuum. So, again, it is the status of all beings as unities that draws them together as all having a kind of 'life', even if they exist in a timeless state like God, or the gross state of a rock. I argue that, interpreted in this way, it is easier to see how Conway can argue that life is communicated from God to his creation, and is then shared out across both organic and inorganic nature. The kind of unity that creatures possess, and thus what constitutes their 'life' for Conway, will be the subject of the next section.

Life and the van Helmonts

Conway's understanding of life as the atemporal or successive existence of a unified system can be fruitfully examined in relation to the vitalism espoused by her friend, Francis van Helmont, and his father, Jan Baptist. The elder van Helmont had proposed a form of monism that moved away from Aristotelian presuppositions, partly by undermining an ontological distinction between matter and form (a principle that unifies and shapes matter so that it is a particular kind of thing). He achieved this by postulating semina transmitted in the form of gas, which are able to form a unified, living being. Given the transmutability of all things, van Helmont argues that we should not understand such semina as bringing life to matter; rather, matter and semina are intertwined in such a manner that a unified organic being is brought about, with the material aspect being a reflection of the spiritual (we can perhaps think of them as 'two sides of the same coin'). The key role in this process is played by the archeus, whose will and imagination operate together to generate the living being (see Pagel 1982: 96–102). The archeus has a seminal idea that offers a schema for the living being to be generated and then continues to act as a vital principle for that creature as it goes through its life. As Pagel (1982: 97f.) notes, the role of the archeus is often couched in political terms, with the internal structure of a living being described as a 'monarchy' under the control of a 'master' or 'internal president' that controls and orders all aspects of a living being, both material and spiritual.

Moving back to Conway, as already mentioned, she proposes a rather complex view of the nature of living beings and one that reveals the potential influence of the van Helmonts. As Hutton (2004: 144) states, it is difficult to state when Conway may have first been introduced to Helmontian ideas, though it may have been in the early 1650s. Regardless of when it first happened, the vitalist and monistic ideas of Jan Baptist van Helmont would almost certainly have been a major topic of conversation at Ragley Hall upon the arrival of his son, Francis (who had largely adopted the theories of his father, though with some additions, most notably a commitment to the possible transmutation of species – see Hutton 2004: 150f.). As noted previously, Conway argues that, given God's omnipotence, he is able to create an infinite number of creatures, and given his overwhelming goodness, he would create as many creatures as he can. Therefore, simply by considering the divine attributes, we can conclude that '[God's] creatures are infinite and created in an infinity of ways, so that they cannot be bounded or limited by number or measure' (3.4; 16).

Such reasoning also applies, Conway argues, to the structure of creatures themselves. There is no obvious contradiction in the idea of God being able to create smaller and smaller creatures inside each other, and so it must be the case that this has happened, whether the beings in question are material or more spirit-like:

> An infinite number of creatures can be contained and exist inside the smallest creatures and that all these could be bodies and in their own way mutually impenetrable. As for those creatures which are spirits and which can penetrate each other, there can be an infinite number of spirits in any created spirit, all of which spirits are as equal in extension to the aforementioned spirit as they are to each other... [So] in every creature, whether spirit or body, there is an infinity of creatures, each of which contains an infinity in itself, and so on to infinity.
> (3.5; 17)

It is possible, then, that God has created an infinite number of creatures, including creatures being contained within each other, and so it is the case that, given that he would create as much as possible, the structure of living beings is such that they contain an infinite number of spirits that are at some point on the spirit–matter continuum.

Seemingly at least partly inspired by the ideas of the van Helmonts, Conway expands upon this account of the nature of living beings by drawing upon the notion of each composite creature being composed of a hierarchy of spirits. She introduces this notion in the *Principia* within her account of the transmutation of individuals across species, arguing that a human individual who lives a 'brutish or animal life' (6.7; 36) may indeed find themselves, in a future life, returning as one of the lower animals. The process in which this takes place is framed as a contest between rival spirits within the unified system of spirits that make up the composite individual. If the individual acts in a brutish, animalistic manner, this is reflective of a brutish spirit having dominion over 'his more excellent part', such that 'the brute spirit is now superior and predominant and holds the other captive' (6.7; 36). Given the new dominance of the brute spirit, it has the primary power to form the creature as it enters a new life, and such a form will be that of a lower animal to reflect its own image: 'This body, which the vital spirit forms, will be that of a brute and not a human, for the brute spirit cannot produce or form any other shape because its formative power is governed by its imagination, which imagines and conceives as strongly as possible its own image, according to which the external body must take shape' (6.7; 36). So, the constitution of a living created being is that of a hierarchy of spirits, and the form of its appearance is set by the nature of the spirit that is currently the most powerful within that system:

> Just as a body, whether of a man or brute, is nothing but a countless multitude of bodies collected into one and arranged in a certain order, so the spirit of man or brute is also a countless multitude of spirits united in this body, and they have their order and government, such that one is the principal ruler, another has second place, and a third commands others below itself, and so on for the whole.
> (6.11; 39)

Conway certainly seems to envision this ruling spirit as the kind of archeus postulated by van Helmont.

In terms of the scheme of divine justice, it is these systems of spirits that are the primary objects of divine approbation and punishment, rather than individual spirits themselves. In Section 8 of Chapter VI of the *Principia*, Conway argues that God's punishment extends to the scheme of transmigration and is not limited to being condemned to suffering in hell. It conforms to divine justice, Conway states, that a human individual who has lived like a brute has to take on that form in a future life:

> When a human being has so greatly degraded himself by his own wilful wrongdoing and has brought his nature, which had been so noble, to a lower

state, and when that nature has demeaned itself in spirit to the level of a most foul brute or animal so that it is wholly ruled by lust and earthly desires and becomes like any beast... what injustice is this if God compels him to bear the same image in his body as in that spirit into which he has internally transformed himself?

(6.8; 36)

The moral destinies of those spirits who make up a single living being are very much tied together: the influence of the overwhelming primary spirit will determine the state of the living being as a whole, and thereby its moral and ontological progress on the spirit–matter continuum. In this manner, all these spirits, in a unified system, are drawn together in one life, extending over many lifetimes and tracking progress either towards God (and greater spirituality) or away from God (and towards greater corporeality).

Finally, we can return to the question of the sort of life enjoyed by God in Conway's system. In the first chapter of the *Principia*, Conway suggests a parallel between divine and creaturely life that reflects the Helmontian view concerning the generation of beings, despite the commitment to divine simplicity. In an analogous manner to the way in which the archeus forms a living being in its imagination through a seminal idea, with regard to divine creation, 'there is an idea which is his image or the word existing within himself, which in substance or essence is one and the same with him, through which he knows himself as well as all other things and, indeed, all creatures were made or created according to this very idea or word' (1.6; 10). As such, it is possible to see how Helmontian ideas regarding the generation of living beings by the archeus could have suggested an account of divine creation to Conway that, amongst other things, allowed her to attribute a univocal sense of 'life' to both God and his creatures, based around the idea of systematic unity and focused on a creative force that generates according to a guiding idea or blueprint, thus expanding even further upon the idea of 'life' as a communicable divine attribute.

What kind of monism?

One of the benefits of investigating Conway's vitalism and her notion of 'life' may be that helps to resolve a longstanding debate about the nature of the monism with regard to creation[5] proposed in the *Principia*. According to the existence–monism interpretation of Conway, there are three existent substances, namely,

God, Christ and Creature. All creatures are modes of the one creaturely substance and do not have their own independent existence as a distinct substance by themselves. In contrast to this is the type-monism interpretation, according to which there are three types of quiddity postulated by Conway, God, Christ and Creature, and that whilst there is only one substance that falls under the kind 'God', and one substance that falls under the kind 'Christ', there are an infinite number of substances that are of the kind 'Creature'. The debate concerning Conway's monism[6] is certainly sparked by the fact that there is a certain amount of ambiguity in the text, compounded by it being the case that we are confined to working with translations of the *Principia* (where errors might have crept in), rather than with the original notes that may have been a little more unambiguous. As an example, Conway states that 'all creatures, or the whole of creation, are also a single species in substance or essence, although it includes many individuals gathered into subordinate species and distinguished from each other modally but not substantially or essentially' (6.4; 31): such a statement, I argue, certainly reveals Conway's monism, but is ultimately ambiguous between existence and type-monism.[7] On the other side, in defence of a type-monist interpretation, we have Conway referring to *a particular creature* remaining 'the same substance' across its different forms (7.1; 43), as well as speaking of 'created substances' (9.9; 69) in the plural.

However, there may be good reasons to prefer one interpretation over the other and thus resolve the textual ambiguity, considering other philosophical commitments that Conway certainly has, and I would argue that her vitalism is one such component of her system that could help settle the matter. Let us reconsider Conway's notion of 'life'. As I argued earlier, the life of a creature, for Conway, consists in its being created as a unified system of spirits that can persist over time. Given the status of 'life' as a communicable attribute, we can draw an analogy between the life of God and the life of a created being. As God exists as a wholly independent unity, each created being is also its own separate system of spirits, though with some caveats given their limited nature, such as the fact that they are wholly dependent on God for their being and that they can causally interact with other created beings. Given the analogy that Conway seems to draw between God and his creatures, with the claim that both enjoy 'life' in a univocal sense, we would do best in our interpretation, I argue, to preserve the independence of each creature in her metaphysics as much as we can. Such independence is more clearly safeguarded on the type-monist interpretation, insofar as all creatures are the same kind of substance but have their own independent being, as they are not mere modes of one creaturely substance. If

Conway were an existence-monist with regard to creatures, then it would not be as clear how life could be equally attributed to both God and his creatures within her metaphysics.

A final, and related, point we can put in favour of type-monism begins with a consideration of Conway's claim, which we considered earlier, that God would seek to create as much life as possible. Given this claim about God's creative nature, we can consider the question of whether type or existence-monism is more likely. It certainly seems that Conway's God would create as much as he is able to create, which would include seeking to create as many creaturely substances as possible. There seems no obvious reason, at least not within the confines of Conway's system, why God could not create more than one creaturely substance, and so the claim that God would create as much life as possible seems to point reasonably decisively towards type-monism, which posits an infinite number of creaturely substances.

In response to this point, Gordon-Roth has suggested (in correspondence) that my argument faces difficulties in explaining why God has confined himself to only creating two kinds of things, namely, Christ and creatures. Surely, God could have created an infinite number of types of things, but did not do so, and the fact that he has not does not seem to count as a limitation on God as far as Conway is concerned. However, I argue in response that we do in fact have good reason for understanding why Conway's God is ultimately confined to creating only beings who have two types of quiddity. Whilst it is conceivable in my view that God could create an infinite number of substances, that does not carry over to the number of species. Recall that what marks out a particular kind of thing is the kind of change it can go through: God cannot change, Christ can only change for the better and creatures can change for better or worse. Given that the capacity for change is what suffices to distinguish a kind of being, what other possible species could there be? There could not be a species that could only change for the worse, as Conway would not allow that God could create such beings (insofar as they would be absolutely antithetical in nature to their source of being – God). So, we have good reason to think that, within the confines of Conway's system, you can at most have three kinds of quiddity, and an infinite number of individual substances – hence, type-monism.

To sum up, I agree with Gordon-Roth (see 2018: 284–8) that much of the textual evidence is at the very least exceedingly ambiguous with regard to the type/existence-monism debate. However, given other claims that Conway makes with regard to God's creative activity and the nature of life, I believe we have good reason to prefer a type-monism interpretation of Conway's system. Gordon-Roth, on the other hand, has recently used the ambiguity of the text to argue for an oscillating interpretation of Conway's monism: there are indeed contradictory claims in the *Principia* regarding monism, but this is a conscious decision given that she wishes to oscillate 'between a view in which there is a proliferation of spiritual substances and just one existing substance in the realm of creation' (2018: 292). Both type-monism and existence-monism are true for Conway, but which is true for you depends upon the perspective you take. When we ask the question of how many spiritual substances there are in creation, we can do so from the imagined perspective of God and the perspective of creation. From God's timeless perspective, all things will appear as one, such that it is right to say that from the divine standpoint, all of creation is one substance, whilst from our perspective, as created beings, there are multiple created substances. Such an interpretation, Gordon-Roth writes, is intended 'not as a knockdown defeat of either the type or existence-monist readings of Conway on creation, but as an alternative to the two interpretations currently on the table' (2018: 294).

For reasons I have already suggested, I believe that a type-monist reading of Conway is to be preferred. In addition, I argue that Gordon-Roth's oscillation interpretation is not, in fact, a new third interpretive option that can be taken as it ultimately collapses into an existence-monist position. If we are considering both the divine perspective upon a particular metaphysical issue and how things appear from our limited standpoint, surely it is how things appear to God (the perfect omnipotent being) that is going to be the correct view. Conway would hold that God, as an omniscient being, cannot be mistaken about the nature of creation. Either existence-monism is true or not, and if it seems to God that it is indeed true, then surely it is. So, I argue that the oscillating position has to collapse into existence-monism, with any passages that point towards type-monism being interpreted as only how it erroneously seems from our limited perspective.

It may be that those who follow this line of interpretation are quite happy with this and so are satisfied with ultimately being left with an existence-monist position. However, this then begs the question as to why Conway makes such misleading statements: in other words, why does Conway assert how things appear from our perspective without more clearly signalling that she thinks how things appear to us is fundamentally wrong? There is a further methodological difficulty for this interpretation, insofar as Conway uses aspects of her experience of the world to argue for her monistic position, which is an approach that would be immediately undercut if she believes that our viewpoint concerning the question of the number of created substances is fundamentally flawed. For these reasons, I think that the oscillation interpretation causes more problems than it solves.

A further suggestion regarding the nature of Conway's monism is offered by Emily Thomas (2020: *passim*), who has suggested a 'priority monist' reading. According to this view, the whole cosmos is taken as ontologically fundamental, with the parts of creation viewed as ontologically secondary to the whole. As Thomas explains, this interpretation neatly incorporates aspects of both type-monism (or 'existence pluralism', as she calls it here) and existence-monism: 'Priority monism agrees with existence pluralism that many things exist. However, priority monism agrees with existence monism that the universe is, in an important sense, one' (2020: 7). The first passage that Thomas points to in defence of her interpretation is as follows:

> God has implanted a certain universal sympathy and mutual love into his creatures so that they are all members of one body and all, so to speak, brothers, for whom there is one common Father… There is also one mother, *that unique substance or unity from which all things have come forth, and of which they are the real parts and members*.
>
> (6.4; 31 – my emphasis)

If we only focus on the latter part of this passage, it certainly appears that Conway is referring to precisely what is claimed by a priority monist, namely, one single substance, encompassing all of creation, that is ontologically prior to the parts that make it up.

However, the way to read this passage is not so clear once we take it in context. Conway is here talking about the sympathetic relations between all creatures, so that we are figuratively brought together into a single unity (signalled by her use of the phrase *ut ita dicam*, 'so to speak'). In the same way that God is our symbolic 'father', the sympathy between all things acts as a symbolic 'mother', bringing all creation together in a harmonious unity. Conway is using metaphorical familial language here to emphasize the unity and similarity of things due to our shared ground in God and our sympathetic relations with each other (we will consider these relations between creatures in more detail in the next section). Thus, we should not use this passage as textual evidence for the metaphysical claim that all creaturely things are composed of one single substance. Furthermore, it is indeed the case that Conway refers here to all things being 'real parts' of 'that unique substance or unity'. However, the point Conyway is making is simply that all things are really contained within the figurative idea we are considering.[8] It is true that, later on, Conway refers to 'reptiles and beasts' being 'real parts of earth and water' (6.6; 34), but here the context has changed, insofar as she has moved from the consideration of the unity of all things to the empirical matter of the spontaneous generation of creatures: as such, it is not too much of a stretch to read Conway as having transferred to a more ontologically heavy reading of the phrase 'real parts'.

Of course, the readings I am proposing of these passages are not conclusive, but the more literal reading proposed by Thomas of the key passage from 6.4 is not necessarily the obvious one.[9] The debate concerning the precise nature of Conway's monism will undoubtedly continue in the literature, and hopefully the points I have raised here will stimulate further scholarly reflection on these aspects of the philosophy presented in the *Principia*. My overall claim is that the textual evidence is ambiguous unless we focus on the wider systematic context of Conway's philosophy, which, as I have argued above, gives good reason to follow a type-monist interpretation of her metaphysics. We must also take great care with regard to the context of particular passages and phrases as we consider the textual evidence available to us.

The sympathy and harmony of all things

On the basis of her views concerning the constitution of creatures, Conway claims that creatures stand in sympathetic, harmonious relations to each other. Her understanding of the unity of creatures is encapsulated in her account of causation, which is introduced very briefly in Chapter III of the *Principia*. There, Conway argues that her claims concerning the infinite divisibility of things, which involves the existence of infinitesimally small spirits, and the structure of creatures are strengthened by also offering us an explanation of possible action at a distance. Given that creatures are constituted by a dynamic system of bundled spirits, it is possible that they can lose and gain spirits without losing their identity. As such, if we were to allow the possibility of action at a distance, we could understand it through the model of one creature emanating a particular spirit (or spirits) and another incorporating it into itself. Conway argues that we can understand 'the causes and reasons of things', as well as 'how all creatures from the highest to the lowest are inseparably united', through the transit of 'subtler mediating parts, which come between them and which are emanations from one creature to another' (3.10; 20). Though this is not to be taken as a general account of causation, it is nevertheless a way of incorporating 'the most secret and hidden causes … which ignorant men call occult qualities' (3.10; 20) into her metaphysics.

This model of sympathetic relations can explain not only the unity between creatures, but also the unity within creatures. Conway holds that individual creatures are composed of bundles of spirits, and what binds these together is what holds all things in nature in sympathetic harmony, namely, mediating spirits. The archeus, as the principal spirit in a given creature, shapes the rest of the bundle of spirits through its emanative activities. Presumably what makes one spirit the archeus rather than another is the dominance it has through its emanations, captured in the extent to which other spirits in that creature are directed by incorporating its mediating spirits. In this regard, we can see that the Neoplatonic reflection of the divine in nature appears again, insofar as the creature forms a mirrored microcosm of the universe as a whole, with a ruling spirit shaping all other things through its emanative activity (though, of course, divine emanation is unique in its creative activity).

However, such a theory of the unity of creatures may seem to pose a problem of individuation for Conway: namely, given that all creatures are connected by the emanation of mediating spirits, how are we to distinguish one creature from another? If such mediating spirits are what ultimately binds individual creatures together, then there is seemingly no easy way of distinguishing between the system of spirits linked within an individual creature and the system of spirits linked together in nature as a whole. At the very least, if we are to ontologically distinguish individual creatures, it can only be in uncertain terms, based on the relatively close relationship between a group of spirits that form a close system, under the control of a single ruling spirit, the archeus.

It is worth noting that the problem of individuating organisms is by no means limited to Conway: indeed, it can sometimes be difficult to exactly demarcate the point where an individual ends and the rest of the world begins. Take the example of digestion: when you eat something, we do not think that the food in question immediately becomes part of you; rather, you are digesting it. However, at some point in the digestion process, at least some of that food is incorporated into your body, at which point you would say that it had become part of you. At which point in the process, though, does this occur? It would seem impossible to pin down a specific moment where the food becomes a part of you, which suggests that in fact your individuation as a being has fuzzy, rather than definite, edges. When viewed from this perspective, Conway's theory of the individuation of creatures, which also seems to allow for fuzzy edges, seems less problematic.

As Thomas has noted (2018: *passim*), the question of identity in Conway's philosophy is a difficult and multi-faceted one: not only do we need to consider the problem of individuation, but also that of the identity of creatures over time. Given Conway's commitment to the possibility of transmutation, the issue of tracking a certain creature over time (particularly from one form of bodily existence to another) becomes rather difficult. Conway allows that the spirit of a particular horse may go on to become another horse after bodily death (see 6.6; 32f.), so we cannot use any bodily criterion for identity over time, but then we are left with the question of how we are supposed to identify this new horse as the same being that existed before.[10] We cannot appeal to any kind of psychological continuity either, as we do not have memories of past lives: Conway stipulates that 'memory requires a body' (6.2; 39) and so memories cannot be retained from one form of bodily existence to the next.

One option is to follow Peter Loptson (see 1982: 41) in interpreting Conway as committed to distinct individual essences, or 'haecceities', which a particular creature has over all of its lifetimes and also serves to individuate it from all other things. On this view, all creatures have an essential, haecceitous property that makes them the unique individual they are: so, I have the essential property of 'Being Jonathan', and that is a property that I will retain across different bodily existences and acts as a marker to track my development on the spirit–matter continuum and ensure that I have an ontologically distinct existence, apart from all other things. An individual being holds this haecceitous property regardless of the kind of thing it is, or what it is composed of: so, two entirely different types of being, composed of entirely different stuff, could be the same creature, as long as one creature has inherited this haecceitous property from the other.

Loptson's haecceity interpretation is challenged by Thomas, who argues that for Conway, creaturely identity over time is secured by there being an individual 'soul substance' that subsists across different lives (see 2018: 140f.). Thomas criticizes the haecceity interpretation on the basis that Conway equates an individual having a particular essence with its substance, rather than with an essential property that is retained across lifetimes. A couple of passages from the *Principia* are used in support of this interpretation. First, in Chapter I, Conway speaks of each creature being created by God as 'a distinct and essential substance' (1.7; 10), which certainly seems to strongly imply that what makes a particular creature the being that it is, and individuates it from all other things, is that it is a particular substance. Second, in Chapter VII, Conway writes of 'the soul of every human being [remaining] a whole soul for eternity and [enduring] without end' (7.4; 55). This seems a very straightforward assertion concerning creaturely identity over time, insofar as we find Conway claiming that it is the 'whole soul', or the 'soul substance', which endures for eternity across lifetimes. So, we can reject Loptson's haecceity interpretation on the basis of the textual evidence, which strongly implies that it is some feature of the material or substance of a creature that makes it the creature it is and distinguishes it from all other things, not just an inherited haecceitous property.

If Thomas's 'soul substance' interpretation is correct, then we have another point in favour of type-monism with regard to creation, rather than existence-monism. What individuates creatures, and secures their identity over time, is that they are their own distinct substance. So, it cannot be the case that creatures, in Conway's philosophy, are only modes of one substance; otherwise, there would be no way to distinguish between them or track their identity over time, according to her own theory of identity. We could perhaps attempt to sustain a sense of identity based on distinct modes of a single substance, but this is not how Conway presents her theory, and so it would require a substantial amount of textual evidence on the side of existence-monism to overturn this (and I have argued that the evidence is simply not there).

Having defended the 'soul substance' interpretation, though, I would not claim that is entirely without its own problems. Thomas builds upon her interpretation by identifying the archeus, or principal spirit, as the soul substance in question, rather than the system of spirits that makes up the creature as a whole. Lascano follows a similar line, stating that 'the principal spirit of an individual … constitutes the personal identity of a creature' (2013: 330). Again, there is certainly textual evidence in favour of Thomas's and Lascano's interpretation, but there is perhaps a tension revealed here with Conway's theory of transmutation. As we saw earlier, a human being can be transmuted into a lower form of existence after bodily death by becoming 'a brute in spirit …, [allowing] his brutal part and spirit to have dominion over his more excellent part' (6.7; 36). Conway seems to be suggesting that, within an individual, which spirit is the ruling one *can change*, with the effect that the individual can become more brutish in the next life. On this reading, it would not seem natural to identify the individual with the ruling spirit, as each creature could conceivably see a change in ruling spirit and yet remain the same individual as part of the overall scheme of divine justice on the spirit–matter continuum.

One way to potentially evade this problem, and this is the route that Thomas takes (see 2018: 143), is to deny that the ruling spirit can change within a creature; rather, when Conway is talking about the brutish and more intellectual parts of the creature gaining ascendance, she is referring to power plays *within* the ruling spirit. The ruling spirit is not a simple being (it has parts, albeit strongly unified ones – see 7.4; 54f.), and thus there can be a shift of power within it, without the unity of that spirit being dissolved. It is through this shifting landscape of dominant inclinations that a ruling spirit can be 'further advanced or diminished', according to 'its current worthiness or unworthiness, capacity or incapacity' (7.4; 55). So, the identity of an individual creature is bound up with a spirit that has parts of various inclinations and can employ other spirits in order to achieve its goals. Thomas summarizes her interpretation of Conway's view of identity and the constitution of creatures in this way:

> I suggest that Conway's creature can be pictured as wheels. The 'principal' or 'ruling' spirit sits at the central hub of the wheel, surrounded by 'ministering' spirits. The outer rim of the wheel is comprised of bodies, and the hub and rim are connected via 'subtle and tenuous' bodies which act as spokes. As it is only the principal spirit or central hub that moves from one body to the next, it is this in which identity consists.
>
> (2018: 143)

With all this mind, Conway's account of the divine scheme of justice looks ever more complicated. We must remember that all things, not just principal spirits, will ultimately be saved and that spirits earn an improved position on the spirit–matter continuum through the way in which they comport themselves as principal spirits. It follows, then, that all those spirits who are not currently principal spirits will presumably achieve that status at some point, so they are able to engage in moral development. Whilst the corporealized spirits that make up your body are currently under the controlling influence of the spirit substance that is 'really you', they eventually will be able to undertake their own journey towards perfection, perhaps bringing other spirits under their own influence on the way. However, we are left in a rather counterintuitive situation, insofar as there are parts of you (as common sense would have it), such as your body, that is not part of what is 'really you', and in fact has its own moral destiny apart from you. Conway also seems to rule out any moral destiny for non-principal spirits, as their unity 'may be dissolved' (7.4; 55), and so there could not be an ongoing identity for them across lifetimes, but this seems to be in conflict with the claim that all things will ultimately be saved.

One potential way of solving this confusion is to delineate different kinds of moral destinies for different things. All creatures in Conway's universe have a moral journey to undertake, but the nature of that journey will be different depending on the kind of being involved. Conway potentially hints at this when discussing the distinction between human and terrestrial spirits in relation to the generation of human beings as a whole:

> Since the human body was made from earth, which, as has been proved, contained various spirits and gave those spirits to all the animals, without doubt the earth gave human beings the best and most excellent spirits which it contained. But all these spirits were far inferior to the spirit of human beings, which they received from above and not from the earth.
>
> (6.6; 34)

Here, Conway clearly distinguishes between two types of spirit, terrestrial and human, that come together to compose a human individual: you have the principal human spirit coming 'from above', using or being provided with the finest of the terrestrial spirits to generate its body. Despite such a distinction, Conway states that, in interaction with human spirits, terrestrial spirits can be aided in their moral development: 'The human spirit ought to have dominion over these spirits, which are only terrestrial, so that that it might rule over them and *raise them to a higher level*' (6.6.; 34 – my emphasis). Such aid can be continued across an infinite number of lifetimes, if, as emphasized by Lascano (2013: 330–3), Conway claims that a ruling spirit will always require some form of body in order to have a rich psychological life (e.g. a body is required in order to retain memories – 6.11; 39) and interact with the rest of creation (a body is required to emanate the subtle spirits used to establish sympathetic relations with other things – 8.5; 61). In order to secure a kind of moral destiny for terrestrial spirits, even if they are ultimately left behind by developing human spirits (as they move on from terrestrial bodies to 'aerial' or 'etherial' ones), Conway speculates that 'this visible earth will not always remain in its present state' (6.6; 33), and so a new state for the earth could provide an environment for developed terrestrial spirits where they can reside and continue developing, in principle apart from human spirits.

The main difficulty I see for Conway here surrounds the question of what grounds this distinction between human and terrestrial spirits.[11] Given her commitment to type-monism, she cannot claim that there is a strict ontological distinction between them, as they are all made out of the same kind of substance. As we saw, Conway claims that human spirits have a kind of unity within them not enjoyed by other spirits, but there is no obvious explanation available as to why we have one kind of spirit that has this unity and another kind of spirit does not. Also, we can ask if terrestrial spirits can gain the kind of unity that human spirits enjoy, such that they can engage in the kind of moral journey available to humans, or whether that path is forever blocked to them, and if so, why. Furthermore, we have a puzzle concerning the transmutation of humans into other species. As discussed earlier, Conway seems to allow that if humans act in a beastly manner, they will take on a beastly form in another life, but would that then mean that we have two classes of animals (one class of fallen humans, and another of those formed by terrestrial spirits)?

The way out of this confusion is to interpret Conway as claiming that by taking on and ruling over lower spirits in the form of a corporeal body, the human spirit is able to facilitate spirits through a development back towards its own level. Thus, these non-human terrestrial spirits are not confined to their lower status; rather, the possibility of their ascent through increasingly higher forms of life is affirmed. After the death of the human being, Conway states that such terrestrial spirits will 'return to earth', but such spirits will not necessarily be trapped in an endless cycle of returning to the earth after forming part of a higher creature, as they will eventually be given the opportunity to be the archeus of a non-human animal. Conway argues that all non-human animals receive both their body and their principal spirit from the earth, so it is not too much of a stretch to assume that a particular spirit would, having perhaps been prepared for this opportunity for development by multiple lifetimes as part of the body of other creatures, be able to take charge of their own moral destiny finally as the principal spirit of their own animal. In this new form, such a spirit is able to act in a manner in accordance with the divine will and thus be viable for further movement up the ontological-moral scale. So, there is no strict ontological divide between human and non-human spirits; rather, they simply lie at different points on the ontological-moral continuum and could in principle exchange places on it. In thus answering the open questions concerning Conway's scheme of divine justice, we can claim that all spirits have their own distinct moral destinies, though this does leave us with the unusual claim that there are parts of us, as individuals, who are not part of what is *really* us, and in fact will go on to have their own independent everlasting existence as a being who is on a different journey back towards the perfect spirit, God.

The original equality of creatures

This interpretation also allows us to preserve Conway's commitment to the finite distance between species and the original equality of all creatures. For Conway, there must be a finite distance between species as there cannot be an upper limit on the perfectibility of a creature. It could be, for example, that a horse that increasingly aligns to the divine will would be continually reborn as a horse and would never have an opportunity to be reborn into another kind of existence. Conway considers and ultimately rejects this possibility, on the basis that there is a limit to the moral progress that can be made as a horse (and presumably the same would apply to any non-human animal): she asks, 'To what further perfection or degree of goodness of being or essence does or can a horse attain after he has performed good services for his master and has done what was and is appropriate for such a creature?' (6.6; 33) Though a horse can do what a horse should do very well (such as being unstintingly obedient to their master), such perfection that can be achieved has a definite upper limit as far as Conway is concerned. Engaging in moral development involves approaching, in one's character and conduct, the perfect moral goodness of God, and it is not too much of a stretch to see that there are forms of life in which this will be achievable to a greater extent that in others: for example, as human beings with rational capacities, we are able to use those for good (in a manner analogous to God) in a way that a creature without those capacities cannot. Conway argues that 'if a creature were entirely limited by its own individuality and totally constrained and confined within the very narrow boundaries of its own species ... then no creature could attain further perfection and greater participation in divine goodness, nor could creatures act and react upon each other in different ways' (6.5; 32). Due to the possibility of transmutation across species, creatures have the capacity to use different forms of life as a means of developing towards the perfection of God and, as we have seen, to aid other created spirits in their moral endeavours by incorporating them as part of the overall structure of an individual creature.

Conway's account also has the implication that no creature is entirely lost to God and to goodness (and thus there is no sense of eternal damnation in her philosophy). No matter how far an individual creature falls down the ontological continuum between pure spirit and gross matter, they will always be able (and in fact positively facilitated) to ascend back up the hierarchy of different forms of life and become closer to the infinite, perfectly good spirit of God. Conway argues that it would not accord with the justice of God to allow for any individual creature to be eternally lost and condemned to estrangement from the divine. In defence of this view, she offers an account of the function of divine punishment. First, a just God, who ultimately wills the best for his creation, will always use punishment in a manner 'appropriate to the deed itself' (7.1; 42). There is no transgression of the divine will by the free will of a creature so great that it would justify eternal damnation; in other words, justice dictates that a temporary, limited sin should be dealt with by a temporary, limited punishment.

In addition, Conway argues that the use of divine punishment will necessarily have a just purpose of redirecting the morally transgressing creature away from their sinful state, and thus it becomes the 'means of which evil turns back again to good' (7.1; 42). On this view, punishment takes on a restorative function in facilitating corrective development of our moral character: 'At this time [of divine punishment] every sin will have its own punishment and every creature will feel pain and chastisement, which will return that creature to the pristine state of goodness in which it was created and from which it can never fall again because, through its great punishment, it has acquired a greater perfection and strength' (7.1; 42). Thus, the nature and function of divine punishment, with the implication that eternal damnation would not be allowed by God, implies the finite distance between species for Conway.

Furthermore, Conway does not wish to allow for there to be a limit to the moral perfectibility of creatures, in that infinite moral progression (understood as approaching the perfect goodness of God) is open to all. It would not only be a lack in divine justice to allow otherwise, but it is also an implication of Conway's account of creation that all creatures have the possibility of transcending their current forms and approach both the moral and the ontological status of the divine. As part of this account, she argues for the original equal ontological status of all non-divine beings. As Conway states, all creatures were made by God 'from one blood', such that 'in their primitive and original state [they] were a certain species of human being designated according to their virtues' (6.4; 31). All creatures, when first created, share the same starting point as a kind of human being, presumably meaning that they have all the capacities available to a human being, including rational and affective faculties. The phrase 'designated according to their virtues' also suggests that all creatures are created at an equal state in terms of moral purity, which is of course to be expected given Conway's fundamental assumption that ontological and moral status are correlated (an equal ontological status will more or less imply an equal moral status). If true, the original ontological and moral equality (in the form of a kind of human being) of all creatures certainly gives a strong reason to believe that individually created beings could move from one species to another across lifetimes. Clearly, many creatures have not remained in their original state and have taken on another form of life as a different species, and so transmutation across lifetimes must be possible. Furthermore, in principle, all these creatures could return to their original status as human beings.

We are then led to the question, though, of why we should believe that all creatures were created equally in the sense proclaimed by Conway – namely, as having an equal moral and ontological status as a kind of human being. Such a view was certainly antithetical to that of the established Church in England at the time, which allowed for the divine creative plan to involve creatures who are not equal to human beings and are therefore not able to enjoy the potential benefits of salvation and becoming close to God. Conway, though, believes that all the communicable attributes must be found to some extent in all creatures and so from that perspective are created equally.

Conway goes even further, though, than the claim that all creatures are created with the same capacities for exemplifying the divine attributes. As we have seen already, Conway claims that all creatures originally have the same moral and ontological status as 'a certain kind of human being'. An implication of this view would be that many creatures have since fallen from such an original status to become lower animals. I argue that Conway's claims in this regard are shaped by her view of the divine creative act as a simple act that is reflective of a fundamentally egalitarian scheme of divine justice. As God desires to communicate his goodness as maximally as possible, it would be contrary to his nature to bring about creatures who are not able to fully share in his goodness and love, to the extent that is possible for an imperfect non-divine being. It stands to reason, then, that each creature would begin their existence at the same starting point, before their exercise of free will takes them either up or down the ontological-moral scale and thereby through transmutations across species.

Such an account of the fall of creatures from an equal status as a 'kind of human being' bears some similarities to the account proposed by Henry More of the creation and fall of souls.[12] More argues that all souls were created as aethereal beings prior to the creation of the physical world: 'The souls of men, and other animals ... as many as ever there were to be of them, did really and actually exist without any dependency on corporeal matter' (1662: *Conjectura Cabbalistica*, 17). It was only until some individual souls began misusing their capacities that they made their descent into physical bodies. More uses the narrative of the Fall of Adam to exemplify the descent that all souls undertake after their first creation. At first, Adam enjoys a blessed existence: 'Adam was first wholly aethereal, and placed in Paradise; that is, in an happy and joyful condition of the Spirit ... the Sun of Righteousness then shone fairly upon him' (1662: *Conjectura Cabbalistica*, 22). However, Adam's will and reason are led astray by the promise of a pleasure-filled life of the body, leading to his loss of a blissful aethereal state (see 1662: *Conjectura Cabbalistica*, 26). More understands the Fall of Adam to be of symbolic significance for all human beings, illustrating the descent that all beings undergo: we begin in an equal state of blessedness and then variously descend to different levels of sin depending on the manner in which the individual strays from the divine will. Thus, Conway's account of the original equality of souls, followed by the descent of souls according to moral worthiness, potentially reflects the influence of More in this regard. Once the original equality of creatures is claimed, the only explanation we have for variety across nature is the possibility of creatures to transmutate across species, and this is precisely what Conway claims.

Conway as process philosopher

As I noted earlier, it has been suggested that Conway can be understood as a process philosopher, but we could not explore this suggestion fully until we had a more complete view of her metaphysics. In this section, I want to explore if there is a sense in which Conway can be legitimately thought of as a process philosopher. One standard definition of a process philosophy is a metaphysics that posits processes as ontologically fundamental. As a counterpoint to this view, we can speak of a 'substance metaphysics' that holds things that are made of a substance as ontologically fundamental. So far, I have assumed that Conway is offering a kind of substance metaphysics, and I will argue for that interpretation in this section. However, I would entirely grant that processes form an important part of Conway's metaphysics, to the extent that we may wish to think of her as a 'moral process' philosopher.

One scholar who has suggested a significant overlap between Conway's metaphysics and process thought is Carol Wayne White, who describes three main claims of process philosophy:

1 'events and relationships – rather than separate substances or separate particles – constitute reality'
2 'becoming, not being, is the central metaphor for understanding reality … nothing is constant, everything is in flux'
3 'contingency, emergence, and creativity are essential elements that take precedence over determinism and fixity'. (2009: 82)

I would argue that whilst Conway would agree to some extent with some aspects of these claims, this is insufficient to establish her as a process philosopher, insofar as she ultimately does not accept (1): in other words, she does not accept that events and relationships are ultimately constitutive of reality. However, there is perhaps enough overlap between Conway's philosophy and modern process thought that there could be instructive comparative study of the two. I will argue that there are close enough parallels such that we could call Conway a 'moral process philosopher', but this is only if we adopt quite a broad understanding of process philosophy.

Whilst Conway would not accept (1), that events and relationships ultimately constitute reality, claims (2) and (3) certainly seem to reflect something of the overall metaphysical picture we find in the *Principia*. Conway's world is one characterized by flux, constituted of individuals who are constantly changing and interacting with each other, and who are constantly being added to by God through his divine action. It is also the case that we cannot fully grasp the universe without focusing on the way it *becomes*, as well as the way it is. Reflection upon God and the divine attributes, whether aided by reason or the inner light, helps us to understand not only that all things are ultimately spirit, but also that they are in the middle of a process of moving closer towards God, the infinite spirit. As we have seen, the becoming of all things is taking place all the time throughout the lives of creatures, as mediating spirits are exchanged and the archeus rules over the dynamic system that is each creature. All of this leads to a worldview that is surprisingly overwhelmingly characterized by its contingency, given its ground in a necessary act of divine will. So, considering Conway's philosophy in very broad strokes, it is certainly the case that her system has an overall tenor that is sympathetic to the kinds of ideas found in process philosophy. However, given that Conway would not accept that events and relationships constitute reality, with her commitment to a substance-based metaphysics, we cannot straightforwardly claim that she offers a process philosophy in the *Principia*.

Another reading of Conway as a process philosopher is offered by Emily Thomas, who offers a more liberal understanding of process philosophy. Thomas sees the difference between substance and process philosophy more as a question of emphasis: 'Entities that we usually conceive as things – such as human bodies or trees – can also be conceived as processes, if we emphasize their changing or happening rather than their persistence through change. In effect, process philosophy emphasizes the primacy of process and change, rather than thing-ness and persistence' (2017: 1005). In this case, we have a wider definition of process philosophy that could perhaps more comfortably accommodate Conway, insofar as it allows for there to be things in our ontology that persist over time, but they are de-emphasized in relation to the importance bestowed upon process and change in our explanation of the constitution of reality.[13] Thomas points to two aspects of Conway's thought that are particularly distinctive of process thought: (1) beings are constantly changing 'bundles of activity' (2017: 1006) and (2) time 'is a grand process constituted by smaller processes: the movements of existing things' (2017: 1007). These two claims are not merely a question of emphasis, in that they are definitive metaphysical claims that rule out other options. So, it seems that Thomas is operating with a more limited definition of process philosophy than it originally appeared. Leaving that aside, would Conway agree with claims (1) and (2)?

Beginning with (1), Conway certainly thinks of individuals in terms of dynamic, constantly changing systems that are always actively sending out mediating spirits to other things and thereby standing in sympathetic relations to them. However, whilst these spirits are active, they are not *constituted* by their activity; rather, they are substances that engage in constant activity, reflecting an ever-changing creation. So, Conway would not agree that there are beings who are simply 'bundles of activity'. As for (2), I argued earlier that Conway defines time in terms of the movement of creatures on the spirit–matter continuum, with an overall journey towards God. Insofar as each creature is undergoing its own process of ontological and moral development, it would be right to say that time is a 'grand process constituted by smaller processes'. Time thus becomes both an ontological and a moral process for Conway.

However, (2) by itself is not sufficient for a process philosophy, insofar as a substance metaphysics can define time in such a way. According to a relational theory of time, time is constituted by things changing, or in other words, it is constituted by the relations between different states of things as they change. Such a view of time is contrasted with a substantivalism about time, according to which time is an independently existing thing apart from events that happen in the world (we can think of time according to this view as a kind of container in which events happen). A substance metaphysics can deny that time has its own kind of independent existence and instead adopt a relationist viewpoint by claiming that time is constituted by change (and I would argue that this is what Conway does). Even if Conway accepts claim (2), then, that does not necessarily imply that she thereby has a process philosophy. As such, I conclude that we cannot conclude that Conway is a process philosopher on the basis of the two essential claims that Thomas picks out: Conway does not accept (1), and (2) does not by itself entail a process philosophy.

As an alternative, I argue that we can think of Conway as a process philosopher insofar as we take the broad definition based on emphasis, though it is a distinctively moral emphasis that is placed on processes. The most fundamental things in Conway's creation are individual spirits, of whom there are an infinite number that naturally congregate as systems under a single overall ruling spirit and use mediating spirits to have sympathetic relations with other such systems. Insofar as that is the case, Conway holds a substance metaphysics. However, from the perspective of morality and salvation, it is ongoing dynamics within spirits and systems of spirits that are crucial. From an ontological perspective, we have two levels (individual spirits and systems of spirits[14]), but from a moral perspective, it is how such a dynamic process plays out between and within spirits that determines the salvation of creatures.

So, taking the broad definition of process philosophy based on the question of emphasis, we can perhaps call Conway a 'moral process philosopher', but not a process philosopher in the more limited sense that takes processes as ontologically fundamental in some way. Given this, I conclude that whilst there is perhaps enough overlap to make comparative research on Conway and process philosophy mutually illuminating, the similarities between the two should not be overemphasized in order to ensure that we are not misconstruing the text of the *Principia*.

The role of suffering

Before we conclude, one final aspect of Conway's account of transmutation that we have yet to discuss in detail is the role that specifically pain and suffering have to play in bringing about the kind of transformations that she postulates in the *Principia*. The most prominent hint of this is found in an argument she offers against the possibility of eternal damnation: she states that it would be impossible for a creature to proceed towards evil and crassness ad infinitum, due to the inevitability of pain and suffering in life. The experience of pain has a physical effect on the being itself, such that 'whatever grossness or crassness is contracted by the spirit or body is diminished' (7.1; 43): in other words, pain has the natural effect of reducing the crassness of the creature that experiences it. On that basis, given the assumption that suffering is an unavoidable part of life, a creature will always ascend overall on the spirit–matter continuum through the natural workings of pain and suffering.

In this way, pain comes to have a fundamentally important soteriological role to play. Conway argues that 'the spirit imprisoned in such grossness or crassness is set free and becomes more spiritual and consequently, more active and effective through pain' (7.1; 43). Pain acts as a kind of moral and ontological purifier, undoing the effects of our original movement from God and also 'stimulates the life or spirit existing in everything which suffers' (7.1; 43). So, the experience of pain is crucial for the overall movement of creatures back towards the infinite spirit, God, alongside Christ, revivifying and re-spiritualizing creatures who have fallen into grossness.

So, it appears that Conway views pain as sufficient for ontological progress on the spirit–matter continuum and inevitable, such that all things will have an overall movement back towards the infinite spirit of God. Is it, however, necessary for such movement? In other words, can one become less gross without undergoing the experience of pain? It would seem that pain is not necessary, for when we considered Conway's view of freedom, we saw that movement towards God can be achieved through the morally worthy exercise of our free will. Unless doing the right thing inevitably involves some form of suffering, then pain is not necessary for positive transformation on the spirit–matter continuum. Conway could perhaps argue that acting in a morally virtuous manner does inevitably involve some form of suffering, though such a wide claim would be difficult to sustain. We may then wonder precisely why suffering is taken to have the ontological effect Conway claims it has. The spiritualizing effect of acting in a morally worthy manner has some intuitive sense, insofar as acting in accordance with goodness would make us more like God. However, given that God does not experience pain (or indeed any passions whatsoever, as far as Conway is concerned), it is not as clear how suffering would necessarily bring us closer to the divine.

It is likely that Conway's view of pain draws upon her own extensive experience of suffering during her bouts of ill-health, as well as the substantial religious tradition of the divinizing power of hardship. Such a view can be found in a letter to Conway from Henry More, in which he argues that a healthy body can in fact act as an impediment to moral and spiritual development: 'I hope your body will not prove a Tomb to you, but rather an holy Temple, an hallowed edifice for your soul to work in, those bodies that are most vigorously in health are the most devouring sepulchres to swallow down the soul into and to bury all the nobler faculties' (L 337). Within the Christian tradition, there is also significance attributed to the suffering of Christ in the final hours of his life, which is seen as a necessary prelude for the forgiveness of sins and the return of creation to God. Conway reflects upon the suffering of the historical Christ and its role in the salvation of creatures in *Principia*: she writes, 'The purpose of all [of Christ's] suffering up to his death and burial, was to heal, preserve, and restore creatures from corruption and death' (5.6; 27). However, there is no clear explanation as to how Christ's suffering achieves this restoration for us and so we are left with no answer as to why pain in general has this ontological effect.

Christia Mercer (2012: 195f.) has offered an explanation for the role of suffering in Conway's philosophy based on the notion of universal sympathy. One way of understanding how pain can revivify creatures is in terms of the sympathy between the creatures that make up our world. Given these sympathetic relations, Mercer appeals to a possible enhancement relation between creatures, where 'an increase in the goodness of one will promote an increase in the goodness of another, although the relation is non-reciprocal' (2012: 195). A suffering creature is able to transmit its revived nature to other things and so the benefits of suffering can be shared out across creation (this might help explain how a creature that did not suffer, or at least not suffer to a great extent, could nevertheless reap the ontological benefit of the overall suffering of creatures). However, this still does not quite explain how suffering *does in fact* revivify creatures in the first place, so that they then can enhance the status of other creatures.

My suggestion for such an explanation, within the confines of Conway's philosophy, returns to the points we considered in Chapter 2 concerning the love that the mind has for the body. When we suffer through a physical illness, we are aware of our body in a much more immediate manner than when we are healthy and simply living through our everyday lives. Given this, it is intuitive that when the body is in pain, the love that the mind has for the body is intensified as it is reminded of the affinity that binds them together. As a corollary, it also reminds the spirit in question of the affinity between all things (including those spirits that are further down on the spirit–matter continuum) and thus the love for all things is increased.[15] In this way, through the experience of suffering, we come to increasingly mirror the universal love that God has for all of creation, and that is why pain has the moral and ontological impact that Conway claims it has. Admittedly, such an argument is not stated explicitly in the text, but I argue that it fits neatly with what Conway claims about the role of suffering and universal sympathy with regard to the question of our salvation.

The communitarian aspect of the transformative power of suffering is also noted by Nelson and Alker, who point to the significance of the comforting presence of Quakers at Ragley Hall in the final years of Conway's life: they argue that 'Conway fashions her encounters with Quakers in the language of healthcare' (2011: 76) in a manner that suggests their company has real medical benefit for her ('I must profess that my converse with them is ... to receive health and refreshment from them' (L 421)), in addition to the spiritual benefits she claims in a letter to Henry More from 1675 (see L 422). Though of course one could take such claims in a less metaphysically substantive sense, Conway's theory of universal sympathy allows for the health benefits conferred by the company of suffering individuals, such as the early Quakers, in quite a direct way. Indeed, due to the unity of individuals and the possibility of enhancement relations, the benefits for Conway and those around her can be shared and multiplied.

The traditional notion that pain brings one closer to God also fits naturally with Helmontian ideas concerning the impact of the mind upon the body in the context of disease. The views of van Helmont concerning the generation of the body by the archeus led to a strong sense of the connection between mind and body, to the extent that the mind is believed to have more substantial control over the body than is generally held today. This theory leads van Helmont to postulate that the mind itself, particularly insofar as it experiences disorder in the passions (such as too strong an imagination or feelings of fear), is the cause of most disease (see 1694: 138). Disorder in the mind brings about disorder in the body, so it stands to reason that disease brought about this way could be treated with a purely psychological cure, including through the experience of pain.

Conway's focus on spiritual purification through pain seems to be based on an alchemical model and perhaps speaks of the influence of her discussions with van Helmont. As Coudert notes, van Helmont explores the possible purification of body through suffering with a chemical analogy of the purification of substances through alchemical methods:

> Substances could be purified, improved, transmuted, and in a word, perfected through the careful ministrations of the alchemist. He applied alchemical theory to medicine, firmly believing that the pain and suffering of a patient was similar to the first step in the alchemical process, a temporary stage during which impure or 'sick' substances were 'mortified' and 'died', only to be resurrected in a purer or... 'healthier' state through the application of appropriate 'medicines'.
> (1999: 161)

On this model, the experience of pain is seen as a preparatory stage on the journey to purification, priming the creature for a potential future life in a higher state. However, it is not clear on this model whether the experience of pain is sufficient for the kind of purification required to be reborn in a higher state of existence: it could be that pain prepares the creature for this rebirth *simpliciter* or that it prepares the creature for further experiences and actions in this life that will ultimately bring about an ascent towards God. Either way, van Helmont sees the experience of suffering as playing an important role in preparing the individual to return to God.

For Conway's part, though we cannot be entirely sure, it is not too much of a stretch to suppose that the role she gives to pain and suffering as a physical and spiritual purifier is more rooted in her own experiences than in her intellectual influences. From her letters and reports we have of her life, her significant illnesses seem to have dominated her life throughout her adulthood and so it would be likely that she would wish to build what she had learned from these experiences into her systematic philosophy.

Conclusion

Many questions remain concerning Conway's vitalism, her theories of identity and the constitution of creatures, and their link to other aspects of her philosophy. In this chapter, I have sought to shed some light on her vitalism and other related topics as presented in the *Principia*, though I realize that the arguments I have proposed are not conclusive and will undoubtedly be challenged. We have been considering what are some of the most cryptic remarks found in Conway's work and they will inevitably lead to further scholarly debate. At the very least, I hope to have expanded the range of interpretive options available to us and offered a fresh perspective upon Conway's philosophy.

In many of the arguments presented in this book, I have looked to Conway's conception of the nature of God to ultimately guide my interpretation. As a strategy for approaching an interpretation of Conway's philosophy, it is certainly apropos for a couple of reasons. First, relative to other parts of her system, the discussion of the nature of God in the *Principia* is reasonably clear and straightforward, and as such, it gives us a more secure basis for interpreting other passages which are perhaps a little more unclear or even ambiguous. Second, such an approach ties with Conway's Neoplatonic assumptions concerning the deep link between God and his creation via his emanative activity. Given certain assumptions about God's nature, and the manner in which creation will reflect the divine, it is possible to 'read off' features of how creatures must be from reflection on God. Indeed, in this chapter, I have used assumptions about the nature of God to argue for a particular interpretation of the notion of 'life' in Conway's system, as well as with regard to considering the type of monism that she assumes with regard to the created universe. Though this strategy may not always clarify interpretive matters, it will inevitably aid scholars in their project of gaining a deeper understanding of the philosophy proposed in the *Principia*.

Conclusion

I believe that it is an incredibly positive step in scholarship concerning the history of philosophy that Conway's philosophy (and those of other early modern women philosophers, such as Margaret Cavendish) is receiving increased attention in the literature. Given the interesting arguments and ideas contained in the *Principia*, it is of great regret that scholarly neglect of Conway has been allowed to continue for so long. Of course, books like this, and the articles I have considered in this work, are really just the beginning of a long journey in re-examining the history of philosophy and retrieving the ideas of those thinkers who have been left out of traditional narratives due to accidents of history.

With regard to Conway, there is still much work to be done in analysing the extant texts we have associated with her, including not just her letters and the *Principia*, but also works published by van Helmont that may have been influenced or even partly written by her. As we have seen throughout this book, there are aspects of her philosophy that are not entirely clear and thus require careful interpretation and discussion, which will undoubtedly continue as the literature on Conway continues to grow. There is also much more that can be done in terms of placing Conway in her historical context and the different currents of thought that were swirling around in the mid-seventeenth century. I have not been able to cover this in any great detail here, as the focus has been on the arguments that Conway proposes in the *Principia*. However, more could certainly be done on investigating Conway's intellectual links to the early Quaker community, as well as to van Helmont and Henry More. It may also be of interest to consider parallels between her thought and other thinkers of the period, even if there is no obvious line of influence between them.

As far as I am concerned, part of the appeal of Conway's philosophy is the way it looks to both the past and the future. Conway is unafraid to investigate and incorporate ideas from diverse, oft-forgotten philosophical and religious traditions, with the result that she extensively challenges the prevailing orthodoxies of her time. We are also offered an intoxicating vision of the future, in which all things are able to transcend their current state of existence and look forward to a time of loving unity with other creatures and the divine. As for the present, Conway offers a perspective upon nature that could help shape our thinking about our place in the environment, particularly as we face the challenges of climate change and pollution. As we have seen, Conway emphasizes the interconnectedness of all things and thus the need for active participation of all beings in preserving and cultivating the world. It is a lesson that we would do well to learn. I hope that this book spurs others to examine Conway's philosophy and retrieve her valuable insights for today.

Notes

Introduction

1. I will refer to this work as the *Principia* throughout.
2. Following established scholarly convention, I will refer to Anne by her married name (Conway) throughout, rather than by her maiden name (Finch).
3. The portrait of Conway's life offered in this section draws upon numerous biographical sources, including the editorial material provided by Marjorie Nicolson in *The Conway Letters* (1992: *passim*) and by Sarah Hutton in her *Anne Conway: A Woman Philosopher* (2004: *passim*).
4. Nicolson claims that this note appended to her will dates from Conway's very final days, when she knew that death was close (see L 450). The basis for this claim is not entirely clear to me: as it is not dated, it seemingly could have been written at any point during the last five years of her life. Conway does make a point of emphasizing that, in a departure from usual practice, she was writing the note herself (see L 481), but she relied on amanuenses for a significant period prior to her death and so this detail does not necessarily help us to achieve a more precise dating.
5. Some years after her death (1697), Leibniz also singles out Conway for praise in a letter, stating that his 'philosophical views approach somewhat closely those of the late Countess of Conway' (1974: 217). The possible influence of Conway's philosophy upon Leibniz is a matter that has received much scholarly attention, including by Merchant (1979) and Duran (1989). Steven Schroeder (2007) also pursues a Leibnizian reading of Conway's philosophy. Given the amount of attention this topic has received elsewhere, and the space required to examine Leibniz's philosophy in order to consider the question properly, I will not discuss it in this work.
6. Those who wish to explore Cavendish's philosophy in detail may consult both David Cunning's (2015: *passim*) and Deborah Boyle's (2018: *passim*) recent books on her work.
7. As Hutton states, there are parallels between *Principia* and *Two Hundred Queries* that suggest Conway may have had a hand in the writing of this text (2004: 206–12). The possibility is worth entertaining particularly due to the collaborative nature of much of van Helmont's work. There is also some overlap with the

Helmontian text *Seder Olam*, published in 1693. We should, however, be very cautious in approaching these texts as potential sources of Conway's ideas, given the uncertainty surrounding their writing. We must also take into account the fact that there are also significant dissimilarities between *Principia* and the Helmontian texts, as well as it being the case that any overlap can be imputed to the intellectual exchange between Conway and van Helmont that took place at Ragley Hall over many years.

8   In the introduction to their translation of the *Principia*, Coudert and Corse do not commit themselves to dating the text beyond saying that it was written 'some time during the last nine years of her life' (xxxviii).

9   As O'Neill argues (1998: 32–9), there are various reasons why early modern women philosophers such as Conway have been overlooked by scholars for so long, including misattribution (the *Principia* has occasionally been erroneously attributed to van Helmont) and the potential political threat to the patriarchal social order that women philosophers embodied.

10 Unfortunately, this edition is long out-of-print and copies are scarce. I was able to consult a library copy during the writing of this work.

11 Despite my best efforts, I have been unable to track down a copy of this edition and so I was not able to consult it during my research.

12 There is also a new edition and translation of the *Principia* in the works by Oxford University Press, co-edited by Marcy Lascano, Christia Mercer, Andrew Arlig, Jasper Reid and Sarah Hutton. It is not entirely clear at the time of writing when this volume will eventually appear.

13 The details of Conway's visit to France are recounted in more detail by Nicolson (see L 116–18).

14 More repeatedly counsels Conway in this manner, as she undergoes various periods of ill-health: for example, in a letter from 1661, he again places the use of reason in philosophy as an important tool in looking beyond this life, to eternity: 'Resolve this with yourself perpetually that this life is but either a pleasing or unquiet dream, and therefore not to be transported nor cast down with anything, but to place one's content solely in the exercise of sound reason and a good conscience, and that Death itself is but the Day Spring of eternal Life' (L 121).

15 Generally speaking, I suspect rather more editorial intervention in Conway's *Principia* than most, certainly more than all of the other Conway scholars I have spoken to on this topic. However, this is mere suspicion, and so I will not explore this question in detail here. I would also certainly not wish to deny that the *Principia* is substantially the work of Anne Conway. It is possible that more evidence will arise in the future that definitively settles this issue of potential editorial intervention.

Chapter 1

1. Conway's acquaintance with Quakers can be dated back to at least 1666, as there is an extant letter from that year from an early prominent Quaker, Henry Bromley, who refers to Conway in appreciative terms (see L 278f.).
2. See Hill (1991: 236) for more on the apologetic perspective of much early Quaker writing.
3. A variant of this passage is also found at Luke 13:28, which have led some to postulate that it is taken from an earlier source (written or oral) of Jesus's sayings available to both Matthew and Luke, often designated 'Q'.
4. The Quakers were highly unusual in having meetings reserved for women, though these were not as powerful or as well-resourced as the general meetings dominated by men (see Lloyd 1950: ch. 8).
5. Quaker women writers often described their drive to write as a kind of compulsion, stemming from the divine. Tarter notes that, from the very beginning of the Quaker movement, there were 'a rising number of Quaker Englishwomen who felt the physical calling – indeed, the very urgency – to inscribe and publish their prophesyings ... [These] authors declared that the Lord had impelled them to record their messages; many describe this spiritual leading as nothing less than God's outright "command"' (2018: 69).
6. This often involved mimicking masculine Biblical prophets (see Gill 2005: 137–9).
7. The situation was perhaps further complicated for Conway by her husband's own antipathy, shared by other members of the nobility and gentry, towards the Quakers on the basis of their threat to the social hierarchy. In a letter from 1659, Lord Conway had painted the Quakers as social malcontents, 'whose design is only to turn out the landlords' (L 161). Ragley Hall, where Conway lived, is located in the county of Warwickshire, which is identified by George Fox as one of the first strongholds of Quakerism, dating back to 1645 (see Barbour & Roberts 1973: 145), so there was a strong and well-established Quaker community in the area where Conway lived.
8. Crocker rightly points out that More's exhortation to pursue self-denial is not intended to argue for the undertaking of strict ascetic paths, but rather more of a middle way that seeks to counteract overemphasis on the pursuit of natural pleasures, and its concomitant impact on the intellect, such that we prioritize immersion in the senses and our base emotions (see 2003: 26n.). In such a way, the soul can be slowly drawn away from the material world towards its rightful position in union with God.
9. See Leech (2013: 44) for details on More's account of the descent and ascent of the soul.
10. Nicolson, in *The Conway Letters*, erroneously states that it is most likely that More is discussing Isaiah 5:24 here. However, this is unlikely, as the verse in question

does not refer to 'hay' and the Old Testament would not have been read in Greek, so the use of the Greek phrase 'δια πυρος' would be out of place. However, the phrase does occur in the Koine Greek version of the passage from 1 Corinthians 3, which does refer to both hay and stubble. We can also construe More's reference to 'other combustible stuff' (L 68) as referring to the wood that is mentioned just before in the same verse. In addition, it makes sense that Conway might enquire as to the reason for 'hay', 'stubble' and 'wood' to be added to the list, following on from 'gold, silver, precious stones' (1 Cor 3:12), and that More would interpret this passage as concerning deviations from the core Christian message.

11 Hutton corrects Nicolson's original rendering of 'holiness' as 'religion' (see L 541).
12 More understands reason as a faculty of deduction, discerning 'one Truth from another, that no man can discover any looseness or disjointedness in the cohesion of the Argument' (1925: 61) by working with the materials furnished to us by commonsense and external perception.
13 The Quakers themselves accepted that the inner light was not to be confused with reason or conscience. Due to the strong sense of divine participation that they connected with the workings of the inner light, they tended to simply identify the capacity with one of the Persons of the Trinity (see Underwood 1970: 94f.).
14 The historian David Byrne (2007: 29) has also suggested that some notion of the inner light acts as an implicit foundation of Conway's metaphysical system, though he does not expand upon this suggestion in detail.
15 'Convincement' is the standard term used within the Quaker community for converting to Quakerism.
16 Allison Coudert gathers a significant amount of evidence for the hypothesis that van Helmont had significant contacts with the Quaker community from around 1659 onwards (see 1999: 36–8), though there is nothing that is entirely decisive on this historical question.
17 Given that Keith's epistemology is intimately bound up with his Christology, I have left this discussion until later in this work, when we come to consider Conway's account of the role of Christ.

Chapter 2

1 See the discussions of the Form of the Good and the 'Divided Line' in Plato (1974: 299–316; 502c–511e).
2 Note that the definition does not go the other way: spirit is not matter. As Conway sees it, material things are a subset of spirits (i.e. those that are more corporeal), so it is very much a spiritual monism we are describing here.
3 We will return to Conway's theory of the systematic interaction between spirits in the final section of this chapter, in relation to her vitalism.

4   Having considered a number of philosophical arguments in favour of spiritual monism, Conway also claims scriptural authority for her theory, citing a number of passages from the New Testament that appear to reject the existence of dead matter (she also claims she could provide supporting passages from the Hebrew Bible too, but does not do so here): for example, we can look at Acts 17:24–5, where it is written, 'God that made the world and all things therein … he giveth to all life, and breath, and all things', and 1 Timothy 6:13, where God is referred to as '[giving] life to all things'. Conway does not spend long going over these passages and only offers brief quotes from them. Clearly, this is only intended to be a very minor part of her overall argument for spiritual monism, though it is at least useful to rebut those who charge her of entirely departing from Christian scripture.

Chapter 3

1   See Reid (2012: 175–81) for a thorough discussion of this shift in More's philosophy.
2   Thomas (2017: 997f.) and Reid (2012: 255) have also pointed out that Conway's *Principia* tends to show her affinities with More's early work from the 1640s and 1650s, particularly the *Poems*, rather than his later texts.
3   It should be noted that God's sustaining activity does not exhaust his creative activity, according to Conway, who argues that the divine 'not only gives to [created things] form and figure, but also essence, life, body, and whatever good they have' (1.3; 9), and as such is no mere ground of being.
4   Conway's account of creation is not entirely Neoplatonic due to the fact that in her system, creation is not limited to sustaining all created beings in existence, and is not blind in the sense suggested by the Neoplatonic creative model of heat emanating from a fire; rather, there is some sense of purpose behind the creative activity of Conway's God.
5   It is worth noting that Swinburne himself, in an early paper, argues for the timelessness of God on the basis that: (1) only a timeless God could be a proper explanation for the universe and its laws and (2) God's continued existence can only be explained if he is timeless (see 1965: 332–5).
6   Hutton (2004: 92) notes that it is not clear when Conway became familiar with Plotinus and the *Enneads*, but it is almost certain that she was by the time she writes the notes that would become the *Principia*, as van Helmont tells us. Given Henry More's interest in Plotinus, and the impact of Neoplatonism upon his early *Poems*, it seems likely that Conway was familiar with Plotinus from early on in her philosophical education.
7   See Reid (2012: 354–6) for an extensive discussion of this argument as found in Glanvill's text and More's annotations upon it.

8   A more in-depth analysis of More's arguments concerning the details of his theory of the pre-existence of the soul can be found in Reid (2012: 349–56).
9   The process of the generation of the Intellect from One is actually a little more complicated than the account I have offered here, insofar as an indefinite intellect, as a first generation, has to be converted into the definite Intellect proper, but this is not important for our purposes here (for a more detailed account, see Emilsson (2017: 94–9)).
10 This is not to say that the Johannine Logos doctrine does not have any basis in the Hebrew Bible. It is likely that the author of this passage (or the possible oral tradition that this passage is based on) is also invoking Proverbs 8:22, where 'Wisdom' (for which we can read Logos) speaks of their creation prior to that of the material universe: 'The Lord possessed [alternate: created] me in the beginning of his way, before his works of old.' In fact, it is possible, as Boyarin (2001: *passim*) has argued, that the Platonic influence upon the author of the Gospel of John was mediated through the impact of Middle Platonism upon Jewish 'Wisdom' theology.
11 Textual analysis shows that the author is indeed evoking the creation narrative as found in the Book of Genesis (see Brown 2010: 276f.).
12 Given More's interest in Philo, it is highly likely that he was a subject of extended discussion within the Conway circle, including Conway herself, More and van Helmont.
13 Whilst Conway certainly follows the Johannine Logos doctrine in broad terms, with regard to Christ playing a role in creation, she does not follow John's Gospel with regard to ideas concerning the nature of time. As Borgen argues (1972: 118ff), the Prologue to the Gospel of John is often taken to be assuming the creation (and thus the finite nature) of time, and in fact posits a kind of primordial time prior to the creation of the material universe. Such an account of time would certainly be rejected by Conway.
14 Emily Thomas (in correspondence) points out that if Conway's definition of time is linked to the development towards perfection alone, then those who engage in moral backsliding might be held (quite absurdly) to be 'stopping time' in some sense. In order to avoid this, we must take Conway's definition of time to be linked to the process of moral development either towards or away from God.
15 Emilsson (2017: 170) notes that the account is not quite as simple as this, as it would perhaps be better to say that time is the 'unquiet power' of the soul, as opposed to simply the motion of the hypostasis Soul, but this is not a significant distinction to make in the context of our discussion here.
16 In this interpretation, I differ from Emily Thomas, who argues that Plotinus holds an absolutist theory of time, in the sense of seeing time 'as a kind of *container* for the things that exist successively in time' (2017: 996n.), and thus sees Conway and Plotinus are at some distance here.
17 The translation of Proverbs found in the Septuagint is rather idiosyncratic, and so other translations (such as that found in KJV, which I have been using in this work) do not quite fit Origen's point here.

Chapter 4

1. This chapter is a revised and expanded version of my paper, 'Anne Conway and George Keith on the Christ Within', published in *Quaker Studies* 23.2 (2018): pp. 161–77. I would like to thank the journal for permission to reuse this material as well as an anonymous reviewer from that journal for their helpful comments.
2. Exceptions to this trend in the scholarship on Conway include Hutton (2004: ch. 9) and White (2008: ch. 2), and I intend to build upon their excellent work here.
3. In this, I follow the usual distinction between substance and quiddity – substance is what a thing is made out of and quiddity is what makes something the kind of thing it is. So, all things are made out of spirit, according to Conway, and there are three types of things that exist. I argue that the differentiating attribute between the three quiddities, for Conway, is the power of change that the being in question holds.
4. As we shall see later (in Chapter 7), there is a current interpretive debate concerning whether there is just one creaturely substance or many. I will argue that there is not just one creaturely substance.
5. An anonymous reviewer rightly points out that the use of the notion of an ontological continuum containing both God and creation might incorrectly suggest that Conway sees God and creatures as potentially interchangeable, with no substantial ontological difference between them. They are right to point out this danger, but I think it is a useful way to think about Conway's ontology as long as we bear in mind that creatures can never reach the end of the ontological continuum at which God sits (due to a difference in essence), and thus they are not, even in principle, interchangeable.
6. This correspondence is discussed in detail in Tollefson (1999: *passim*).
7. See Gabbey (1990: 23–32) for an in-depth discussion of the role that the Spirit of Nature plays in More's metaphysics.
8. However, More did later adopt a more conciliatory attitude towards the Quakers, due to efforts on the part of Conway to encourage dialogue through correspondence and meetings at Ragley Hall. As Hutton points out (2004: 187f.), More praises the piety to be found in some of the Quaker writings he engaged with, particularly favouring George Keith, who he believes to be the 'absolutely best Quaker of them all' (L 513).
9. In addition, Keith seems to have been impressed by More's notion of the Spirit of Nature, which we have already had occasion to discuss. In a letter from 1674, following a visit from Keith, More states of him that, 'He is very philosophically and Platonically given, and is pleased with the notion of the Spirit of Nature' (L 392f.).
10. In a similar manner, More holds his doctrine of the Spirit of Nature to be self-evident, with the certainty of mathematics, in the light of reason: 'the principle we speak of is neither obscure nor unreasonable; nor so much introduced by me,

as forced upon me by inevitable evidence of reason', and to doubt it would be 'as ridiculous, as to doubt of the truth of any one plain and easy demonstration in the first Book of Euclid' (1712: 205f.).

11 More is seemingly unconvinced by Keith's developing Christology, writing a manuscript in 1875/6 entitled 'Examination or Confutation of G.K.'s opinion touching the extension of the soul of Christ' (see the reference to the manuscript at L 417), which unfortunately has not survived.

12 Conway states that Christ 'is like God in all his attributes' (5.4; 26) but does not expand much further on the extent to which the divine attributes are communicable to him.

13 For a more detailed exploration of Malebranche's theory of causation, see Nadler (2000: *passim*).

14 Also note how salvation is opened up to all creatures, who can join in with the overall progress towards the good, in contrast to the traditional Christian picture in which redemption is confined to human beings.

15 An in-depth narrative of the events leading to, and following from, the Keithian schism can be found in Cody (1972: *passim*).

16 As noted by an anonymous reviewer, the beginnings of Keith's schism can already be seen through an emphasis on the historical Christ in his correspondence with Knorr von Rosenroth, dating from the mid-1770s, at the same time as responding to many critiques of Quakerism on this question. I am grateful to the reviewer for bringing this to my attention.

Chapter 5

1 This chapter is a revised and expanded version of my paper, 'Anne Conway on Time, the Trinity, and Eschatology', published in *Philosophy and Theology* 29.2 (2017): pp. 277–95. I would like to thank the journal for permission to reuse this material, as well as an anonymous reviewer from that journal for their helpful comments.

2 The classic understanding of the interaction between ontology and epistemology found in the immanent Trinity and economic Trinity has been helpfully summed up by Lee: 'The economic Trinity is the ground of cognition for the [immanent] Trinity, and the [immanent] Trinity is the ground of being for the economic Trinity' (2009: 92).

3 Later on, Conway reiterates such an overall movement towards spirituality in more secular terms: '[Nature] always works toward the greater perfection of subtlety and spirituality since this is the most natural property of every operation and motion … These spirits, whether good or bad, always advance to a greater subtlety or spirituality' (8.5; 61f.).

4   I will return to the question of the role of pain and suffering in Conway's philosophy in Chapter 7.
5   We can see here the beginnings of Conway's eschatology, which I shall consider in more detail in the following section.
6   However, Conway is still clearly concerned to appeal to Christian readers, for she makes numerous references to the New Testament for support throughout the *Principia*.
7   The notion of Christ as the Word or Logos was introduced in Chapter 3.
8   The editors of the CUP translation clearly imply that they believe the 'Annotations to the First Chapter' to be the work of Conway (see the editorial footnote on 10).
9   Such beings also enter into a progressively more loving relationship with God, in that 'those creatures which are most like God love him more and are more loved by him' (7.3; 47).
10 One of the main problems facing the timeless view of God is that of the apparent incompatibility between divine foreknowledge and creaturely freedom. If God is outside of time, then he knows all my actions from his eternal standpoint and so what I do is 'fixed' in advance. It seems an intuitive part of our understanding of freedom that one could have acted otherwise, but this is apparently ruled out by such a model of God and so none of my actions can be free. Whilst Conway does not entirely avoid this problem, its philosophical sting is rather reduced insofar as our salvation is no longer at stake: all creatures will be saved, so the question of the extent to which we can be held responsible for our actions is not as important as it is when we invoke some doctrine of divine moral judgement. I will return to the question of freedom in Conway's philosophy in the following chapter.

Chapter 6

1   One notable exception to this scholarly omission is Lascano (2017). Whilst Lascano does briefly discuss the relationship between More and Conway on freedom (see 2017: 168–9), I wish to explore this relation in more detail.
2   This chapter is a revised and expanded version of my paper, 'Anne Conway and Henry More on Freedom', published in *International Journal of Philosophical Studies* 27.5 (2019): pp. 631–48. I would like to thank the journal for permission to reuse this material, as well as Ruth Boeker and anonymous reviewers from that journal for their helpful comments.
3   Most recent major studies of Henry More's philosophy mainly overlook his theory of freedom, though a notable exception is Reid (2012: 179–81 *et passim*) and I will have cause to consider his account later in the discussion.

4   By a broad 'libertarian' understanding of freedom, I understand a power to self-determine without external influence. Beginning with this notion of freedom is apt as it is a kind of freedom often attributed to God, and as Reid points out (2012: 179), More is committed to a strongly libertarian approach to freedom throughout his philosophy.

5   We do not have to think of freedom primarily in this way, but it is a useful approach to capture common-sense notions related to freedom, and it is how the debate was often framed in the seventeenth century.

6   As Crocker notes, More strikes a contrast between a free spiritual world and the material realm: he proposes 'a simple vision of the primal intellectual dichotomy between the intelligence, freedom and bliss of spirit, and the deadness, immobility, ephemeral nature and "otherness" of materiality' (2003: 37).

7   See Pink (2011: 543–5) for a more in-depth examination of Hobbes's account of freedom in the sense of self-determination. It is also worth noting that Hobbes speaks of free action in the sense of action that is unimpeded, which is compatible with a will that is always determined to a particular course of action (see van Mill 1995: 444–6).

8   See Reid (2012: 180) for a fuller explanation of Hobbes's argument concerning the determinate necessity of future events.

9   More's rejection of any view that sees animal nature as inherently sinful is at least partly inspired by his early repudiation of Calvinism, which emphasizes the complete moral infirmity of the soul due to original sin and thus our complete reliance on grace for salvation (see More's autobiographical remarks concerning his Calvinist education and his reaction against it in Ward (2000: 15–17)).

10 It was suggested by an anonymous reviewer that More could be simply claiming that a good person will not choose the bad as long as they are a good person, whilst leaving open the possibility that such an individual could morally 'backslide' to being a bad person again. The main point I would raise against this reading is that More is clearly talking about the possibility of action being compelled by one's nature, in the manner that God cannot do anything other than pursue the good. Such a position seems to suggest a kind of perpetual virtue, for if one has achieved that state, how *could* one morally backslide? If we do morally backslide, then we have clearly not yet reached the point where we are being compelled by our own good nature. Granted, the text here is not decisive, but it is difficult to see why More would invoke the analogy with divine action here if one does not follow my interpretation of this passage.

11 The voluntarist approach can be contrasted with the intellectualist view that Conway propounds, which claims that divine agency is determined by a recognition of that which is good.

12 See, for example, Mawson (2001: *passim*) and Kaufman (2003: *passim*) for differing views on the nature of Cartesian indifference.
13 For more on Conway's and More's respective approaches to the question of salvation, see Hutton (1996: *passim*).

Chapter 7

1 With regard to the question of the notion of life in Conway's philosophy, as well as the individuation of creatures (which I will consider later on in the chapter), it is the case that the *Principia* does not necessarily explicitly address these issues. However, I argue that there are interesting theoretical assumptions regarding these issues that we can tease out of the text and use to address other interpretive questions regarding Conway's philosophy.
2 See Chapter 5 for more details on this soteriological process that involves both Christ and creatures.
3 See DeWeese (2004: 139–42) for a defence of an atemporal reading of Boethius.
4 In Chapter IX of the *Principia*, Conway refers to the 'more excellent attributes' shared by God and creatures as 'spirit or life and light' (9.6; 66). She states that she means by these 'the capacity for every kind of feeling, perception, or knowledge, even love, all power and virtue, joy and fruition' (9.6; 66). This passage does not conflict with the interpretation offered here, as it is the unified system of spirits that make up a living being that allows it to have such capacities.
5 In this section, I am only going to focus on the question of the kind of monism attributable to the created universe, apart from Christ: in other words, the monism of the world comprised of creatures specifically.
6 John Grey (2017: 8) points out that part of the significance of the question of Conway's monism is connected to her critique of Descartes, in that if she is indeed an existence-monist, her rejection of the Cartesian philosophy is far more radical than has often been appreciated.
7 Grey also argues that the passages called upon in defence of an existence-monist interpretation are fundamentally ambiguous (see 2017: 8f.).
8 As Wilson notes, the notion of real parts in early modern philosophy is not limited to the strict ontological question of substances, but also extends to the analysis of ideas: so, something can be a real part of another thing if it is 'really and wholly present in the thing analysed' (1994: 181).
9 Thomas also claims that passages in which Conway 'compares the parts of the universe to the parts of a living body' are 'indicative of priority monism', due to the Aristotelian idea that 'a living body is prior to its parts' (2020: 8). Whilst Conway does refer to Aristotle's form–matter distinction very briefly at one point in the

Principia (see 7.4; 51), there is otherwise no evidence that Conway's philosophy is substantively shaped by Aristotelian philosophy and so in the absence of an explicit claim by Conway, we should not read her as following an Aristotelian model of the part–whole relation with regard to the body.

10 Thomas (2018: 135) points out that securing a sense of personal identity over time is important for Conway due to the divine scheme of justice that she proposes, which tracks the moral development of a creature over many lifetimes through their changing position on the spirit–matter continuum (see 6.2; 29).

11 Karen Detlefsen has also noted the difficulty of distinguishing between humans and non-humans in Conway's system, arguing that ultimately the human mind is distinguishable by being at 'a level of moral perfection exhibited by the one kind of substance in the created world, and it is an especially high level of moral perfection' (2018: 145).

12 For a more detailed examination of Henry More's account of the creation, descent and redemption of souls, see Reid (2012: 349–81).

13 Thomas (2017: 1005f.) offers Leibnizian thought as an example of a philosophy which satisfies this broader definition (and thus we could perhaps consider Conway as something of a proto-Leibnizian).

14 As Detlefsen points out, we can potentially provide an ontological ground for distinguishing systems of spirits based on relations of sympathy between individual spirits: 'Each of us is a single individual because of the greater degree of love and sympathy among our internal parts than any of those parts have with any other part of creation' (2018: 146). However, I would stress that this does not imply that systems of spirits are ontologically fundamental for Conway.

15 Mercer (2012: 196) also discusses the cognitive achievements that accrue to us as we morally develop, insofar as we come to a deeper understanding of the unity of all things.

Bibliography

Barbour, Hugh and Roberts, Arthur O. (1973) *Early Quaker Writings 1650–1700*. Grand Rapids, MI: William B. Eerdmans.
Boethius (2000) *The Consolation of Philosophy* (trans. Walsh). Oxford: Oxford University Press.
Borcherding, Julia (2019) 'Loving the Body, Loving the Soul: Conway's Vitalist Critique of Cartesian and Morean Dualism'. In Donald Rutherford (ed.) *Oxford Studies in Early Modern Philosophy, Volume IX*. Oxford: Oxford University Press: pp. 1–35.
Borgen, Peder (1972) 'Logos Was the True Light: Contributions to the Interpretation of the Prologue of John', *Novum Testamentum* 14.2: pp. 115–30.
Boyarin, Daniel (2001) 'The Gospel of the *Memra*: Jewish Binitarianism and the Prologue to John', *Harvard Theological Review* 94.3: pp. 243–84.
Boyle, Deborah (2006) 'Spontaneous and Sexual Generation in Conway's *Principles*'. In Justin E.H. Smith (ed.) *The Problem of Animal Generation in Early Modern Philosophy*. Cambridge: Cambridge University Press: pp. 175–93.
Boyle, Deborah (2018) *The Well-Ordered Universe: The Philosophy of Margaret Cavendish*. New York: Oxford University Press.
Broad, Jacqueline (2002) *Women Philosophers of the Seventeenth Century*. Cambridge: Cambridge University Press.
Brown, Jeannine K. (2010) 'Creation's Renewal in the Gospel of John', *The Catholic Bible Quarterly* 72.2: pp. 275–90.
Byrne, David (2007) 'Anne Conway, Early Quaker Thought, and the New Science', *Quaker History* 96.1: pp. 24–35.
Byrne, David (2016) 'Ragley Hall and the Decline of Cartesianism', *Restoration* 40.2: pp. 43–57.
Cody, Edward J. (1972) 'The Price of Perfection: The Irony of George Keith', *Pennsylvania History: A Journal of Mid-Atlantic Studies* 39.1: pp. 1–19.
Conway, Anne (1996) *The Principles of the Most Ancient and Modern Philosophy* (eds Coudert and Corse). Cambridge: Cambridge University Press.
Coudert, Allison (1975) 'A Cambridge Platonist's Kabbalist Nightmare', *Journal of the History of Ideas* 36.4: pp. 633–52.
Coudert, Allison (1999) *The Impact of the Kabbalah in the Seventeenth Century: The Life and Thought of Francis Mercury van Helmont (1614–1698)*. Leiden: Brill.
Crocker, Robert (1997) 'The Role of Illuminism in the Thought of Henry More'. In Rogers et al. (eds) *The Cambridge Platonists in Philosophical Context*. Dordrecht: Kluwer Academic: pp. 129–44.

Crocker, Robert (2003) *Henry More, 1614–1687: A Biography of the Cambridge Platonist*. Dordrecht: Kluwer.
Cunning, David (2015) *Cavendish*. New York: Routledge.
Davies, Adrian (2000) *The Quakers in English Society 1655–1725*. Oxford: Clarendon Press.
Descartes, René (1968) *Discourse on Method and the Meditations* (trans. Sutcliffe). Harmondsworth: Penguin.
Descartes, René (1971) *Oeuvres de Descartes*. Vol. 3 (eds Charles Adams and Paul Tannery). Paris: Librairie Philosophique J. VRIN.
Descartes, René (1984) *The Philosophical Writings of Descartes: Volume 2* (trans. Cottingham, Stoothoff and Murdoch). Cambridge: Cambridge University Press.
Descartes, René (1985) *The Philosophical Writings of Descartes: Volume 1* (trans. Cottingham, Stoothoff and Murdoch). Cambridge: Cambridge University Press.
Detlefsen, Karen (2018) 'Cavendish and Conway on the Individual Human Mind'. In Copenhaver (ed.) *Philosophy of Mind in the Early Modern and Modern Ages: Vol. 4*. London: Routledge: pp. 134–56.
DeWeese, Garrett J. (2004) *God and the Nature of Time*. Aldershot: Ashgate.
Duran, Jane (1989) 'Anne Viscountess Conway: A Seventeenth Century Rationalist', *Hypatia* 4.1: pp. 69–77.
Duran, Jane (2006) *Eight Women Philosophers: Theory, Politics, and Feminism*. Urbana; Chicago: University of Illinois Press.
Emilsson, Eyjolfur K. (2017) *Plotinus*. London; New York: Routledge.
Fouke, Daniel C. (1997) *The Enthusiastical Concerns of Dr. Henry More: Religious Meaning and the Psychology of Delusion*. Leiden: E.J. Brill.
Frankfurt, Harry (1977) 'Descartes on the Creation of the Eternal Truths', *The Philosophical Review* 86.1: pp. 36–57.
Gabbey, Alan (1990) 'Henry More and the Limits of Mechanism'. In Sarah Hutton (ed.) *Henry More (1614–1687): Tercentenary Studies*. Dordrecht: Kluwer Academic Publishers: pp. 19–36.
Garrett, Aaron (2013) 'Seventeenth-Century Moral Philosophy: Self-Help, Self-Knowledge, and the Devil's Mountain'. In Crisp (ed.) *The Oxford Handbook of the History of Ethics*. Oxford: Oxford University Press: pp. 229–79.
Gerson, Lloyd P. (1994) *Plotinus: The Arguments of the Philosophers*. Abingdon; New York: Routledge.
Gerson, Lloyd P. (2014) 'Plotinus'. In Zalta (ed.) *The Stanford Encyclopedia of Philosophy*, Summer 2014 Edition. http://plato.stanford.edu/archives/sum2014/entries/plotinus/.
Gill, Catie (2005) *Women in the Seventeenth-Century Quaker Community: A Literary Study of Political Identities, 1650–1700*. Farnham: Ashgate.
Gordon, Robert (1671) *Christianity Vindicated, or, the Fundamental Truths of the Gospel Concerning the Person of Christ and Redemption through Him*. London: R. Boulter.

Gordon-Roth, Jessica (2018) 'What Kind of Monist Is Anne Finch Conway?', *Journal of the American Philosophical Association* 4.3: pp. 280–97.

Grey, John (2017) 'Conway's Ontological Objection to Cartesian Dualism', *Philosophers' Imprint* 17.13: pp. 1–19.

Hamilton, Edith and Cairns, Huntington (1961) *Plato: Collected Dialogues*. Princeton: Princeton University Press.

Hatfield, Gary (2003) *Routledge Philosophy Guidebook to Descartes and the Meditations*. London; New York: Routledge.

Helmont, J.B. van (1662) *Oriatrike, or Physick Refined*. London: L. Loyd.

Helmont, F.M. van (1694) *The Spirit of Diseases*. London: S. Howkins.

Henry, John (1990) 'Henry More versus Robert Boyle: The Spirit of Nature and the Nature of Providence'. In Hutton (ed.) *Henry More (1614–1687): Tercentenary Studies*. Dordrecht: Kluwer Academic Publishers: pp. 55–76.

Hill, Christopher (1991) *The World Turned Upside Down: Radical Ideas during the English Revolution*. London: Penguin.

Hobbes, Thomas (1962) *The English Works of Thomas Hobbes: Vol. 5*. London: Scientia Aalen.

Hobbes, Thomas (1985) *Leviathan*. London: Penguin.

Howgill, Francis (1656) *The Inheritance of Jacob Discovered*. London: G. Calvert.

Hutton, Sarah (1996) 'Henry More and Anne Conway on Preexistence and Universal Salvation'. In Baldi (ed.) *Mind Senior to the World: Stoicismo e origenismo nella filosofila platonica del seicento inglese*. Milan: Francoangeli: pp. 113–26.

Hutton, Sarah (2004) *Anne Conway: A Woman Philosopher*. Cambridge: Cambridge University Press.

Hutton, Sarah (2005) 'Platonism and the Trinity: Anne Conway, Henry More and Christoph Sand'. In Mulsow and Rohls (eds) *Socianianism and Arminianism: Antitrinitarians, Calvinists and Cultural Exchange in Seventeenth-Century Europe*. Leiden: Brill: pp. 209–24.

Kane, Robert (1996) *The Significance of Free Will*. Oxford: Oxford University Press.

Kaufman, Dan (2003) 'Infimus gradus libertatis? Descartes on Indifference and Divine Freedom', *Religious Studies* 39.4: pp. 391–406.

Keith, George (1668) *Immediate Revelation, or Jesus Christ the Eternall Son of God, Revealed in Man and Revealing the Knowledge of God, and the Things of His Kingdom, Immediately*. Aberdeen.

Keith, George (1692) *A Discovery of the Mystery of Iniquity & Hypocrisie Acting and Ruling in Hugh Derborough*. Philadelphia: W. Bradford.

Kenny, Anthony (1970) *Descartes' Philosophical Letters*. Oxford: Clarendon Press.

Kieffer, René (2010) 'John'. In Muddiman and Barton (eds) *The Gospels: The Oxford Bible Commentary*. Oxford; New York: Oxford University Press: pp. 960–1000.

Kirby, Ethyn Williams (1942) *George Keith (1638–1716)*. New York: D. Appleton-Century.

Lascano, Marcy P. (2013) 'Anne Conway: Bodies in the Spiritual World', *Philosophy Compass* 8.4: pp. 327–36.

Lascano, Marcy P. (2017) 'Anne Conway on Liberty'. In Broad and Detlefsen (eds) *Women and Liberty, 1600–1800: Philosophical Essays*. Oxford: Oxford University Press: pp. 163–77.
Lee, Seung Goo (2009) 'The Relationship between the Ontological Trinity and the Economic Trinity', *Journal of Reformed Theology* 3: pp. 90–107.
Leech, David (2013) *The Hammer of the Cartesians: Henry More's Philosophy of Spirit and the Origins of Modern Atheism*. Leuven: Peeters.
Lloyd, Arnold (1950) *Quaker Social History 1669–1738*. London: Longmans, Green and Co.
Loptson, Peter (1982) 'Introduction'. In Peter Loptson (ed.) *The Principles of the Most Ancient and Modern Philosophy*. The Hague; Boston: Martinus Nijhoff: pp. 24–59.
Mawson, T.J. (2001) 'Eternal Truths and Cartesian Circularity', *British Journal for the History of Philosophy* 9.2: pp. 197–220.
McRobert, Jennifer (2000) 'Anne Conway's Vitalism and Her Critique of Descartes', *International Philosophical Quarterly* 40.1: pp. 21–35.
Mercer, Christia (2012) 'Knowledge and Suffering in Early Modern Philosophy: G.W. Leibniz and Anne Conway'. In Sabrina Ebbersmeyer (ed.) *Emotional Minds: The Passions and the Limits of Pure Inquiry in Early Modern Philosophy*. Berlin: De Gruyter: pp. 179–206.
Mercer, Christia (2019a) 'Anne Conway's Metaphysics of Sympathy'. In O'Neill and Lacano (eds) *Feminist History of Philosophy: The Recovery and Evaluation of Women's Philosophical Thought*. Cham: Springer: pp. 49–73.
Mercer, Christia (2019b) 'Anne Conway's Response to Cartesianism'. In Schmaltz Nadler and Antoine-Mahut (eds) *The Oxford Handbook of Descartes and Cartesianism*. Oxford: Oxford University Press: pp. 707–20.
Merchant, Carolyn (1979) 'The Vitalism of Anne Conway: Its Impact on Leibniz's Concept of the Monad', *Journal of the History of Philosophy* 17: pp. 255–69.
Mill, David van (1995) 'Hobbes's Theories of Freedom', *The Journal of Politics* 57.2: pp. 443–59.
Moore, Rosemary (2000) *The Light in Their Consciences: Early Quakers in Britain 1646–1666*. University Park, PA: Pennsylvania State University Press.
More, Henry (1642) *Psychathanasia Platonica: Or a Platonicall Poem of the Immortality of Souls, Especially Mans Soul*. Cambridge: R. Daniel.
More, Henry (1647) *Philosophical Poems*. Cambridge: R. Daniel.
More, Henry (1653) *An Antidote against Atheism*. London: R. Daniel.
More, Henry (1659) *The Immortality of the Soul*. London: J. Flesher.
More, Henry (1660) *An Explanation of the Grand Mystery of Godliness*. London: J. Flesher.
More, Henry (1662) *A Collection of Several Philosophical Writings*. London: J. Flesher.
More, Henry (1668) *Divine Dialogues Containing Sundry Disquisitions & Instructions Concerning the Attributes and Providence of God*. London: J. Flesher.
More, Henry (1679) *Cantabrigiensis Opera Philosophica: Volume 2*. London: J. Maycock for J. Martyn & W. Kettilby.

More, Henry (1682) *Annotations upon the Two Foregoing Treatises, Lux Orientalis ... and the Discourse of Truth*. London: J. Collins.
More, Henry (1690) *An Account of Virtue, or, Dr. Henry More's Abridgement of Morals Put into English*. London: B. Tooke.
More, Henry (1708) *Theological Works*. London: J. Downing.
More, Henry (1712) *A Collection of Several Philosophical Writings*. London: J. Downing.
More, Henry (1878) *The Complete Poems of Dr. Henry More* (ed. Grosart). Edinburgh: Edinburgh University Press.
More, Henry (1925) *Philosophical Writings of Henry More* (ed. Mackinnon). New York: Oxford University Press.
More, Henry (1995) *Manual of Metaphysics: Vol. 1* (trans. Jacob). Hildesheim: Olms.
Nadler, Stephen (2000) 'Malebranche on Causation'. In Nadler (ed.) *The Cambridge Companion to Malebranche*. Cambridge: Cambridge University Press: pp. 112–38.
Nelson, Holly Faith and Alker, Sharon (2011) 'Conway: Dis/ability, Medicine, and Metaphysics'. In J.A. Hayden (ed.) *The New Science and Women's Literary Discourse*. New York: Palgrave Macmillan: pp. 65–83.
Nicolson, Marjorie Hope and Hutton, Sarah (1992) *The Conway Letters*. Oxford: Clarendon Press.
O'Neill, Eileen (1998) 'Disappearing Ink: Early Modern Women Philosophers and Their Fate in History'. In Janet A. Kourany (ed.) *Philosophy in a Feminist Voice: Critiques and Reconstructions*. Princeton, NJ: Princeton University Press: pp. 17–62.
Pagel, Walter (1982) *Joan Baptista Van Helmont: Reformer of Science and Medicine*. Cambridge: Cambridge University Press.
Parageau, Sandrine (2018) 'Christ in Anne Conway's *Principia* (1690): Metaphysics, Syncretism, and Female *Imitatio Christi*', *Journal of Early Modern Christianity* 5.2: pp. 247–65.
Pink, Thomas (2011) 'Thomas Hobbes and the Ethics of Freedom', *Inquiry: An Interdisciplinary Journal of Philosophy* 54.5: pp. 541–63.
Plato (1974) *The Republic* (trans. Lee). Harmondsworth: Penguin.
Plato (2005) *Meno and Other Dialogues* (trans. Waterfield). Oxford: Oxford University Press.
Plotinus (2018) *The Enneads* (ed. Gerson). Cambridge: Cambridge University Press.
Rabinowitz, Celia E. (1984) 'Personal and Cosmic Salvation in Origen', *Vigiliae Christianae* 38: pp. 319–29.
Reay, Barry (1985) *The Quakers and the English Revolution*. London: Temple Smith.
Reid, Jasper (2012) *The Metaphysics of Henry More*. Dordrecht: Springer.
Remes, Pauliina (2014) *Neoplatonism*. Abingdon: Routledge.
Rust, George (1682) *A Discourse of Truth*. London: J. Collins.
Schroeder, Steven (2007) 'Anne Conway's Place: A Map of Leibniz', *The Pluralist* 2.3: pp. 77–99.
Sorabji, Richard (1983) *Time, Creation and the Continuum*. London: Duckworth.

Swinburne, Richard (1965) 'The Timelessness of God: I', *Church Quarterly Review* 116: pp. 323–37.

Swinburne, Richard (1993) *The Coherence of Theism* (revised ed.). Oxford: Clarendon Press.

Taliaferro, Charles (2005) *Evidence and Faith: Philosophy and Religion since the Seventeenth Century*. Cambridge: Cambridge University Press.

Tarter, Michele Lise (2018) 'Written from the Body of Sisterhood: Quaker Women's Prophesying and the Creation of a New Word'. In Tarter and Gill (eds) *New Critical Studies on Early Quaker Women, 1650–1800*. Oxford: Oxford University Press: pp. 50–68.

Thomas, Emily (2017) 'Time, Space, and Process in Anne Conway', *British Journal for the History of Philosophy* 25.5: pp. 990–1010.

Thomas, Emily (2018) 'Anne Conway on the Identity of Creatures over Time'. In Thomas (ed.) *Early Modern Women on Metaphysics*. Cambridge: Cambridge University Press: pp. 131–49.

Thomas, Emily (2020) 'Anne Conway as a Priority Monist: A Reply to Gordon-Roth', *Journal of the American Philosophical Association* Online First View: pp. 1–10.

Tollefson, Deborah (1999) 'Princess Elizabeth and the Problem of Mind-Body Interaction', *Hypatia* 14.3: pp. 59–77.

Trevett, Christine (1991) *Women and Quakerism in the Seventeenth Century*. York: The Ebor Press.

Trigg, Joseph W. (1998) *Origen*. London: Routledge.

Tzamalikos, Panayiotis (1991) 'Origin and the Stoic View of Time', *Journal of the History of Ideas* 52.4: pp. 535–61.

Underwood, T.L. (1970) 'Early Quaker Eschatology'. In Toon (ed.) *Puritans, the Millennium and the Future of Israel: Puritan Eschatology 1600 to 1660*. Cambridge: James Clarke: pp. 91–103.

Ward, Richard (2000) *The Life of Henry More* (ed. Hutton et al.). Dordrecht: Kluwer.

Wedderburn, A.J.M. (1973) 'Philo's Heavenly Man', *Novum Testamentum* 15.4: pp. 301–26.

White, Carol Wayne (2008) *The Legacy of Anne Conway (1631–1679): Reverberations from a Mystical Naturalism*. Albany, NY: SUNY Press.

White, Dorothy (1661) *An Epistle of Love*. London: R. Wilson.

Whittaker, Thomas (1961) *The Neo-Platonists: A Study in the History of Hellenism*. Hildesheim: Olms.

Wilson, Fred (1994) 'Substance and Self in Locke and Hume'. In Barber and Gracia (eds) *Individuation and Identity in Early Modern Philosophy: Descartes to Kant*. Albany: SUNY Press: pp. 155–200.

Yandell, Keith (2009) 'How Many Times Does Three Go into One?' In McCall and Rea (eds) *Philosophical and Theological Essays on the Trinity*. Oxford: Oxford University Press: pp. 151–69.

Index

Adam and Eve 52–3
Adam Kadmon 111, 120–2, 125
affinity 63–5, 67, 179
Alker, S. 179
animals 194 n.9
   Descartes and 66
   kinds of 63
   lower 158, 173
   non-human 170
   passions 136
   souls of 61
Antidote against Atheism, An (More) 38–9, 136
apocalypticism 28–31
apocatastasis 131
archeus (ruling spirit) 151, 156, 158, 159, 165, 167–70, 175, 177, 180
autexousion 136, 137, 140
automata 66

Bible 25–6, 29, 30, 36
Boethius 154
Borcherding, J. 55, 59
Borgen, P. 190 n.13
Boyle, D. 61
Byrne, D. 3, 188 n.14

Cambridge Platonism 4, 33, 103, 136, 150
Cartesianism 14, 100, 102, 112, 149, 150
Cavendish, M. 8
Christ 27, 38, 42–3, 97
   and 'Christ Within' 42, 43, 93, 96, 102–6, 109, 110, 112, 113
   creatures and 82–6, 119, 154, 161
   freedom 148–9
   God and 115–16, 154
Christianity 17–18, 41, 47, 90, 111
   and Judaism 85
   Neoplatonism and 46–8
   truth of 116, 120
Christian orthodoxy 38, 40, 70, 77, 104, 111, 117, 131

Christology 82, 84, 86, 95, 96, 102, 105, 106, 113, 125–7
Church 11, 22, 85
   'inner light' 30
   Quakers 30–1
   and scripture 25–8, 36, 103
Church of England 6, 7, 173
communicable attributes 48–9, 99
conceivability and explanation 59–60
Conjectura cabbalistica (More) 4
Consolation of Philosophy, The (Boethius) 154
convincement 41, 102, 103, 188 n.15
Conway Letters 9–18
Corse, T. 10
Coudert, A. 10, 41, 74–5, 120, 126, 127, 180, 188 n.16
creation
   creatures and Christ 82–6
   divine 59, 86, 141, 151, 159
   eternity of 73–9
   God and 47–9, 53, 58, 67, 111, 118, 124, 145, 181
   infinite time 69–73
   of souls 79–81
   time and motion 86–92
creature 97–100, 106–9, 116, 118, 143–8, 154–5, 160, 163, 179
   and Christ 82–6, 119, 128, 129, 154, 161
   constitution of 63, 65, 88, 151, 164, 168, 181
   God and 48, 58, 97, 120, 148, 154, 160
   identity and 168
   infinity of 157
   life of 152
   love between 53–5
   moral and spiritual development 147, 148
   original equality of 170–4
   sympathetic relations 165
   time and 92
   unity of 165

Creed, A. 122
Crocker, R. 32, 34, 36, 187 n.8, 194 n.6

Davies, A. 26
dependence thesis 50, 51
Descartes, R. 17, 45, 50–2, 55, 56
   and animals 66
   Conway and 14–15, 50, 51, 61
   God and the physical universe 100–1
   voluntarism 142
Detlefsen, K. 196 n.11, 196 n.14
DeWeese, G. J. 74
divine
   attributes 22, 40, 48, 49, 52, 78, 99, 134, 155, 157, 173, 175
   and human freedom 134–43
   immutability 97, 153
   justice 118, 119, 158, 167, 170, 172, 173
   punishment 118, 119, 171, 172
Divine Dialogues (More) 72, 134
dualism
   argument against 52, 55, 58, 60
   More and 100–2
   substance 14, 45, 46, 50–2, 60–5, 67, 96
Duran, J. 66, 100

Emilsson, E. K. 83, 90, 190 n.15
Enchiridion Ethicum (More) 133, 137, 140–1, 147, 149
Enneads (Plotinus) 77, 83, 88, 90, 189 n.6
enthusiasm 38–9
eschatology 25, 29–30, 79, 128–32
eternity 72–9, 81, 116, 128, 131, 154
existence-monism 151, 159–63, 167
Explanation of the Grand Mystery of Godliness (More) 85, 101, 103, 104, 136

Fall of Adam (More) 173–4
Forms, the 47, 48
Fouke, Daniel C. 24, 31
Foxcroft, E. 4
Frankfurt, H. 142
freedom 133–4, 149–50, 194 n.5
   Christ 148–9
   divine and human 134–43
   God 142–5, 148
   libertarian 134, 135, 194 n.4
   More and Conway 140–8

Gabbey, A. 191 n.7
Garrett, A. 136
Gerson, L. P. 75, 89
Gill, C. 27–8
Glanvill, J. 79
God 14, 21–5, 32–5, 37, 45, 58, 97, 140, 153, 160, 161
   atemporal 119, 128
   and Christ 115–16
   and creation 47–9, 53, 58, 67, 106, 111, 118, 124, 145, 181
   and creatures 58, 97, 120, 148, 154, 160
   eternity of 73–9
   freedom 142–5, 148
   goodness of 47, 81, 96, 99, 119, 130, 134, 143, 145, 149, 154, 155, 171, 173
   and humans 146
   and infinite time 69–75, 78, 79, 86, 130
   life 153–6
   love of 53
   and monism 45–51
   and the physical universe 100–1
   soul and 37, 40, 42
   timeless 73–7, 162, 189 n.5, 193 n.10
   and world 121
Gordon, R. 104
Gordon-Roth, J. 161, 162
Gospel of John 84, 91, 190 n.10, 190 n.13
Grey, J. 50, 51, 195 n.6, 195 n.7

habit 137, 138
harmony, sympathy and 164–70
Helmont, F. M. van 2–5, 7, 19, 28, 41, 42, 65, 111, 120–3, 180, 181, 183, 185 n.7, 188 n.16
   life and 156–9
Helmont, J. B. van 41–2
Henry, J. 101–2, 134
Hobbes, T. 135–6, 139, 194 n.7
holenmerism 76
Holy Spirit 35–7, 101, 115, 121, 122
Howgill, F. 24–5
human being 66–7
   capacity 38
   Christianity and 131
   divine and human freedom 134–43, 146
   humans and non-humans 196 n.11

moral development of 147
and terrestrial spirits 168–9
Hutton, S. 4, 9–10, 84, 105, 107, 108, 124, 125, 131, 157, 185 n.7, 189 n.6, 191 n.8

identity
　and creatures 168
　over time 166, 167
　in *Principia* 151–2
illumination 37–42, 145
Immediate Revelation (Keith) 103, 105
immortality 36, 37, 64
Immortality of the Soul, The (More) 135
immutability 97, 99, 118, 153
incommunicable attributes 48–9, 99
incorporeal substances 135
infinite time 69–75, 78, 79, 86, 130
inner light 21–5
　benefits 37
　Christ and 105–6
　church and women writers 25–30
　Fouke and 31
　Quaker 23–32, 34–43, 188 n.13
Intellect 83, 89, 90, 117, 190 n.9
intellectual prejudices 79–80
interpretation 19, 34, 59, 72, 76, 115, 119, 120, 125, 142, 153–6, 160, 162–4, 166–8, 170, 174, 190 n.16

Jesus of Nazareth 106, 110, 111, 125

Kabbala Denudata (Helmont and Rosenroth) 3–4, 19
Kabbalism 3–4
Kane, R. 135
Keith, G. 4, 43, 95, 96, 102–7, 110–13, 188 n.17, 191 n.9, 192 n.16
Kieffer, R. 84

Lascano, M. P. 143, 145, 167, 169, 193 n.1
Leech, D. 33
Leibniz, G. W. 185 n.5
Letter of Resolution Concerning Origen, A (Rust) 17
Leviathan (Hobbes) 135
libertarian freedom 134, 135, 194 n.4
liberum arbitrium 139
life 65, 151, 160

of Christ 38
defining 152–6
and education 1–8
God 153–6
and Helmonts 156–9
of soul 89–90
Lloyd, A. 26
Logos 84–6, 105, 121, 123–6
logos ousios 84, 110, 123–5, 128
logos proforikos 110, 123–6, 128
Loptson, P. 9, 10, 166, 167
love
　and affinity 67
　between creatures 53–4
　of God 53
　and interaction problem 52–60
　and pain 58–60
　universal 54–5, 179
Luria, I. 3–4

McRobert, J. 59
Malebranche, N. 108
material extension 107
materialism 46, 50, 52, 67, 135
matter
　epistemological 21, 41, 42
　of false enthusiasm 38
　and form 156
　mind and 50, 51
　spirit and 49–51, 56–8, 61–3, 99, 100, 102, 115, 132, 152–7, 159, 166–8, 176–9
Mercer, C. 52, 123, 179, 196 n.15
metaphysical system 8, 21, 22, 33, 45, 46, 70–1, 83, 86, 88, 95–9, 115, 119, 120, 125, 128, 130
mind 8, 19
　and body 56, 60, 62, 64, 180
　and matter 50, 51
　and pain 55–6
modalism 111, 115, 121
monism 96, 155
　existence-monism 151, 159–63, 167
　God and 45–51
　priority 163
　spiritual 45, 46, 49, 51–2, 54, 60–5, 67
　type-monism 151, 160–2, 167, 169
Moore, R. 104
morality 87, 92, 136, 141, 177

More, H. 2–5, 7–8, 14–17, 21, 22, 28, 61, 65, 66, 173, 186 n.14, 188 n.12, 191 n.10, 192 n.11, 194 n.9, 194 n.10
   Conway and the Quakers 37–42
   and Conway on freedom 140–8
   divine and human freedom 134–40
   dualism 100–2
   illumination 37–42
   Neoplatonism and knowledge 31–7
   religious epistemology 104
   soul, pre-existence of 79–81
   spirit and matter 56–8
motion 57–8
   time and 86–92
   transmission of 108

Nelson, H. F. 179
Neoplatonism 31–7, 42, 45, 47, 77, 78, 90, 102
   and Christianity 46–8
   emanationist model 75
Nicolson, M. 9, 185 n.4, 187 n.10

occasionalism 108
O'Neill, E. 11, 186 n.9
ontological-moral continuum 170, 173
Oriatrike (Helmont) 41–2
Origen 17, 91–2, 116, 125
   universal salvation and 130–2

Pagel, W. 156
pain. See suffering/pain
Parageau, S. 127
Penn, W. 17–18, 23
Philo 84, 85, 124, 125, 190 n.12
Philosophical Poems (More) 65, 72
Pink, T. 194 n.7
Plato 47, 48, 70
Plotinus 33, 69, 75, 77, 83, 88–91, 190 n.16
priority monism 163
problem of interaction 56, 61, 62
process philosophy 87, 88, 152, 174–7
prophecy 29
Psychozoia (More) 32, 34

Quakerism 4–6, 9, 18, 21, 23, 27, 29–31, 36, 40–2, 112
Quakers 187 n.4, 188 n.13
   Church's role 30–1
   community 23, 25, 27–31, 37, 40–2, 112
   inner light 39, 42
   personal impact 6
   position of 5
   theology 103, 105, 112, 113
   women 27–8, 187 n.5

Rabinowitz, C. E. 131–2
Reid, J. 65, 122–3, 136, 139, 189 n.2, 189 n.7, 194 n.8
relational theory of time 176
Remes, P. 47–8
revelation
   Church and 30
   divine 13, 23
Rosenroth, C. K. von 3, 19
Rust, G. 17, 134

salvation 108, 126–8, 146, 149–50, 173, 177, 179, 192 n.14
   and Origen 130–2
scepticism 36, 39, 41
Schroeder, S. 185 n.5
scripture 13, 25, 26, 29, 30, 36, 67
'second substance' 124
Son and Spirit 116, 117, 121, 122
'Son of God' 111
Sorabji, R. 71
soteriology 91, 92, 108, 110, 112, 115, 116, 128–30, 132
soul 17, 21, 34, 55
   of animals 61
   creation of 79–81
   and God 37, 40, 42
   immaterial 135
   immortality 36–7
   Intellect and 89–90
   and pain 55
   substance 166–7
spirit 46
   and body 49, 61, 63, 65, 66
   Christ and 18, 102–6
   human and terrestrial 168–70
   and matter 49–51, 56–8, 61–4, 99, 100, 102, 115, 132, 152–7, 159, 166–8, 176–9
   and perfection 119
   ruling 167–8

'Spirit of Nature' (More) 101, 102, 112, 191 n.9, 191 n.10
spiritual monism 45, 46, 49, 51–2, 54, 60–5, 67, 189 n.4
spontaneity 138–9, 146
spontaneous generation 60–5, 67, 164
subordinationism 111, 115, 117
substance 51
    creaturely 151, 160, 161
    dualism 14, 45, 46, 50–2, 60–5, 67, 96
    immaterial 76
    incorporeal 135
    metaphysics 174, 176, 177
    purification 180
    and quiddity 191 n.3
    second 124
    soul 166–7
    spiritual 162, 168
    types 96–100
suffering/pain 8, 16, 55, 56, 110, 119, 126, 127, 152, 177–81
Swinburne, R. 77, 189 n.5
sympathy 55, 56, 152, 163–70, 179, 180, 196 n.14

Taliaferro, C. 33
Tarter, M. L. 187 n.5
Thomas, E. 76, 163, 164, 166–8, 175, 176, 189 n.2, 190 n.14, 195 n.9, 196 n.10, 196 n.13
Timaeus (Plato) 70
time 129–30, 153, 176, 193 n.10
    beginning of 72–4, 91
    definition 87, 88
    eternity of 73–9
    infinite 69–73
    and motion 86–92, 116
    over 19, 166, 167, 196 n.10
Trevett, C. 27, 29
Trinitarianism 84, 85, 90, 111, 116, 124, 125, 128
Trinity 24, 41, 69, 85, 111, 115–17, 119–23, 125, 192 n.2
Triune God 116–28
type-monism 151, 160–2, 167, 169
Tzamalikos, P. 91

universal salvation 130–2
'universal seeds and principles' 82–3, 85, 86

virtual extension 107
virtue 33, 49, 136–40, 147, 150
vitalism 45, 63, 65–7, 151, 159, 160, 181

Ward, R. 39–40
White, C. W. 87–8, 174
White, D. 29
Whitehead, A. 88
Whittaker, T. 75
Wilson, F. 195 n.8
women writers 26–9, 187 n.5

Yandell, K. 117

Ingram Content Group UK Ltd.
Milton Keynes UK
UKHW022034140323
418579UK00005B/193